English for the future

MARY HARTLEY

*Former Head of English, St Peter's Catholic Comprehensive
School, Guildford and Assistant Examiner for
GCSE and A-level English*

Nelson

Thomas Nelson and Sons Ltd
Nelson House Mayfield Road
Walton-on-Thames Surrey
KT12 5PL   UK

Nelson Blackie
Wester Cleddens Road
Bishopbriggs
Glasgow
G64 2NZ   UK

Thomas Nelson Australia
102 Dodds Street
South Melbourne
Victoria 3205 Australia

Nelson Canada
1120 Birchmount Road
Scarborough Ontario
MIK 5G4 Canada

First published by Thomas Nelson and Sons Ltd. 1996
I(T)P Thomas Nelson is an International Thomson Publishing Company
I(T)P is used under licence

ISBN 0-17- 490010-4
NPN 9 8 7 6 5 4 3 2 1

Acknowledgements
Acquisitions: Alex Bridgland/Steve Berry
Administration: Jenny Goode
Editorial: Gaynor Roberts
Marketing: Jane Lewis
Production: Liam Reardon
Staff design: Maria Pritchard
Design: DP Press Ltd

Printed in Great Britain by Hobbs the Printers Ltd, Totton,
Hampshire

CONTENTS

Preface

PREFACE

If you are a student in a further education college or a sixth form following a GCSE course in English, probably within one year, then this book is intended to help you. Whether you have already taken an English examination and are hoping for a higher grade, or are taking the course for the first time, you will find the material and activities helpful for exam preparation and for compiling a coursework folder.

writing

speaking

drama

tape-recording

working in pairs

working in groups

The following icons are used throughout the book to denote different types of activity: writing; speaking; drama; tape-recording; working in pairs; working in groups.

The book is divided into five thematic chapters, in line with the five half-terms of the course. However, you do not need to treat it as a formal coursebook and follow it through from the beginning. In every chapter there is a range of reading material followed by questions to test your understanding and suggestions for oral and written work. At the end of each chapter is an end-of-chapter assignment which is based on all the material in that chapter, a summary sheet which shows you what has been covered, a revision exercise and further suggestions for coursework. If you do work through the book systematically, you may like to know that the last two chapters contain more demanding reading material.

A good way to use the book would be to discuss your individual learning requirements with your tutor and decide which activities would best suit your needs. Against this background you should be able to work through the book on your own or in a pair or group and select the work that you want or need to cover. There are frequent self-checks to help you judge your progress and, where relevant, answers are denoted by the symbol *a* and given at the end of the book.

Throughout the book you will find instruction and advice on aspects of grammar, punctuation and spelling and a range of material aimed at developing your understanding of and skill in the use of language.

If you work through as much of the material as you can you will be in a good position to put together a coursework file which demonstrates your skill in a number of areas. You will also be able to approach the examination with a firm background in reading and responding to a variety of material and an increased accuracy and confidence in your use and understanding of language.

A final word: don't forget to look at the section on raising your grade at the end of the book!

TAKING IT EASY

Your viewing habits

You may have noticed that the same television programmes regularly appear in the ratings lists. It may be the case that your own favourites never appear at all. This assignment gives you an opportunity to discuss the programmes you particularly enjoy and to find out how far others agree with your choice.

ASSIGNMENT

1 Think about your favourite television programmes. Decide which are the ones you never miss if you can help it, the ones you nearly always watch and the ones you quite like. Think about why you enjoy them. List them (up to 10) in your order of preference and beside each title give a brief reason for your choice.

Example:	Programme	Reason
1	Brookside	Strong drama, realistic situations
2		
3		
etc.		

2 In pairs or small groups compare your lists. Each person in turn should talk through their list and say more about the reasons, giving examples to illustrate the point.

Guidelines *Listening to other people*

Good listening means more than just keeping quiet while someone else is speaking. Good listeners show that they are listening by their body language and by the way they acknowledge what people are saying. Listening is a vital skill which enables discussion to be more focused and effective, because more points are heard and understood. Good listeners:

make eye contact;
nod;
smile where appropriate;
make encouraging responses like 'yes' and 'mmm';
concentrate on the speaker;
acknowledge what is said even if they disagree;
do not interrupt;
make responses which show they have heard and understood.

Writing a soap

The viewing public love soap operas, and some would say that the best of them are actually examples of excellent drama. The most popular ones certainly capture the public's imagination, and their characters have become very familiar figures whose names are

recognised even by people who do not watch that particular programme. Some of the characters seem so believable that they are treated like real people and receive letters giving them advice and asking them to family weddings!

ASSIGNMENT

The media studies department in your college is running a competition for the best original drama in the soap opera tradition. As an entrant you should submit:

a) an outline of the idea, with descriptions of characters and setting;
b) a sample scene.

They have stipulated that there should be no more than four main characters and that the setting should suitable for their studio or the immediate location.

The person who submits the best idea with the best example of writing will have their scene filmed and screened during the college arts week.

Here are some suggestions to get you going.

1 Choose a drama or soap opera from your list of favourite programmes. Make notes on it under the following headings.

Characters: Think about the important characters and how they are presented.

Name	Age	Clothes and appearance	Job	Three-word description	Main relationships
1					
2					
3					
etc.					

Language: Think about how the characters speak.

Name	Accent/dialect	Typical phrase(s)
1		
2		
3		
etc.		

Setting: Think about the setting (or settings) and what they contribute.

Country	City	Kind of area(s)	Meeting place(s)

Stories: Think about the kinds of plots.

Different stories going on at once	Conflict between characters	Major events

2 Using the same headings, make notes for your own programme.

3 With the notes as a basis:

(a) write up a full description of the main characters, their appearances and personalities, their jobs and relationships.

Example Andy is nineteen and in his second year at college. He wears a lot of leather and wants to look tough but is really very unsure of himself and easily led. He looks up to Jed, who dropped out of their course at the end of the first year and who tries to persuade Andy that college is for kids.

(b) describe the setting(s), giving enough details of interiors and exteriors to enable the television group to prepare them.

Example Pauline's kitchen is shabby and lived-in, with piles of ironing on chairs and used cups and mugs on the table.

(c) give some idea of the kind of stories that will develop.

Example Pete is so determined to win a place in the team that he makes sure his rival Jon will miss the trial. He does this by......but ....

4 Now choose a scene to write. It doesn't have to be from the beginning, just choose something which will show your characters and how they behave in a certain situation. Write about three pages of script. You could use this example as a guide for setting it out.

SCENE 1

INTERIOR. LINDSEY'S HOUSE, HALL, MORNING

Lindsey picks up the post from the mat and flicks through it until she finds the letter she's been waiting for. She opens it and reads it.

LINDSEY: That's that, then. How on earth am I going to tell the others?

MARK and RANIA hurry downstairs, laden with bookbags etc.

MARK (joking) Come on, out of the way, we'll miss the bus. (Pause) What's the matter?

Read carefully through your outline and your scene before you hand them in. Even if you are not able to film, your class could spend a lesson reading the submissions and choose the best.

Language Link

Accent and Dialect

Dialect is the technical term used to describe special ways of speaking. It is usually used to refer to the way people speak in a certain area, but can also describe how people in particular social groups or particular occupations speak. Every dialect has its own vocabulary, accent and order of words.

The kind of English you read in books and newspapers, which is used in Parliament, in law, in national television and radio broadcasts, is the dialect known as Standard English. The use of Standard English means that everyone shares the meanings of words and uses the same grammar and spellings.

Standard English is the formal English appropriate for most writing tasks.

Accent is the term used to describe the way words are pronounced. It usually applies to areas, but like dialect, can also be associated with social class.

More suggestions for coursework

- Choose your favourite character from a soap opera or similar drama (include programmes like *Casualty*). Write a description (300 to 500 words) of the character and say what you like about him or her.
- Popular dramas often tackle current social issues , e.g. unemployment or racial prejudice. Choose an issue you think could be dealt with in a television drama. Write a short proposal (350 to 500 words) saying what the issue is, why you think it should be used, and which programme you think would be most appropriate. Give an outline of the way it could be introduced in the programme.

A bad influence?

Some people are very worried about the bad effects of television, particularly on children. Here is an article from *Good Housekeeping* magazine which claims that television is not necessarily bad, and that in fact children should watch television!

Television is bad for children; it must be. Experts of every kind – politicians, doctors, teachers- are constantly telling us so. Last year the Schools Minister lambasted 'junk television', including soap operas like *Neighbours*, for turning children into unimaginative voyeurs, and a primary school teacher protested this year that television was robbing children of their innocence.

This bad press creates a climate in which television is seen, where children are concerned, to be at best a necessary evil. No one seriously challenged the Prince of Wales when he attacked the "utterly gratuitous violence on television"; we tend to take at face value all those statements that when children commit violent crimes it is solely because they have been watching *Teenage Mutant Ninja Turtles*.

The Minister's objection to *Neighbours* implies that if children weren't watching what he calls 'junk', they would necessarily be doing more homework, or something else improving. But children can't do homework all night, and as journalist Katherine Whitehorn has pointed out, without television, we would not necessarily be spending "our entire time playing the recorder, making collages and reading one another's poems out loud. She is grateful to television programmes like *Magpie*, *Blue Peter*, and later *Tomorrow's World*, *Horizon* and *QED* for fostering her son's interest in electronics, now his career.

Not only overtly educational programmes are of benefit, either. The dismissal of *Neighbours* is unfair. A recent study by Christopher Crouch, a lecturer in communication studies, has suggested that one reason girls like *Neighbours* so much is that they identify with the way that most of the households are headed by strong, independent women and even the younger female characters are assertive. "Women have a higher status than in many soaps," he says.

One of the two big objections to television is that it blunts children's brains and slows their language development; that it stops them reading and prevents them from learning as much. However, there is no evidence that television watching is entirely devoid of the skills needed for reading. As Dr Messenger Davies points out in her book *Television is Good for your Kids*, to follow a *Postman Pat* story "children must have an ability to understand the underlying logic of events: that when Pat abandons his van, it is because a tree has fallen across the road earlier".

Underlying the 'junk' objection is a rather strange notion – that television should constantly be teaching people things. As adults we watch television primarily to relax, yet we seem to need to justify television in terms of its capacity to 'improve' the young.

The other big objection to television is that it inculcates the 'wrong' values. Politicians like to blame it for violent behaviour; teachers for bad language. Bad language is the commonest cause of adult complaints to both the BBC and ITV – yet research for the Broadcasting Standards Council this year concluded that teenagers were much more offended by the sight of horses injured in the Grand National or by racism.

American studies have suggested that television is responsible for both violent behaviour and fear of crime, but America is a much more violent society than Britain, with more violence on television, and far fewer programmes made specifically for children. Other research suggests that a violent personality comes first, and leads to a taste for violent programmes. Also, Japanese television has a great deal of crime and violence in it, yet research shows that children in Japan are less aggressive than those in other countries.

A Leicester University study found that nearly half of mothers actively encouraged their children to watch television, and in another study mothers listed some of the things they thought their children learnt from television: numbers, letters and shapes, songs and rhymes, vocabulary, imaginative play, general knowledge, concentration, craft activities, games.

All this is not to say that television is always beneficial, nor that watching all day, every day would be desirable. But television is not a drug: significantly, children's viewing figures are halved in the summer. If they seem to be watching too much, it would be worth asking what else is on offer. And just as programmes featuring kindness and unselfishness cannot compensate for growing up in a brutal and violent household, neither can violent programmes override decency and good manners in a household in which these attributes are constantly valued and practised.

Dr Messenger Davies says that television "informs children; it helps to structure their lives; it gives them common interests with their friends and other members of the family; it provides an occasion for family togetherness, discussion, and sometimes argument. Above all, children use television primarily as entertainment – a valuable and valued form of leisure-time activity which they can choose to do or not to do."

ASSIGNMENT

You have been asked to write a contribution to a collection of articles, addressed to parents, about the effects of the media on children. You can choose to write about either the good influence of television or the bad influence. Your article should be between 350 to 500 words. Use the passage above to get some ideas.

Guidelines *Writing an article*

- List all the points in the article which show that television is a bad influence.

- List all the points which show that television is not a bad influence.

- What point does the writer make about the connection between TV and violence in the paragraph about American and Japanese TV?

- Add further points, ideas and examples of your own. Decide which side you want to present.

- Select the points you will use. Look at each one and think how you can present it convincingly. You could:
    explain it and give reasons for it;
    give examples from your experience;
    give examples from other people's experience;
    give examples from what you may have read or heard discussed.

- Organise your points into paragraphs. Group together similar ideas and decide on the best order.

- The first paragraph will be the introductory paragraph. Make it clear what the article is about. Try to think of an opening sentence that will catch the interest of your readers.

Example 'Television has been called a drug – but don't worry, it is not harmful, and may actually do your children good!'

or

'What would you say is the most harmful drug available to your children? I think it's television.'

- In the second paragraph, make your first point and back it up with explanation, comment and example.

- In paragraphs three to five start each new paragraph with a main point which adds to your argument. Begin each one with a phrase like:

'Another point is that...'

or

'My third reason for warning you...'

- Your last paragraph should summarise what you feel the article has said.

- Read through your first draft and ask yourself:

Is the argument clear?
Have I shown that each new paragraph is making a new point?
Are all the points clear and easy to understand?
Have I used appropriate language, bearing in mind the audience and the purpose of the article?
Are the spelling, punctuation and grammar as accurate as I can make them?

You could ask a friend to read it through with you to see if it's clear and to check for mistakes.

- Now write the final version.

Punctuation Mark

Full stops

The full stop is used to indicate the end of a sentence.

Look at these examples from the article you have just read.

'The other big objection to television is that it inculcates the 'wrong' values.'

'Other research suggests that a violent personality comes first, and leads to a taste for violent programmes.'

Sometimes it shows that a word has been abbreviated.

Example	Wed. (Wednesday), I.o.W. (Isle of Wight)
Exceptions	An abbreviation does not need a full stop if:
	a) it is made up entirely of capital letters;

Example	BBC ITV
	b) it ends with the last letter of the word which is being abbreviated.
Example	Mr Dr

SELF CHECK

1 Insert full stops and capital letters where appropriate in the following sentences.

Television's role is very important it is a major force it is up to us how we use it. Television is widely used as a sedative I have seen it turned on early in the morning for very young children turning the set on to quieten them down is commonplace

2 Think of six abbreviations which do not need full stops.

a

Broadcast news

International, national and local news is broadcast on television throughout the day. What is news? Who decides what are the most and the least important items? What is the main purpose of television news? How are different items presented?

ASSIGNMENT

1 You can do this activity by yourself or with a group.

(a) Divide up the four main TV channels so that someone takes BBC1, someone takes ITV, someone takes BBC2 and someone takes Channel 4.

(b) Watch the same day's evening news broadcast and as you watch make notes on how the news is presented. You could use this chart to help you.

News item	Studio/film report	Interviews	Your comments
1			
2			
3			
4			
5			
etc.			

(c) Compare your findings. Jot down your responses to the following questions.

Were there significant differences in the items and the order in which they were presented?
Which items do you think were dealt with most effectively?
Which items do you think were dealt with least effectively?
Did you learn anything from the news programme?
Did it make you think about any issue?
Did any part of it entertain you?

(d) Devise a chart to show your findings. On the chart you need to show the four channels, the range of aspects on which you are assessing them (use your chart and the points for discussion above) and a system (such as numbers of stars or ticks) to show how each channel performed in each category.

2 Your group has to choose the items and write the script for a three minute national news bulletin. You have to choose six

items from the following ten and decide the order in which they should go and the number of seconds each should have. The items are given to you in note form for you to turn into appropriate sentences for the script.

a) Murderer, born in Britain, due to be executed in the USA next week. Was condemned in 1983 for shooting and killing middle-aged man in course of robbery. Reprieve requested by lawyers. Prime Minister asked to intervene.

b) Princess Diana on skiing holiday with sons – complained about photographers – intrusion of privacy.

c) Safebury- giant supermarket chain – closing 17 stores. Hundreds of jobs will be lost. Just announced – details to follow.

d) Two Tory MPs suspended for receiving payment in return for asking questions on payers' behalf in House of Commons.

e) Spanish Prime Minister thrown out fisheries deal drawn up by EU and Canada. Canada recently seized Spanish trawler fishing in international waters. Accused Spain of overfishing and endangering species.

f) Great-grandmother from Luton celebrated 100th birthday with train ride through Channel Tunnel. Thoroughly enjoyed it.

g) 10-year-old girl, child B, (the child's real name cannot be used and in all reporting she should be referred to as 'Child B') being treated for leukaemia doing well after operation. Anonymous donor paid for treatment. Has slim chance of survival.

h) Policeman shot in stomach – west London – happened during routine enquiry. Stable after surgery. Age 27, has been in police force 18 months.

i) Passenger train in Chile crashed killing six people and injuring 15. Two Britons thought to be among injured.

j) Romanian airbus crashed killing 60 passengers. Crash could have been caused by explosion.

 When the script is finished, read it in what you judge to be an appropriate tone and at an appropriate pace. You may find that after your first reading you need to change some expressions which do not sound right. Make any necessary changes until you are satisfied, and tape the final version.

Points of view

Television critics sometimes agree about the programmes they review, but just as often they have widely differing opinions. Here are two reviews of the first ever *The Big Breakfast* on Channel 4.

No appetite for a breakfast with Bob

The short history of breakfast television has demonstrated that the very name is a contradiction in terms. At this time of day we are attempting, most of us, to get up and get out. Thus is radio the obvious, logical, backdrop - and thus does *The Big Breakfast* attempt to sell itself as 'radio TV'. The term comes from the press release, a ghastly mix of pretentious nonsense and ludicrous imagery: "This is a show that curdles your milk and sends your fried eggs running for their shells."

That is at least fair preparation for the programme itself, a ghastly mix of pretentious nonsense and ludicrous imagery. Channel 4 is rightly committed to the pursuance of minority audiences, but how large a minority do the terminally moronic constitute?

The show is set not in a studio but in three east London lockkeeper's cottages which have been knocked into one. The result is the pre-existing three breakfast shows, knocked into one. The colours are primary - yellow, red, blue - on the presumed argument that at 7 am we need cheering up.

Naturally the presenters are horribly cheerful. They banter back and forth with the crew, the crew throws things at them. The news comes every 20 minutes, no more than 10 seconds per story, nothing (yesterday) foreign.

There are cartoons: boy, are there cartoons. There is a competition: 'Whose washing line is it anyway?' Five items are hung on the line and people call in to guess to whom they might belong. Yesterday they belonged to Kylie Minogue.

Shortly after 8 am comes Bob Geldof. He describes what he has seen so far as 'rubbish', and I am not here to disagree with him. We cut to the first of Geldof's much-hyped interviews, to be shown in segments of a couple of minutes down the week. Paul Keating, the Australian prime minister, talks to Geldof about putting his arm around the Queen - he says that he didn't. And about being a republican - he says he is.

Keating, in fact, says nothing new to Geldof, who has shaved for his live appearance on the programme but not for his recorded interview with Keating. Old Bob,

so perverse, dontcha love him? Shortly afterwards, Bob's wife Paula Yates arrives to interview Joanna Lumley, for a reason I now forget.

Breakfast television has been on a slippery slope. I had thought Roland Rat marked the bottom. Not quite.

Peter Barnard, *The Times*

ASSIGNMENT

By yourself, or in pairs or small groups, can you sum up what Peter Barnard disliked about the programme? Pick out any words and phrases that you feel convey his feelings effectively.

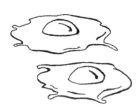

Bright young things for breakfast

Channel 4's *The Big Breakfast* is vibrant to the point of pain. Even the decor is high decibel. Not everybody is ready for fried eggs on the wall at 7 am. The colour is like catching your head between a couple of cymbals. Anyone under 25 will love it.

Bob Geldof, whose production company makes the show, is a notoriously late riser himself, but for *The Big Breakfast*'s big day he stole in from the garden like a cartoon wolf and silently loped off, all legs and black leather. If he wasn't the boss, you'd have said he was the burglar. Perhaps because of this early rising bleariness, he has adopted an oh-what-the-hell-with-it style of shaving, which leaves designer tufts here and there. Looking as if he had spent the night under Sydney Bridge, he interviewed Paul Keating, Prime Minister of Australia, who undoubtedly fancies himself a bit of a wild colonial boy but beside Geldof looked as flash as a rat with a gold tooth.

The first programme was effervescent and cheerfully chaotic. Presenters tended to get hit by flying objects, even a candy floss pink Paula Yates, who deftly made the first page of *The Sun* ("TV Paula's Licence Dodge Charge"). And far be it from me to hint at anything in the nature of a stunt here.

Among the flying fish and fried eggs and wacky faxes, Gaby Roslin sort of interviewed Kiranjit Ahluwalia ("You then set fire to your husband, didn't you?"). Until this minute I didn't think it was possible to be too young.

Among the celebratory faxes there was a warning from TV-am "Good luck. You'll need it." *The Big Breakfast Show* will be in competition with GMTV, which takes over TV-am's franchise next year.

Nancy Banks-Smith, *The Guardian*

ASSIGNMENT

By yourself, or in pairs or small groups, pick out any words or phrases from Nancy Banks-Smith's review which suggest enjoyment. Can you find two comparisons she uses, not necessarily ones to convey enjoyment?

ASSIGNMENT

1 Both reviewers comment on some of the same aspects of the programme. Under the following headings, by yourself or in pairs or small groups, pick out the words and phrases they use, comment on their effect and explain what they tell us about the writer's feelings.

Audience	Colour	Bob Geldof's appearance	Interviews	Paula Yates

Example Under 'audience' you could note that Peter Barnard uses the phrase 'terminally moronic' and Nancy Banks-Smith says 'Anyone under twenty-five will love it'. What does this suggest about each writer's attitude to the programme?

2 Choose a programme you strongly like or strongly dislike. Write 300 words about the programme making your views quite clear. (If you're working in a group you could team up with someone who holds the opposite view of the same programme and compare your reviews.)

Language link

Similes

'He stole in from the garden like a cartoon wolf'.

This kind of comparison is known as a simile. A simile is a comparison which is introduced with the words 'like' or 'as'.

We often use similes in everyday conversation. 'His wit is as sharp as a razor.' 'She was as quiet as a mouse.'

Writers use similes to make us see what they are describing in a fresh way. The picture the comparison gives us helps to make the meaning clearer or more lively.

In the example, the writer compares Bob Geldof to a cartoon wolf.
What does a wolf in a cartoon look like?
How would it move into view?
What feelings are associated with it?
How is a cartoon wolf different from a real one?
What kind of movement does the word 'stole' suggest?

SELF CHECK

1 Write a sentence commenting on the effect of the simile you have just looked at.

(You could begin "This simile is effective because it makes you see....)

2 Make up similes of your own to complete the following sentences:
She was as disappointed as someone who.........
He was a pleased as someone who.......
He slunk into the room like....
The room was as crowded as....

Spelling check

Adjectives to adverbs

The *Big Breakfast* presenters were called 'horribly' cheerful. 'Horribly' is an adverb (a word which describes how something is done) formed from the adjective (a word which describes what something is like) 'horrible'.

There are some spelling rules to follow when you turn adjectives into adverbs.

a) To turn an adjective into an adverb add 'ly' to the adjective.

Examples rough + ly = roughly
clever + ly = cleverly
final + ly = finally

Exceptions due + ly = duly
true + ly = truly
whole+ ly = wholly

b) When the adjective ends in a consonant and 'le', change the final 'e' to 'y'.

Examples noticeable = noticeably
subtle = subtly

c) When the adjective ends in a consonant and 'y' change the 'y' to 'i' and add 'ly'.

Examples icy = icily
grubby = grubbily

d) When the adjective ends in 'ic' add 'ally'.

Examples emphatic + ally = emphatically

Exception publicly

THE TELEPHONE CALL

This poem tells a story about someone receiving a telephone call telling them they have won a lottery.

They asked me 'Are you sitting down?
Right? This is Universal Lotteries,'
'You've won the top prize,

the Ultra-super Global Special.
What would you do with a million pounds?
Or, actually, with more than a million –
not that it makes a lot of difference
once you're a millionaire.' And they laughed.

Are you OK?' they asked – 'Still there?
Come on, now, tell us, how does it feel?'
I said 'I just...I can't believe it!'
They said 'That's what they all say.
What else? Go on, tell us about it.'
I said 'I feel the top of my head
has floated off, out through the window,
revolving like a flying saucer.'

'That's unusual.' They said. 'Go on.'
I said 'I'm finding it hard to talk.
My throat's gone dry, my nose is tingling.
I think I'm going to sneeze – or cry.'
That's right,' they said. 'don't be ashamed
of giving way to your emotions.
It isn't every day you hear
you're going to get a million pounds.

Relax, now, have a little cry;
we'll give you a moment...' 'Hang on!' I said.
'I haven't bought a lottery ticket
for years and years. And what did you say
the company's called?' They laughed again.
'Not to worry about a ticket.
We're Universal. We operate
a Retrospective Chances Module.

Nearly everyone's bought a ticket
in some lottery or another,
once at least. We buy up the files,
feed the names into our computer,
and see who the lucky person is.'
'Well, that's incredible.' I said.
'It's marvellous. I still can't quite...
I'll believe it when I see the cheque.'

'Oh,' they said, 'there's no cheque.'
'But the money?' 'We don't deal in money.

Experiences are what we deal in.
You've had a great experience, right?
Exciting? Something you'll remember?
That's your prize. So congratulations
from all of us at Universal.
Have a nice day!' And the line went dead.

© Fleur Adcock 1986. Reprinted from *The Incident Room*
by Fleur Adcock, 1986, by permission of Oxford
University Press

ASSIGNMENT

 1 Work on the poem in pairs. Some of you are going to record the poem, so that only the voices will be heard, and the others will act it out, using movement and maybe props to create a setting. Whichever version you are going to present, it will help you to think about the following points:

(a) The person making the phone call

What kind of voice is it?
Does it change throughout the poem?

Here are some words which might describe the caller's tone of voice at different points:

bright	dignified	understanding	encouraging
cheerful	probing	explaining	joking

Add your own words, and decide how the caller's lines will be spoken.

(b) The person receiving the phone call

What kind of person is she or he?
What kind of voice is it?
Where are there changes of feeling in the poem?

Here are some words which might describe this character's voice at different points:

hesitant	excited	disappointed	angry
disbelieving	grateful	cautious	tense

Add your own words, and describe how the person's lines will be spoken.

(c) The setting and background

What is the person doing when the phone rings?
What time of day is it?
How does she or he react when the phone rings?
What kind of room is it?
What kind of actions might accompany the different feelings?

2 Practise your presentation of the poem and when you are ready, either read it with actions for the rest of the group, or play them your recorded version.

3 Discuss the different effects created by the reading and the dramatised reading. Which did you find more successful?

Language link

Words ending in 'ce' and 'se'

You have just been asked to 'practise' your presentation.

Words such as practice and practise, advise and advise, are sometimes confused.

(a) Remember that 'ice' is used for nouns.

Examples   I received sound advice about my career.
Regular practice of scales has helped to improve my piano playing.

(b) Remember that 'ise' is used for verbs.

Examples   I advise you to think carefully before making a decision.
If you practise regularly your performance will improve.

SELF CHECK

Which is the correct word to use in these sentences?

1 It is time to renew my television licence/license.

2 I was asked to devise/device a new schedule.

Winners and losers

Six out of ten people play the national lottery and a handful have become millionaires. The lottery has become a part of our lives in the mid-nineties and is a topic of conversation all over the country in all walks of life.

Read the following statistics and comments.

Sales exceeded £1 for every UK citizen in the lottery's first ten weeks.

It is estimated 58 % will play every week and a further 6 % at least once a month. The average spend is £2.08 per head.

Two groups with relatively high incomes, the 25 to 34 pre-family group and the 45 to 59 post-family group, will become key to the lottery's success.

Before the lottery there were 15 million regular gamblers in the UK. Now there are 25 million.

The lottery has created up to 12 million new shopping trips each week; sales in shops with terminals are up 20 per cent.

Foodstores have gained 5000 customers per week; confectionery, tobacconists, newsagents and convenience stores 2700.

Saturday night TV-viewing has risen by 20 per cent because of the BBC1 draw programme.

Pools firm takings have fallen by 10 to 15 per cent a week and Saturday bingo attendances are down.

Charities expect donations to drop by £172 million.

Source: Lottery Fallout (Henley Centre and GAH Partnership)

I think the lottery is good because it raises money for the arts.

I think gambling is wrong, so I won't take part.

I wouldn't bet on a horse that was 14 million to one, so I certainly wouldn't bet on the lottery!

The lottery exploits the working-class and they don't realise it. The money is in the hands of the elite.

It's good fun gives you something to hope for. After all, someone's got to win!

I do it every week without fail. If I won, all my problems would be over.

ASSIGNMENT

1 From the statistics and the quotations, make notes under these headings:

Good things about the lottery	Bad things about the lottery

2 Using these ideas and your own views, write 300 to 350 words giving your opinion of the national lottery.

"I inherited £100,000!"

Charlotte's story

I was really looking forward to my 18th birthday because my mum and dad had said I could have a party at our house and they'd never let me before. As my birthday fell on a Saturday mum said she'd take me shopping during the day to buy me something to wear that evening. It was going to be such a cool day.

When I woke up I went downstairs and mum had laid out this breakfast with champagne and smoked salmon bagels, which I love. As well as mum and dad, my brother and my gran, who had been staying with us for a while, were there too. When I'd finished opening my presents, my gran gave me a card. But when I opened the envelope I realised it was a cheque - and it was made out for £100,000!

I remember I had a mouthful of bagel at the time and it just stuck in my throat. I looked at gran and she just smiled at me like she'd given me a jumper, like it was nothing. I looked at everyone else and could tell from their faces that they had no idea I was getting this cheque. When I told them what it was my dad looked really shocked and my brother started jumping about the place but my mum was very quiet.

I didn't know what to do then because I couldn't believe what was happening. Gran told me she'd already put the money in a special account for me and the cheque was just for show. My brother was to get the same when he was 18 too. I tried to get gran to take the money back, but it just felt pathetic. It's not as if she'd done it lightly. You don't hand over £100,000 to someone without really thinking about it.

I wanted to ask gran where she'd got the money because she had never seemed that rich to me. I suppose I knew she was quite well off because she'd inherited quite a bit from her father and my uncle too. He was single and had done really well for himself, and had made everything out to her before dying suddenly.

It might sound strange to some people, but the money really freaked me out. I never once thought "Whoopee, I'm rich!" like I thought I would when I've daydreamed about having lots of money. I go to a private school but only because my dad teaches there and the fees are subsidised, otherwise my parents couldn't afford it. The school's only small and there aren't any millionaires' daughters there, so it isn't like I'm used to the high-life or anything.

When I went shopping with mum later on that day I tried to talk to her about it but she wasn't keen because she's always had a difficult relationship with gran.

Gran's always given us a lot of attention and presents but she's never really done that for mum, even though she's her own daughter. I felt as though she was somehow trying to get one up on mum by giving me the money.

At my party I didn't tell anyone about the money. I put it to the back of my mind and pretended I was poor like everyone else! Most of the money has just sat in a bank account since then - in fact, apart from buying a new stereo and a new bed, I haven't touched it - but I suppose I'll use some when I go to university. Even now nobody knows about it apart from my family. I suppose I'm afraid my friends would treat me differently if they knew.

Mum and dad have told me I should buy a house with the money but they've never given me any other advice. Gran never mentions it either. I often think about giving loads away to charity, but I worry about what my mum and dad would say.

I've decided I want to go travelling when I'm a bit older so I could use some of it then. I suppose I'll be glad of it when I have a family and need to buy somewhere to live but I try not to think about it now. It's already turned me off bagels! Somehow the money seems more like a curse because I know it's upset my mum and I feel strange about spending it anyway."

Mizz : Reader's True Experience

ASSIGNMENT

1 Write your responses to the following questions.

(a) What do you learn from the article about Charlotte, her family and her way of life?

(b) How has the money changed Charlotte's life?

(c) Do you agree that it seems like a curse?

(d) What examples can you find to show that Charlotte was telling her story, rather than writing it? (Think about the kinds of expressions and words we use when we are talking which would not be appropriate in formal writing.)

2 Imagine that you have inherited or won £100,000! Write between 300 to 500 words describing your reaction and the way you think the money will change your life. You could begin as Charlotte did, establishing something about yourself and what you are doing when you receive the news.

Nouns

Nouns are naming words. They name:

	Example
physical objects you can touch	chair
people	woman
places	town
collections of animals, people or things	herd, class, bunch
feelings and emotions	love
ideas you understand with your mind	science
names of actions	decision

Real names such as Asia, John Brown, Edinburgh Castle are called 'proper nouns' and have capital letters. So do the names of books, plays, films, songs, television programmes.

SELF CHECK

(a) Find as many nouns as you can from 'Charlotte's Story' to fit the above categories.
(b) Write down three nouns naming things you can touch.
(c) Write down three nouns naming places.
(d) Write down three nouns naming collections of people or animals.
(e) Write down three nouns naming things you can see but not touch.
(f) Write down three nouns naming things you can hear but not touch.

More suggestions for coursework

- Write a story in which gambling plays an important part.
- Write a story about someone who wins the national lottery.

In the ring

Boxing is a sport which has attracted much controversy in recent years. Here are comments from three different newspapers about a boxing match in which one of the participants almost died, and a song about a boxer who did die.

Passage A

The Sun says

The cry went up almost as Gerald McClellan went down on the canvas.

Ban boxing! It's too dangerous!

Doctors have known for decades that the noble art can cause serious damage to the brain. The fighters understand the risks, too.

But the fear of injury, or even death, has to be put aside.

To them it is a job, a way of life. Of course it is brutal and cruel – few of us would dare try it. But we must never forget that no one forces them to box.

They do it for the money.

What happened to Gerald McClellan is a tragedy – just as it was for Michael Watson and Bradley Stone.

But there was no clamour to ban motor racing after Ayrton Senna died. How many jockeys are seriously injured falling off horses? How many rugby players are paralysed with broken necks? Why should boxing be banned when all those sports continue?

You cannot nanny people, however tragic the consequences of their actions might be.

ASSIGNMENT

1 Does the writer think that boxing is a dangerous sport? Pick out the words and phrases which show his opinion. (Begin: 'The writer does/does not think that boxing is dangerous. This is clear from/He says that....)

2 What does the writer say about boxers' reasons for fighting?

3 Does the writer think boxing should be banned? What reason does he give?

Passage B

Today comment

From the very start, the odds were that the Nigel Benn-Gerald McClellan fight was a tragedy waiting to happen.

Two of the most aggressive boxers in the business – and it is a business – were matched in a championship fight with a fortune at stake for them, the promoters, big money punters and future television fees.

The hype verged on the hysterical well before Saturday. McClellan, with a record of putting down his opponents in early rounds, was predicting a win in round three. Benn, desperate to defend and enhance his reputation as the Dark Destroyer, was saying he would win in a later round.

All that was guaranteed to produce a bloody fight. Add to it the hysteria of fans on the night and it is no surprise that it was the most brutal and frenzied for many years.

McClellan's terrible injuries have led to renewed and understandable calls for boxing to be banned. That is not the answer. Boxing is indisputably dangerous, and sometimes deadly.

But a ban would drive it underground.

The yearning of young men for fame and fortune they could not achieve elsewhere, the spice of illegal matches and heavy betting would ensure its survival. Rules governing boxing, protection which can be given and medical help which is at hand would disappear. There would be far more tragedies.

McClellan was half an hour from death on Saturday night. Without the skill of medical teams at the ringside and waiting in hospital, he would have died then.

But there could be one extra medical check. Boxers can show signs of distress a referee may not see or, within the rules, act upon. Boxing authorities should urgently consider ensuring that doctors check each man between every round for any distress.

Nobody can know whether such a system would have saved McClellan but it could undoubtedly protect boxers in the future.

ASSIGNMENT

1 Does the writer think that boxing is a dangerous sport? Pick out the words and phrases which show his opinion.

2 What does the writer say about the boxers' reasons for fighting?

3 Does the writer think boxing should be banned? What reason does he give?

4 The writer suggests a way to give boxers more protection. What is it?

Passage C

The Guardian: Comment

Ignore the undisputed medical evidence on the damage which boxing wreaks. Consider instead what the sport's aficionados were saying yesterday. Even the boxing correspondents were finding it hard to defend the game at the end of the Benn v McClellan fight – the last in a long line to end in a hospital with one of the fighters on a life support machine. Hugh McIlvanney asked whether "any of us outside the ropes deserve to ask so much of the men inside".

Britain's boxing rules have been tightened for over 300 years since the first bare-knuckle fight was recorded. Yet the sport continues to produce pain, permanent injury and death. Every precaution was taken before this fight: five doctors by the ringside including specialists in resuscitation, two teams of paramedics, two ambulances plus key surgeons at one of the country's top neurological hospitals on standby. The speed with which the medics worked undoubtedly avoided an immediate death. Boxing promoters and medics continue to learn lessons, but they will never be able to avoid deaths and permanent brain damage while the sport continues.

There are many more dangerous sports than boxing like rock climbing, motor racing and rugby. Ten climbers in the Scottish highlands alone have died this winter. Moreover, unlike boxers, climbers put rescuers' lives at risk. Yet there is a unique difference between boxing and other sports: the main purpose of boxing is to inflict pain and injury. People who try this in rugby – by stamping or gouging – get sent off. Boxing continues to ignore the longterm brain damage that its followers suffer. Boxing should not be allowed to ignore the victims who do not die from a dramatic blow in the ring but are permanently damaged over the longterm.

Boxing's dwindling band of defenders claims it would go underground if banned. That is always possible, but it hasn't happened in Sweden. The same argument was used against banning bear-baiting, cock-fights and bare-knuckle boxing. None of these is thriving now. Boxing remains a brutal sport that degrades not just the combatants but the spectators too. A civilised society would insist it was stopped.

ASSIGNMENT

1 Does the writer think that boxing is a dangerous sport? Pick out the words and phrases which show his opinion.

2 Does the writer think boxing should be banned? What reason does he give?

ASSIGNMENT

Passages A to C

In passage A the writer points out that there is no pressure to ban other dangerous sports. What point does passage C make about this?

b) In passage B the writer says that a ban would drive boxing underground. What two points does passage C make about this?

c) Passage A calls boxing 'the noble art', passage C calls it 'a brutal sport'. Think of as many points as you can to support each description:

noble art	brutal sport

Newspaper articles, campaigns and television appearances are some of the ways people make their feelings heard. Another way is through poetry and song. Here is a poem by Bob Dylan about a boxer called Davey Moore who was knocked out by Sugar Ramos on March 23 1963 and died two days later without regaining consciousness.

Who Killed Davey Moore?

Who killed Davey Moore,
Why an' what's the reason for?

"Not I," says the referee,
"Don't point your finger at me.
I could've stopped it in the eighth
An' maybe kept him from his fate,
But the crowd would've booed I'm sure,
At not getting their money's worth,
It's too bad he had to go,
But there was a pressure on me too, you know.
It wasn't me that made him fall,
No, you can't blame me at all."

Who killed Davey Moore,
Why an' what's the reason for?

"Not us," says the angry crowd,
Whose screams filled the arena loud.
"It's too bad he died that night
But we just like to see a fight.

We didn't mean for him to meet his death'
We just meant to see some sweat,
There ain't nothing wrong in that.
It wasn't us that made him fall.
No, you can't blame us at all."
Who killed Davey Moore,
Why an' what's the reason for?

"Not me," says his manager,
Puffing on a big cigar.
"It's hard to say, it's hard to tell,
I always thought that he was well.
It's too bad for his wife an' kids he's dead,
But if he was sick, he should've said.
It wasn't me that made him fall.
No, you can't blame me at all.

Who killed Davey Moore,
Why an' what's the reason for?

"Not me," says the boxing writer,
Pounding print on his old typewriter,
Saying," Boxing ain't to blame,
There's just as much danger in a football game."
Saying,"Fist fighting is here to stay,
It's just the old American way,
It wasn't me that made him fall.
No, you can't blame me at all."

Who killed Davey Moore,
Why an' what's the reason for?
"Not me," says the man whose fists
Laid him low in a cloud of mist,
Who came here from Cuba's door
Where boxing ain't allowed no more.
"I hit him, yes it's true,
But that's what I am paid to do.
Don't say "murder" don't say "kill".
It was destiny, it was God's will.

Who killed Davey Moore,
Why an' what's the reason for?

Bob Dylan

ASSIGNMENT

1 Does the writer actually state in the song what he thinks of boxing?

2 How does he make his feelings clear?

3 Look at the people in the song who justify their positions. What do you think of the excuses each one gives? Are they the same people who were referred to in the newspaper comments?

4 In the song these people appear to 'speak'. What is the effect of this?

5 The same question is asked throughout the song. Does the song suggest an answer? What do you think the answer is?

ASSIGNMENT

1 Using the points from the passages and your own ideas, write 350 to 500 words giving your own views on whether boxing should be banned.

2 A local hall stages boxing matches regularly and they are very popular. A group of people opposed to boxing starts a campaign to get them stopped. Imagine that you are either one of that group or one of the supporters of the matches. Design a leaflet which gives your group's point of view in order to get support.

Guidelines *Writing a leaflet*

Title
Think of an eye-catching title which makes clear what the campaign is about. Choose a name for the campaign. You might be able to think of a good slogan.

Audience
Remember who you are writing for. In this case, you will be handing out leaflets to people going to watch the matches and to passers-by.

Content
You have limited space so decide which are the crucial points you want to include. Try to have a mixture of facts, examples and

proposals. Make it clear how you want the reader to support you – by signing a petition, or writing to an MP.

Structure
Organise your leaflet carefully. Divide the content into clear sections, with an introduction, main section and conclusion. The introduction should make the point of the campaign clear. The main section should give the reasons for the campaign and say what the campaign wants to happen. The conclusion sums up the argument and says what the reader could do to help.

Style
A leaflet is designed to be read quickly, so do not include too many words. Choose words which are hard-hitting and catch the attention and interest of the audience. You could use some phrases from the articles you've read.

3 You are going to present a talk show on the subject of boxing and you will need to be in groups of about ten people.

(a) Choose four people to lead the discussion.

(b) One person will be the presenter. It's her or his job to invite people to speak, to draw them out if they are hesitant, to stop them if they go on too long and to make sure everyone in the audience has a chance to contribute. This is the person who opens the show by welcoming the audience, saying what the subject of discussion is and introducing the main speakers, and who closes it at the end.

(c) Three others will be 'experts', or people with very strong views on the subject who are prepared to give their views and defend them. You could have someone acting the part of a boxer, or perhaps someone could be a relative of a fighter who has been injured.

(d) The rest of the group will be the audience. The presenter will ask you individually to speak. You can ask questions or give your own views.

(e) Arrange the room so that the panel is sitting at the front and the rest of the group is in a semi-circle facing them. The presenter should open the show from the front and then move into the audience as people put up their hands to speak.

(f) The presenter should open the show and ask each of the panel in turn to state their point of view. The audience are then invited to make contributions.

More suggestions for coursework

- Do you think competitive sport should be compulsory in schools? Write 350 to 500 words giving your opinion and the reasons for it. If you prefer you could have a debate or a discussion on the subject.

-

Write a story in which a sports player has a leading role. It could be about a tennis player desperate to win a championship, or about bribery in the sport you choose, or about an athlete being tested for drugs....

- A friend who is very good at a certain sport is thinking of taking it up professionally. Write the conversation you have when you discuss the decision.

Saturday night

Saturday night is traditionally thought of as a night for going out and having fun. Here is a short play about what happens when Donna and Toby spend Saturday evening together.

TOBY AND DONNA

SCENE ONE

(Night. Just before eleven o'clock. A quiet street. TOBY and DONNA, waiting for the bus.)

DONNA: We were standing at the bus stop, and I was looking down the road and thinking that if you could go drinking, there were places you could go while late on a Saturday night, when Toby said –

TOBY: You've missed it.

DONNA: I haven't. It doesn't come while five to.

TOBY: Gone that.

DONNA: It hasn't.

But of course he has to check on his digital watch that lights up in the dark.

TOBY: Four minutes to. I tell you, it's gone early. They do, Saturday nights, so they don't have to pick up drunks coming out at closing time.

DONNA: Give it a bit longer.

·So he walks about a bit, kicking at stones and stuff and I watched for the bus. I didn't want it to have gone.

(Pause)

TOBY: I'm bored.

DONNA: You're always bored.

TOBY: Not my fault.

DONNA: He is always bored, Toby. He's always wanting to be doing something different. He's the sort that turns the telly over before the programme's finished, just because he's sick of watching that side.

TOBY: I'm going.

DONNA: I didn't want him to go. it's lonely by yourself at that bus stop. Trees and stuff. Houses miles from the road.

I'm cold.

I thought that might make him cuddle me, but he kept his hands in his pockets.

TOBY: Why don't you come back then, if you're cold?

DONNA: I'm catching the bus.

TOBY: I'm going.

DONNA: Don't.

TOBY: What's the point freezing, waiting for a bus that's gone?

DONNA: You said, when we first went out, that you'd always see me
home.

TOBY: Yeah, well...

DONNA: I made him promise because it isn't always nice for girls on
the street at night, but boys don't seem to realise that.
Well what?

TOBY: You might have said it were a lousy bus route where you
lived.

DONNA: 'Tis from your house. Not from anywhere else. You
promised.

TOBY: Wouldn't have, if I'd known.

DONNA: It's horrible, waiting at this stop by myself.

TOBY: If you come up, me dad'll take you when they get back.

DONNA: But I knew his dad had gone out drinking.
He'll have had a few. I'm not driving with him.

TOBY: My mum'll be okay. She's driving him. She'll drop you back.

DONNA: Will she?

TOBY: Yes.

DONNA: Sure?

TOBY: Yes. She will. You know she will. She always offers. She
doesn't like you going home by yourself, you know that.

DONNA: I wouldn't have to go home by myself, if you took me.

TOBY: She'll take you.

DONNA: His mum, Debra, she does always offer. Sometimes I let her
take me. She talks to me on the way home and it's a bit
embarrassing. My mum doesn't ask me the sort of questions Debra
does and she's the one that's supposed to. Toby's mum asks me
things like 'Do you know how to take care of yourself?" – things like
that. And other things about sex. It's embarrassing when you don't
hardly know somebody. She once told me why she'd been married
four years before she had Toby's brother. She said, first there was the
Berlin Wall and then there was Cuba and that's why her generation
took to the Pill the way they did. I thought she was going to ask me
about contraception and then she asked me if I thought I was going
to die in my bed and I said that depended if they dropped the atomic
bomb while I were asleep.

(Pause)

I felt a bit silly after saying that. She didn't say anything else 'til we
got to my house. There's three boys in their family. She doesn't know
about girls. She asks me to try and find out. Half the time I never
know what to tell her.

Will you come with us when she takes me?

TOBY: Yes. I'm going. You coming or staying?

DONNA: Don't have much choice, do I?

TOBY: You wanted to see to the end of the film. If we'd watched the football, you could have caught the ten o'clock.

DONNA: If you'd watched the football, I'd have got the eight o'clock.

(Pause)

DONNA: He walked right up to me to kiss me.

(Clock begins to strike eleven.)

You know I don't like it in the street.

TOBY: Goodnight kiss.

(They kiss)

DONNA: He does kiss nice.

(The clock stops)

I must have missed it.

TOBY: Told you that ages ago.

DONNA: Might as well come up to your house then, mightn't I?

TOBY: Come on, then.

DONNA: What time your mum and dad coming in?

(They start to go)

TOBY: Not late.

DONNA: I'll have to telephone.

They don't wait up in our house, not like some parents. My dad leaves this alarm clock in the hall. it's set for half-past midnight. If we're not in by then to turn it off, it wakes him and there's hell to pay. My sister goes in, turns it off, and goes out again. It's okay for her. There's loads of places she can go. Clubs and that.

SCENE TWO

(TOBY's home. Kettle is whistling. DONNA is dialling her home.)

DONNA: (as she dials) I tell them if I'm going to be late. Saves arguing with them later.

(Phone is answered.)

It's Donna, dad. I'm at Toby's. The bus never came. We did. We waited ages. His mum'll bring me up when she gets home. She always offers. Yes. He says they'll be in by half past.

Yes. Okay. You know I always take enough money for a taxi. Okay. Bye.

(Phone down)

TOBY: Your coffee.

DONNA: Ta. He says, if it gets to after twelve, I'm to take a taxi. They'll be in by then, won't they?

TOBY: Probably. You didn't want sugar, did you?

DONNA: No. I didn't know you could make coffee.

TOBY: Why not?

DONNA: Haven't ever seen you, that's all.

TOBY: Never given me the chance.

DONNA: You didn't offer when I was getting up and down in the middle of the film.

TOBY: It was the ads.

DONNA: Never time to boil a kettle during the ads. You always miss the first bit after.

TOBY: You kept saying, "Shall I make a coffee?"

DONNA: Didn't notice you offering.

TOBY: Didn't want one.

DONNA: You drank them.

TOBY: Only because you'd made them.

DONNA: I didn't want them neither. Me dad says to my mum, "Put the kettle on, lass". They have a cup of tea nearly every break. Mum keeps saying she's going to bring the tea things in the lounge. Me dad says the pile'll come out of the carpet if it gets boiling water on it. He doesn't ever make his own.

TOBY: I'm really domestic. I can make omelettes and stuff, you know.

DONNA: You've never made me one.

TOBY: Didn't know you wanted one. Make you one now, if you like.

DONNA: This is fine, thanks.

(She drinks her coffee.)

TOBY: It's proper coffee, you know.

DONNA: It was nice coffee. Hot milk and everything. I knew he was trying to be nice to me.

          It's okay.

(They sip)

TOBY: I'd like to be a chef.

DONNA: You what?

TOBY: You know, cooking things.

DONNA: What do you want to do cooking for?

TOBY: It's a good job.

DONNA: No-one told you there aren't going to be any jobs?

TOBY: People always have to eat. They need people to cook for them.

DONNA: They want fancy cooking. How are you going to learn that?

TOBY: I'm going to college for it.

DONNA: Where?

TOBY: Haven't decided. Away from here. I'd like to go to London.

       Somewhere like that.

DONNA: What'd happen to us?

TOBY: I could come home weekends.

DONNA: Oh.

(Pause)

       You really want to go away?

TOBY: Not much point in going to college if you stop at home, is there?

DONNA: No.

TOBY: Be awful.

DONNA: I thought he was going to be a butcher like his dad and brother. Didn't know he wanted to go away. We'd never talked about it. I thought I'd miss him if he went. Girls whose lads have gone to college have an awful time. They know the lads are playing the field. They can't because they've stopped at home, everybody'd know.

       You'll have to stop here while you do your A-levels.

(Pause)

TOBY: Will you miss me?

(He fumbles with her.)

DONNA: Don't!

TOBY: Won't you?

DONNA: I'm trying to drink my coffee.

He was trying to get his hand between my cardi and my blouse.

TOBY: I like you, Donna. I really do.

DONNA: So you say. Hey!

TOBY: Shall I put a record on?

DONNA: If you like.

TOBY: Anything particular you want?

DONNA: Don't mind.

(TOBY puts on record.)

TOBY: You'll like this.

DONNA: I knew it was going to be something romantic. They've got dimmer switches and everything at his house, and Tiffany lampshades – they haven't got round to paper ones at our house. He turned the dimmer switch till it was pitch black.

       What are you doing? I feel like I'm in a coal mine.

(TOBY gropes his way to the settee)

       Mind!

TOBY: Sorry.

DONNA: What are they going to say when they get back and find us in the dark?

TOBY: What?

DONNA: You can see from the street whether the light's on or not.

TOBY: Nice in the dark.

DONNA: I hate the dark. Can't we just have it dim?

TOBY: Okay.

(He gets up and bangs into something.)

DONNA: What have you done?

TOBY: Nothing. Banged the table, that's all.

DONNA: So then, he turns the light up like it's floodlighting at
Hillsborough.

Don't be daft. Like that. It's nice, like that. I bet from the
street it looks like we're watching TV.

TOBY: (back to sofa) You comfortable?

DONNA: Yes.

TOBY: You sure?

DONNA: Yes.

TOBY: You can stretch yourself out a bit if you want.

DONNA: I'm very comfortable thank you.

TOBY: Good.

DONNA: Yes.

TOBY: I really fancy you.

DONNA: I fancy you and all.

TOBY: Really?

DONNA: Yes.

And I do because he isn't bad to look at. He doesn't have sort of
spots or anything. He's got a blackhead on his nose but you can only
see that when you're close up. And most of the time you're kissing
him you don't really notice. A lot of girls at school fancy him
because he's quite nice. He's a good dancer as well.

(TOBY lights gas)

What are you putting the fire on for?

TOBY: Thought you might be cold.

DONNA: I'm fine.

TOBY: I'm a bit cold.

DONNA: I'll have to take my cardigan off. You'll have to mind.

It was an excuse to make him move. I'd got cramp in my arm from
him lying on it.

(Takes off cardigan)

TOBY: That nice?

DONNA: Yes.

TOBY: Good.

DONNA: It was nice lying there, listening to the record. In films, they
always smoke when they're listening to music, but we don't.

DONNA: Hey, what do you think you're trying to do?

TOBY: What's it feel like?

DONNA: It felt like he'd got his hand half-way up my leg.

TOBY: Like that?

DONNA: It's alright.

TOBY: That all?

DONNA: Your hands are cold.

TOBY: Cold hands, warm heart.

DONNA: Could just be because you don't wear gloves when you go out.

(Pause)

TOBY: Nice music, isn't it?

DONNA: Yes.

(Pause)

Do you always put this on when you're with girls?

TOBY: Do you mean my shirt or the music?

DONNA: It's a nice shirt. Sort of soft. Brushed cotton.

TOBY: My gran got it me for Christmas.

DONNA: I've never seen you wear it before.

TOBY: Been saving it.

DONNA: What for?

TOBY: Special occasion.

DONNA: Such as?

TOBY: Tonight.

DONNA: We haven't even been out.

TOBY: You were coming round.

DONNA: You dressed up just for me coming round?

TOBY: Yes. Thought you'd like it. I had a bath as well.

DONNA: Did you?

TOBY: You smell really nice. Why don't you take your shoes off?

DONNA: Why?

TOBY: You could put your feet up if you took your shoes off.

DONNA: Okay.

(Sound of DONNA taking off shoes and dropping them)

TOBY: Nice and wide this settee, isn't it? Like a bed almost.

DONNA: Yes.

TOBY: Pulls out into a bed you know.

DONNA: Does it?

TOBY: When people stop.

DONNA: We've got a put-u-up. It's not as comfortable as this.

TOBY: Do you want me to show you how it makes into a bed?

DONNA: It was so obvious what he was getting at.

Your mum and dad'll be back.

TOBY: They're stopping over at me Auntie Jean's.

DONNA: What? You told me they were coming back.

TOBY: They are – tomorrow.

DONNA: You said your mother would take me home.

TOBY: She will, when she comes back.

DONNA: You said she was coming back tonight.

TOBY: I never did.

DONNA: You lied.

TOBY: Never said they were coming back tonight. You just assumed that.

DONNA: You didn't tell me different.

TOBY: Didn't ask me.

DONNA: How am I supposed to get home?

TOBY: You can stay.

DONNA: Maybe I don't want to.

TOBY: You can get a taxi.

DONNA: Where am I going to get the money for a taxi?

TOBY: Told your dad you had the money for one.

DONNA: Only so he didn't worry. Where'd I get money for taxis?

TOBY: Lend it you then.

DONNA: Lend it me?

TOBY: All right. I'll go halves with you.

DONNA: Why should I have to pay anything?

TOBY: You wanted to come back.

DONNA: You said your mum would run me home, Toby Jordan.

TOBY: I'll give you the money for a taxi then.

DONNA: You got a number?

TOBY: Don't ring for one yet.

DONNA: Get off.

TOBY: Donna.

DONNA: Leave off.

TOBY: What have I done now?

DONNA: I were so mad I could have killed him.

TOBY: Give us a kiss, Donna.

(He tries to kiss her)

DONNA: You've a blackhead on your nose. You know that?

TOBY: Donna....

DONNA: It's horrible to look at.

TOBY: You mad at me?

DONNA: What do you think?

TOBY: I thought you'd like it with no-one here.

DONNA: There's been no-one here all night.

TOBY: You kept saying you wanted to watch the film.

DONNA: I was. I like seeing the end of them.

(Pause)

TOBY: You could have a drink if you wanted.

DONNA: Don't they mind?

TOBY: No. So long as I don't go mad, they never notice what's gone. You can have anything you like.

DONNA: You having one?

TOBY: Might as well.

DONNA: Yes. What you got then?

TOBY: Most things.

DONNA: I don't want one that makes your breath smell. What you having?

TOBY: Vodka and lime.

DONNA: I don't mind that. I want a lot of lime.

TOBY: Okay. The lime's in the fridge. I won't be a minute.

(Exit TOBY)

DONNA: (shouting after him) I'm only staying while twelve. I mean it. He was really ages getting the lime. When he came back, he had these two great nail marks on his nose where he'd squeezed his blackhead.

TOBY: Vodka and lime. You can lie back down now.

DONNA: I can't drink lying down.

TOBY: Donna...

DONNA: I'm going at twelve.

TOBY: Go later.

DONNA: I've got to work tomorrow morning.
Sunday mornings I help out at this hotel. making beds and such. Better than a Saturday job. Means you can go to town on Saturdays. I like it. But sometimes you get odd men. You have to watch them. Some of the other girls have seen it all. You wouldn't believe it.

TOBY: I think you're really attractive.

(She giggles)
I'm not just telling you that. Do you love me?

DONNA: I don't know.

TOBY: I love you.

DONNA: He'd only had two sips of his drink.

TOBY: Donna...

DONNA: He put his hand up my skirt.

TOBY: Do you love me?

DONNA: Don't know.

TOBY: What you going out with me for, if you don't?

DONNA: I like going out with you.
I do as well. It's nice to have someone to go out with. Everyone else has.

TOBY: I really do fancy you.

DONNA: You keep saying.

TOBY: D'you believe me?

DONNA: I believe you. Will you move?

(He moves)

So he moved. I got one breath and he was squashing me again.

TOBY: Will you then?

DONNA: I can't breathe.

TOBY: Will you "all the way"?

DONNA: What?

TOBY: You know.

DONNA: I knew what he meant but...

TOBY: If you love me.

DONNA: I didn't say that.

TOBY: Don't you?

DONNA: I'm not sixteen.

TOBY: Doesn't stop other girls.

DONNA: Have you been with other girls?

TOBY: Well...

DONNA: Well?

TOBY: No.

DONNA: Never know if you're telling the truth or not.

TOBY: I haven't.

DONNA: Truly?

TOBY: Promise. I'll be really careful.

DONNA: I don't know.

TOBY: You can't get pregnant first time, you know.

DONNA: That's not what they taught at school, is it?

TOBY: You can't.

DONNA: Who says?

TOBY: Nobody gets caught first time.

DONNA: I know girls who have.

TOBY: They've been lying then.

DONNA: Who says?

TOBY: Just the first time they got caught. Probably been doing it for ages. Donna...

DONNA: He was really squashing me and breathing right in my face.

TOBY: Donna...

DONNA: I don't know...

TOBY: Don't you fancy me?

DONNA: Yes.

TOBY: Come on then.

DONNA: I don't want to.

TOBY: Won't take long.

DONNA: Not that.

TOBY: You have to begin sometime.

DONNA: No.

TOBY: You'll be okay. I'll make sure.

DONNA: (frightened) I don't want to.

TOBY: Most girls would.

DONNA: Thank you.

TOBY: Donna...

DONNA: I'm not sixteen.

TOBY: Couple of months you will be.

DONNA: That's two months. Can't you just wait two months?

TOBY: Why?

(Pause)

             You saying you will in two months?

DONNA: But I didn't know if I'd even be seeing him then.
             Perhaps.

TOBY: You just said you would.

DONNA: I never did.

TOBY: I get other girls throwing themselves at me.

(Pause)

             Susan really fancies me.

DONNA: Susan had said that. She was really jealous when she knew
Toby was seeing me.

DONNA: She's a slag.

TOBY: I think she's very sexy.

DONNA: I don't want to.
So he got up off the settee.

TOBY: (getting off settee) You might as well go home then.

DONNA: I will.

(Pause)

             Can I have the money for the taxi?

(Pause)

             You said you were giving me the money for the taxi.

TOBY: After the way you've just treated me?

DONNA: You said if I stayed, you would.

TOBY: You haven't stayed.

DONNA: There's staying and staying, isn't there?

TOBY: There is and you haven't.

DONNA: Why should I have to, for my taxi fare?

TOBY: Shouldn't have come then, should you?

DONNA: You said your mum would take me up.

TOBY: Well, I was wrong.

DONNA: You mean, you lied.

(Pause)

             Will you walk me home, then?

TOBY: It's too cold. And we're not seeing each other any more, are
             we?

DONNA: Aren't we?

TOBY: No point, is there?

DONNA: Isn't there?

TOBY: Not that I can see.

DONNA: Five minutes ago you were saying you loved me.

TOBY: Well...

DONNA: He just looked at me. He is attractive. Lots of girls say so. Really pretty ones. Better looking girls than me. They think he's attractive. I'm lucky really, going out with him. And he is a lovely kisser.

Up music.

Louise Page

ASSIGNMENT

1 Presenting the play

(a) Choose three or four pages from the play that you would like to work on. In pairs, work out how you are going to present the scene to an audience. You will need to discuss the relationship between Toby and Donna, and what is going on between them in the scene you have chosen.

Some things to think about:
    positions;
    movements;
    costumes;
    props;
    tone (the tone of voice in which the lines are spoken);
    pace (where the lines are said quickly, or slowly, or with pauses).

When you have discussed the scene and practised it, present your version to another pair, or to a larger group.

(b) Now work on the same scene, only this time you will use voices only. You could either record your reading on an audiotape, or ask your audience to sit with their backs to you so that they just listen to the dialogue.

Some things to think about:
    tone;
    pace;
    sound effects.

(c) Talk about the differences in the two versions.

Was there anything you found more effective in the stage version?
Was there anything you found more effective in the voices-only version?

2 Talking about the characters

(a) Discuss these points in pairs or small groups.

What kind of person is Donna?
What different feelings does she experience during the play?
What different pressures is she under?
What kind of person is Toby?
What does he really think of Donna?
What do you think happens next?
What do you think about the way the male-female relationship is shown in the play? Do you recognise the attitudes of Donna and Toby?

(b) Now write about 250 words on each character. Use the ideas you have discussed, and any others which occur to you from your reading of the play.

3 During the play Donna speaks her thoughts directly to the audience.

Take either the scene you have already worked on or another one that appeals to you, and read it aloud, missing out Donna's 'asides'. Instead, make up lines for Toby to speak to the audience.

Example

TOBY: I'm going to college for it.
DONNA: Where?
TOBY: Haven't decided. Away from here. I'd like to go to London. Somewhere like that.
I could tell she didn't like that. She looked at me like I'd hit her or something instead of just saying I'd like to go away to college.

Write up one of the pages with Toby's words to the audience instead of Donna's.

4 What happens next.

Imagine that Donna and Toby are each talking to a friend about what happened that evening. Think about who each friend is (will Donna talk to Susan?) and the way Donna and Toby will talk about the evening and the relationship. Think about how the friend will respond.

Now write two short scenes:
(a) Donna and her friend;
(b) Toby and his friend.

Language link

Dialect and colloquial expressions

Toby and Donna speak in a dialect which is different from Standard English. They also use colloquial expressions, as we all do in friendly and informal conversation.

Colloquial language is the kind of chatty language we use in speech, and not in formal written English, unless for a particular purpose. The word 'colloquial' comes from Latin, *col* meaning 'together' and *loqui* meaning 'to speak'.

Words that contain the letters 'loqu' or 'logu' will have something to do with speaking.

SELF CHECK

(a) Here are some words from this family.

colloquial	monologue	loquacious
dialogue	soliloquy	eloquent

From the list above choose the best word for the gaps in the following sentences:

i) I enjoyed the play because the characters were believable and the ....was lively.

ii) Ruth enjoyed listening to Tara's stories and opinions, but Tariq thought she was too .... and was annoyed when he couldn't get a word in edgeways.

iii) The barrister's defence speech was........and persuasive, and convinced the jury that her client was innocent.

iv) A well-known.......in *Macbeth* is the speech in which Macbeth imagines he sees a dagger in front of him.

v) No-one else said a word as Matt delivered an angry.......about the state of the flat after the party and their selfishness in not helping to clear up.

vi) "It's a good letter of complaint," said Maria, "but it's a formal communication, and some of your expressions are too........."

(b) Look at the following example of a dialect expression taken from *Toby and Donna*. Find three more examples in the play.

Dialect	Standard English
It doesn't come while five	It doesn't come until five

Spelling check

Suffixes

Look at 'believable' in item (i) above. This word is made by adding 'able' to 'believe'.

There are some spelling rules to follow when you change words which end in a silent 'e' by adding 'able', 'ible', 'ing' or 'ment'. (These syllables are called 'suffixes'.)

1   If the suffix begins with a vowel, the 'e' is normally dropped.

Examples   use + able = usable

                          advertise + ing = advertising

Exceptions   When a word has a soft 'g' (pronounced like 'j') or 'c' (pronounced like 's') the 'e' is kept.

Examples   change + able = changeable

                          notice + able = noticeable

2   If the suffix begins with a consonant the 'e' is normally kept.

Examples   excite + ment = excitement

                          achieve + ment = achievement

Exceptions   argue + ment = argument

SELF CHECK

Add the suffix 'ing' to the following words to make new words.

plunge + ing =   discharge + ing =

enlarge + ing =   sponge + ing =

a

More suggestions for coursework

- Write a story or description based on one of the following titles;
  First date; Girls' night out; Boys' night out; Stags and hens.
- Describe your ideal Saturday evening.

END-OF-CHAPTER ASSIGNMENT

 You have been asked to contribute to a collection of articles about social and leisure activities and issues. Write an article dealing with any of the aspects covered in this section. Refer to a range of extracts from this chapter.

SUMMARY

In this section you have covered the following aspects of GCSE requirements.

SPEAKING AND LISTENING

group discussion
argument and opinion
participating in a talk show

READING

magazine articles
television reviews
statistics
newspaper leading articles
song lyric
poetry published since 1900
complete play published since 1900

WRITING

soap opera
opinion
review
comprehension
leaflet

imaginative account
about character
drama script

LANGUAGE STUDY

full stops
accent
dialect
Standard English
nouns
similes
patterns of spelling

REVISION AND FURTHER ASSIGNMENTS

1 Write out the following sentences inserting full stops and capital letters.

(a) when we arrived at the cinema the film had already started we stood about wondering what to do we decided to go for a pizza

(b) he has been very moody recently he stormed out of the room for no reason at all

2 What is the name of the figure of speech in this sentence? Her skin was as smooth as silk.

3 Write a sentence about each of the following using a simile:
hair
a cold morning
a pet animal

4 Change the following words by adding 'ly' and use each in a sentence:
annual
busy
safe
frantic

5 Use the following topics as a starting point for writing. You could use them as the basis of a story, or personal writing, or argument and discussion, or a play.... If you have time you could treat the same subject in two different ways to help you practise your range of writing.

- Living without television.
- Developments in communication – mobile phones, the Internet etc.
- Your favourite character in a television series or book.
- The lottery ticket.
- Choose a sport you are interested in playing or watching. Give clear instructions about how it is played. Aim your description at youngsters of 10 or 11 years old.
- Write about a sporting event from different points of view. You could write a couple of paragraphs as a player, then a couple from the point of view of a spectator. You could develop some conflicting attitudes. What might be the thoughts and feelings of a close friend or family member watching someone playing rugby, or motor racing?
- Collect some accounts of the same sporting event from different newspapers. Write a comparison of the accounts. Discuss matters like the type of language used, the length of sentences, the tone of writing.

HOME AND AWAY

A guide to St John

The following extracts are taken from different books about St John, which is one of the US Virgin Islands in the Caribbean.

For a small place it is full of history, from the arrival of Columbus, through to Drake and a pride of pirates; to battles between the French, the Danes and the British, who then became allies to crush a rebellion of the slaves. There is little of St John that is not bay-forest, beautiful beaches, silent coves and curling hills. It has become a US National Park through the efforts and the money of the Rockefeller family.

There are 3,000 people on St John. Here, in the wooded sunshine, the zebra butterfly, the wild donkey and the mongoose live together with the golden orb spider whose web is as strong as a fish net. Orchids, hibiscus, the oyster plant, the lipstick flowers bloom together with the yellow-trumpeted Ginger Thomas, the emblem flower of the Virgin Islands. Nests of termites, as large and round as footballs,

* double-entendre means double meaning.

bulge from trunks. The bay tree casts its shade and so does the manchineel, whose fruit is poison and whose sap, which drips from its branches, burns the skin. Its 'death apple' killed some of Columbus's men.

Limes grow by the sea at Lameshur, a Danish version of Limeshore, called so by the British seamen who came there to eat the fruit as a precaution against scurvy (which is why they were first called Limeys). The old Danish roads across St John are still favoured footpaths and go deep into and over the top of the island where there are meadows alive with blue morning glory.

St John, however, for all its sweetness, has an unpleasant past. It was here that slaves imported by the Danish West Indies were first landed to be 'acclimatized' before being transhipped to sugar plantations. The shadow of this tragedy still lurks in the sunlit ruins of the Annaberg estate – the tight slave houses, the mill, the dungeon, the sugar crusher and the spirit crusher, which has a grim double-entendre.*

A contemporary account relates, 'Slave auctions were the most exciting events of any month. When the slaver entered port, the white inhabitants rushed to the water's edge and took to boats in order to get a preview of the living cargo....'

The inevitable rebellion flared in November 1733. The slaves marched and overcame their guards and their owners. It took months and a combined force of Danes, British and French soldiers to subdue them.

In the schoolyard at Cruz Bay, after returning from those haunted ruins, I watched the descendants of those slaves, infant children, hilariously trying to play volleyball with a white teacher and a solitary white boy. In the end the rebellion was worth it.

Leslie Thomas, **My world of islands**

ASSIGNMENT

1 What does Leslie Thomas think about :
   (a) the natural landscape;
   (b) the island's history of slavery?

2 Write a paragraph giving your own impression.

Nearly half of the island of St John is a National Park, largely due to Laurance S. Rockefeller, who bought up some five thousand acres of unspoilt land in the fifties and gave it to the nation. Gradually, the park has been added to and it will eventually cover two-thirds of the island. The result is worthy, but dull. As one drives through the centre of the island, it is a pleasure to see the huge mangoes, the mass of mahogany and some fine kapok trees but, somehow, the regimented beaches, with large plastic rubbish bags every hundred yards, and the streams of visitors and campers lend a falseness to what should be natural. The Annaberg plantation ruins are probably the best arranged and explained example of the workings of a sugar estate in the whole Caribbean, but ... I began to wish that the hordes of tourists would settle down for a picnic among the extensive groves of manchineel trees.

I far preferred the late eighteenth-century church built by the Moravian missionaries, who campaigned with passion and courage against slavery. It was an odd building with a pink roof, white gutters, pale ochre upper walls, dark red lower walls and pale, blue-grey shutters. Strangely, the wall of the external stairway was painted on the outside with steps, corresponding to the actual steps on the other side of the wall. Here the missionaries taught the slaves to read and write. This church was built on the site of the Great House of the plantation where, in the great slave revolt of 1733, the rebels murdered the owner, Judge Sodtmann and his twelve year old daughter. So raw a deed naturally created a *jumbie* or ghost, which haunts the site, coming each full moon in the guise of a large billy goat.

On our way back to the ferry I realised that, as we neared the American continent, we were seeing many new birds, ones we had not seen before, most of which I could not identify. I particularly admired a thrush, speckled like ours, but not so plump and with a far longer beak, much more elegant. As we passed the old Danish customs post I reflected upon the absurdity of all those changes of ownership in the eighteenth century. Twice St John had been British, once for as long as seven years. Of course, then it was a matter of economics, but were those economics worth all those lives? Who cares now if one of those minute specks was once Danish or Dutch, or Spanish or French, or English or Swedish? No one, but it still affects the people's lives without their knowing it.

Quentin Crewe, **Touch the happy isles**

ASSIGNMENT

1   What does Quentin Crewe think about:
   (a) the natural landscape;
   (b) the tourists;
   (c) the island's history?

2   Write a paragraph giving your own impression.

ASSIGNMENT

1 Write a couple of sentences describing any differences and similarities in the two writers' impressions of the island.

2 Note down under these headings the information you have found about
(a) landscape;
(b) buildings;
(c) natural details (birds, flowers etc.);
(d) history.

3 Your task is to write a brief (about 150 to 200 words) factual description of St John for inclusion in a reference book.

Guidelines *Factual writing*

• Remember you are turning **personal** writing into **impersonal**. This means that you, the writer, are not 'taking part' in what you describe but are 'standing back' from it. You are giving information, not your opinion.

• Do not use 'I' – you are not saying what you think.

• Do not refer to either of the passages or the writers, just use the factual details you have gathered from them.

• Be careful with adjectives (describing words). For example, do not refer to the kapok trees as 'fine' because if you use this word you show what you, personally, think of them.

• Be careful with any words or phrases which show an attitude to what is being described. For example, when you write about the rebellion of the slaves, do not say, as the writer of the passage does, that in the end the rebellion was worth it.

• Keep your sentences short and straightforward.

• Use headings and sub-headings.

4 Prepare and write a tourist guide to a place you know well. It may be somewhere you have been on holiday, or it could be a guide to your home town. You could make your guide specifically for students. Remember you will have to include facts and make your guide clear and straightforward, but you are also encouraging people to visit, so you will want to present the place you are writing about in an appealing way. Write about 300 to 500 words.

Guidelines *Writing a guide*

- Gather information. You could visit your nearest tourist office. There may be leaflets and information available in your local library. If you are writing about a place you go to on holiday you could write to their tourist office for material to refresh your memory.

- Decide what you want to include in the guide. Write down the headings you will use. You could use 'Where to stay' and 'Where to eat' to begin with.

- Select the information which will go under each heading and write notes.

- Write your first draft. Remember you are encouraging people to visit, so use suitable descriptive words and phrases. Include a couple of sentences at the beginning which give your audience a general idea of the place.

Example You will enjoy every minute of your stay in this peaceful, unspoilt corner of the country.

- You may want to include maps or photographs, but remember, your use of language will be the basis of your assessment.

- Check your draft carefully for spelling and punctuation. Make sure it creates the impression you want. You could ask a friend to read it through.

- Write your final draft.

Grammar box

Adjectives

Adjectives are describing words. In the passages you have just read, the ruins are described as 'sunlit' and the beaches are described as 'regimented'. Adjectives work with nouns and help to make the meaning of a noun more precise.

adjective	noun
sunlit	ruins
beaches	regimented

They answer questions like:

which?	those books
how many?	four apples
what kind of?	the steep hill

SELF CHECK

Write down as many adjectives as you can to describe the following nouns:

a car, the weather, a film, a journey, a building, a baby.

Comparison of adjectives

Be careful when you are using different forms of an adjective. For example, you might describe someone as 'tall', and someone else as 'taller', and someone else as the 'tallest'. This is the most common way of forming the comparison of adjectives.

long	longer	longest
thin	thinner	thinnest

Be careful to use the word in the second column (longer, thinner) when you are comparing something with **one** other, and the word in the third column (longest, thinnest) when you are comparing something with **more** than one other.

Example Jane is taller than Gina.

This book is the heaviest in the library.

With some words, however, we do not change the word itself but put the words 'more' or 'most' in front of the adjective.

beautiful	more beautiful	most beautiful

Some words change completely when you use the comparative form.

bad	worse	worst
good	better	best

SELF CHECK

Write down the comparative forms of these adjectives. You might need to check some of the spellings.

1	2	3
noisy		
lovely		
easy		
stupid		
little		
many		

Tourist arrangements

Your relatives who live in America are visiting England this summer, and want to spend a week in the West Country. They will hire a car. You have offered to find out about the area and to book accommodation for them. Their family consists of your aunt, uncle, and two daughters, one aged thirteen and one ten. Your aunt is keen on nature and wild life and your uncle is interested in history. Both girls like animals. They are all very active and enjoy most sports.

ASSIGNMENT

Read the following tourist information:

Somerset, Avon and Wiltshire

The county of Avon stretches north and south of the River Avon; from the Severn estuary eastwards to the Cotswolds and the Wiltshire border; and from the Mendip Hills north to the Vale of Berkeley. Within these boundaries are two ancient and historic cities; one of the West Country's leading seaside resorts; and two areas designated 'of astounding natural beauty'.

Bristol, the largest city in the West Country, is situated south of the M4/M5 interchange. Rich in history and seafaring traditions, the city has many links with the early colonisation of America. The quayside area has fascinating old taverns, notably the seventeenth century 'Llangoder Trow' in King Street. Brunel's famous suspension bridge is here too, spanning the breathtaking Avon gorge at Clifton, and his iron masterpiece SS Great Britain is situated in the city docks.

One of Britain's most historic cities can be found 10 miles Southeast of Bristol: the city of Bath. Bath's 2000 year history as a

popular resort started with the Romans, followed by a second great era in the eighteenth century. Rich in Roman remains and Roman architecture, Bath has enjoyed this popularity due, in the main, to its famous warm mineral springs which served the Roman baths. Today the museum adjoining the baths houses many important finds and relics.

The largest seaside resort in Avon, situated on the Bristol Channel, is Weston-super-Mare. Donkey rides on the sands have been a feature here since the mid nineteenth century and, in addition to a full calendar of events, Weston has over two miles of golden sands.

From the heather-covered heights of Exmoor to the sea-level marshes of Sedgemoor, Somerset is a county of contrast. The far-west of the county forms most of the Exmoor National Park. The moors which rise to1707 feet, at Dunkery Beacon, are superb walking and pony-trekking country, with free-roaming ponies and deer. Some of England's prettiest villages lie within the park, including Dunster, where the main street with its octagonal Yarn market and old world cottages is dominated at one end by the castle and at the other by the tower on Conygar Hill. Minehead is a fine resort just outside the park boundary, and makes a perfect centre for exploring the area.

To the east of the county the woods and moors of the Quantocks stretch from the coast near the ancient port of Watchet to the Vale of Taunton Deane.

The other area of outstanding beauty in Somerset is the impressive limestone heights of the Mendip Hills. Here man lived at the dawn of human history in the caves of the Cheddar Gorge, and today you can marvel at the illuminated wonders of stalagmites and stalactites, while adventurous potholers explore yet deeper into the dark depths of the Mendips.

GOOD BEACHES

There are some fine beaches in this delightful part of the country, including some of the West Country's most popular family holiday resorts.

Minehead

Family fun activities: Ancient harbour with sea fishing trips and cruises on the Balmoral and Waverley; thatched cottages and many floral displays especially at Blenheim Gardens; steam train trips on the West Somerset Railway; large sea front fun fair, ten pin bowling and Odeon cinema at Somerwest World, go kart track. A day visitor ticket to Somerwest World includes 3 swimming pools, flume rides, live entertainment, snooker, fun for children; Aquasplash Leisure Pool on Seaward Way features flume, wave machine and 25 metres swimming pool; town centre shopping and Regal Cinema/Theatre; deer spotting safaris on to Exmoor; horse riding, cycle hire, mountain bike tours.

Minehead Strand beach. Wide sandy beach with access down steps from sea wall. Safety and maintenance: cleaned daily. Beach facilities: cafe and several takeaways.

Weston-super-Mare

Family fun activities: Tropicana Pleasure Beach family leisure complex centred around heated fun pool with wave machine and larger water chutes, activity equipment, indoor bouncy Play Isle, solarium, bar and cafeteria; marine lake with canoes, pedalos and water trikes; donkey rides; amusement arcades; parks and gardens, tennis, putting; bowls; pitch and putt; ten-pin bowling; riding and pony-trekking; rugby; football; cricket; angling; golf courses (2); cinema (3 screens); museum; shows and films at playhouse; numerous night spots and discos; Hutton Moor Leisure Centre with squash, badminton, multi-gym, sauna, solarium and new indoor swimming pool.

Beach. 2 miles long, sandy with rockpools and shingle at Anchor Head. Promenade and two piers with amusements, refreshments and toilets. Safety and maintenance: cleaned daily in season by Local Authority. Beach facilities: deck chairs; donkeys and pony carts; sand stalls; marine lake and fun castle; ice-cream kiosks, snack bars, numerous restaurants and pubs; toilets.

AROUND AND ABOUT

Avon Valley Railway, near Bristol. Working railway museum with locos and coaches.

Bristol Zoo, near Clifton Suspension Bridge. Extensive and fascinating collection including pygmy hippos and gorillas.

Cheddar Gorge, 13 miles from Weston. Famous for its caves and underground pools, is in a deep winding fissure in the Mendip Hills.

Longleat Safari Park, Warminster, Wilts, 45 miles from Weston. 100 acre reserve for lions, giraffes, monkeys, zebras and tigers roaming free.

SS Great Britain, Great Western Dock, Bristol. Splendid six-masted ocean-going vessel dating from 1843 and associated with engineering genius Isambard Kingdom Brunel.

The Woodspring Museum, Burlington Street, Weston-super-Mare. Friendly museum with varied collections including Victorian Life at the Seaside and dolls.

HOME FARM

Little Sutton, Near Bath

Listed farmhouse in beautiful valley between Bath and Wells. Perfect centre for outdoor pursuits; sightseeing. A working smallholding with a variety of animals to delight the children. All rooms TV, tea/coffee making. Bed and Breakfast from £15.

Contact Mrs A. Conway

MARLFORD GUEST HOUSE

51 Stoke Street, Bath, Avon

Comfortable Edwardian House – just 15 minutes' walk to city centre. Six bedrooms, all with TV and central heating. Parking. Garden. Bed and Breakfast from £14 to £18

Contact Mr R. Morgan

CAMBOURNE HOTEL

Sea Front, Weston-super-Mare

Family run hotel for 35 years, situated near the Marine Lake with its safe beaches, we will enjoy looking after you and your family! We have a gourmet restaurant and can offer an early evening meal for children if you wish. We also have a games room and bar and can offer free admission for the children to Weston's new Tropicana Leisure Centre. Colour TV in your room, weekly Bar-B-Que, weather permitting

Contact Mrs J. Mitchell

Rose Cottage
Bed & Breakfast
VACANCIES
Col TV/ ensuite all rooms.

1 Bearing in mind the family's interests, make a list of the places you think they would like to visit and the things they would like to do. Plan three days' activities for them.

2 Choose accommodation for them for the first two nights. You should think about what sort of place would suit them, and

about what will be convenient for the activities you have suggested.

3 Now you have two letters to write:

(a) Write a letter to the hotel you have chosen, booking accommodation for your relations for two nights. Remember to state the number and type of rooms required and the dates of arrival and departure.

(b) Write a letter to your relations telling them the arrangements you have made, and giving them your suggestions about what they could do in the West Country. Describe the three days' activities you suggest.

Guidelines *Formal letters*

The letters you write for purposes such as applying for jobs, complaining about goods or services are known as formal or business letters. There are many variations in the layout of business letters. The guidelines given here show you one version.

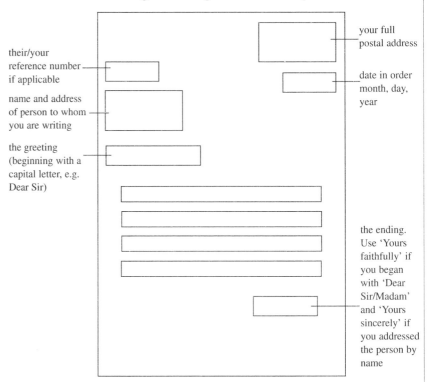

NOTE: It is common practice nowadays not to punctuate addresses. The body of the letter, however, should be fully punctuated.

- It is important to arrange your comments clearly and logically so that the point of your letter is effectively communicated. Most formal letters are written to achieve something – to book a holiday, to apply for a job, to ask for your money back, to request action on some issue.

(a) The first paragraph of your letter should indicate what the letter will be about. State if you are writing to complain, request information etc.

(b) Organise the body of the letter into clear coherent paragraphs, each dealing with one main point.

(c) Your last paragraph should briefly remind the reader what the letter has been about.

Punctuation mark

Commas

Commas are used to indicate a pause.

1 They separate parts of a sentence to make the meaning clear.

Example Colin said the supervisor was responsible for the mistake.
Colin, said the supervisor, was responsible for the mistake.

The use of commas in the second sentence changes the meaning entirely, stating that the supervisor said that Colin was responsible for the mistake.

2 Commas are used to separate items in a list.

Example ice-cream kiosks, snack bars, numerous restaurants and pubs. (Notice that the last two items are usually linked with 'and' instead of a comma.)
They are also used to separate each adjective in a list.

Example This part of the country is peaceful, unspoilt, beautiful.

3 Commas are used to separate phrases which are side-by-side in the sentence.

Example The new ordering system will result in more efficient service, speedier deliveries, greater accuracy and improved customer relations.

4 Commas are used to mark off words which break into the flow of the sentence.
Example The deadline for this work, as I said last week, will not be extended.

a

5 Commas are used to mark off the name if you are speaking to someone.

Example " I've got some good news for you, Jason."

SELF CHECK

Insert commas where appropriate in the following sentences.

(a) The facilities we require are en-suite rooms cable television a baby-sitting service an indoor pool.

(b) The speaker was very persuasive having a good grasp of her subject a clear voice convincing examples a lively delivery.

(c) "If you are not in on time tonight mark my words Donna you will be grounded for a week."

Disastrous holiday

Read the following two documents which give you information about a holiday in the Swiss Alps.

This advertisement appeared in a holiday brochure.

HOLIDAY IN THE SWISS ALPS

For fifty years we have offered to discriminating holidaymakers unforgettable holidays in the Swiss Alps near Geneva – an unspoilt idyllic part of Europe off the main tourist routes. The holidays can now be offered at a price well within the family budget: we charge only £350 per person per week full-board (25 % reduction for children under 14) inclusive of the flight and hiring of equipment.

Flight to the holiday resort is by well-equipped charter flight to Cointrin (the main air port at Geneva) and quaint Swiss trains and buses convey you effortlessly through breathtakingly beautiful mountainous scenery to your comfortable chalet-hotel surrounded by rugged slopes.

In the village close by you may visit the tenth-century church, the Roman ruins and the modern weekly cattle market. Nearby there are bars open until late, a heated swimming pool and a discotheque for the young and old. Dozens of welcoming shops offer you souvenirs of your visit free of local taxes.

The chalet-hotel itself offers you five-star quality at one-star prices.

All the comfortable rooms are centrally heated, have their own showers and private wcs; colour television is available at a small extra charge. The beds have interior-sprung mattresses and ensure a sound night's sleep before beginning the next exciting day on the ski slopes. There are challenges for all: safe nursery slopes for beginners and downhill slalom runs for would-be Olympic champions. Bilingual instructors make the learning easy and enjoyable.

The restaurant offers local dishes cooked in Swiss hygienic kitchens and the atmosphere is lively and filled with music from the Alps. Savour the fruity headlines of the new wines; relish the *noisette d'agneau aux chanterelles* (succulent lamb cooked with mountain mushrooms) or the *sorbet de framboises* (raspberry water ices). You will never forget them. Come home refreshed, the better for your holiday break.

A comprehensive personal and medical insurance is included in the overall price.

Ask for Holiday AGST 129(i) at your local agency.

Rob and Jenny Stanley liked the look of the holiday advertised and booked it for themselves and their two children, Stephanie (aged 13) and Mark (aged 12). Rob kept a diary of their holiday.

Sunday January 3

Aeroplane was overbooked; delayed at London airport for three hours. The weather was good and the flight excellent once we took off – we saw Paris and Dijon as we flew over. Connections in Switzerland missed. The coach when it finally arrived was old and we had to wait for a relief driver. Little Stephanie was exhausted and sick.

Monday January 4

The skis issued were in poor condition; hired others for the children from the local shop at enormous expense. Jenny and I have decided to abandon the idea of skiing. The children cannot understand the instructor who speaks French and German fluently but uses only broken English. Stephanie is still exhausted from the journey out.

Tuesday January 5

Little sleep. The beds are hard and the radiators only lukewarm; central-heating pipes crack all night long. At least the sun is shining today. We tried to find the Roman ruins – they consisted of a few bricks and tiles at the bottom of a deep hole, well out of sight. The medieval church, too, had been rebuilt in the eighteenth century.

Wednesday January 6

Our rooms are cramped. Lorries revving up at six o'clock in the farm next door put paid to any chance of sleep. The tap on the wash-basin drips constantly – it cannot be turned off. The village is more than four miles away; no public transport there and the taxi costs the equivalent of fifteen pounds. The swimming pool was out-of order, and the night life, such as it was, had shut down by seven o'clock!

Thursday January 7

Stephanie broke her leg. The afternoon and evening were spent in the local clinic. At least the ambulance came quickly and the Swiss doctors were efficient. Stephanie had been put in a group on the wrong slope and fell after only a few minutes!

Friday January 8

Jenny and Mark were very ill after eating our usual meal of sausages and sauerkraut. The menu has been the same since we arrived. So much for continental cooking! It will be good to go home for a rest tomorrow.

Saturday January 9

A much better trip this time. Arrived home 9.15 pm in a state of exhaustion. Stephanie must go to the General Hospital on Monday to check her leg.

A later entry

Saturday January 30

Still no acknowledgement of our insurance claim for Stephanie's accident! I must sit down tomorrow morning to set out what happened to us. I'm sure I ought to claim substantial compensation. The holiday was a disaster.

ASSIGNMENT

1 Rob Stanley decides to write to the travel company to claim compensation for his spoilt holiday on the grounds that the brochure had been totally misleading. Using only the facts given in the brochure entry and the diary, write the letter he sends. The letter itself, not counting the addresses etc., should be about 200 words.

Guidelines *Preparing your material*

- Make two columns:

  What the brochure said   **What actually happened**

  Go through the brochure and the diary entries and find examples which show that the brochure was misleading.

  Example

  What the brochure said   **What actually happened**

  bars open till late, discotheque   closed down by seven o'clock
  for young and old

- Use this material to compose your letter. You should mention as many of the disappointments as you can and relate them to the promised attractions in the misleading brochure.

- Refer to the guidelines for formal letters (given in the previous section) for advice about structure and organisation.

- In your final paragraph make it quite clear what you want to happen. Say something like "I would be grateful if you would write to confirm..."

- Think carefully about tone. The letter should be polite and factual, calculated to get a sympathetic response from the travel company, but at the same time should firmly insist on compensation. Be careful not to exaggerate or be sarcastic.

2 (a) In small groups of three or four choose one person to be Rob Stanley and one to be Jenny – or you could choose two people to be Stephanie and Mark. The others in the group are their friends who they spend an evening with shortly after their return from the holiday. In your roles, develop the conversation that takes place. Here the people being members of the Stanley family (and their friends) can exaggerate, use slang and colloquial language, build up their stories – do all the things we do when we're talking to friends!

(You might find it helpful to tape the conversation.)

(b) Write two headings:

The letter   **The conversation**

Jot down the differences you notice between the language used in the letter and the language used in the conversation. Write a short paragraph describing the main differences.

3 Imagine that you are on a holiday you are not enjoying. It might be because the weather is stopping you doing what you want, or you are not getting on well with the people you are with, or everything is more expensive than you thought, or you are homesick for a particular reason .... any combination of ideas!

Write eight diary entries (about 300 words) which make clear your thoughts and feelings. Try to build it up from day to day so that the reader becomes involved in what is happening to you.

4 Write an account of a holiday you really enjoyed, or of a holiday you did not enjoy.

Guidelines   *Writing a personal account*

- On a sheet of rough paper note down all the ideas that occur to you. Do not worry about putting them in a particular order. Do not include just the things that happened but also your feelings, descriptions of the place, descriptions of the people involved, any details you remember which will make your account lively and interesting.

- Group your ideas together.

Example aching muscles; hills; the worst cycling; going more slowly than the others; feeling inadequate.

- Once you have your groups of ideas you should have an idea of what each paragraph will be about.

- Decide on the order in which you will write the account. Try to begin in a way which will interest the reader.

Example Here are some different ways of beginning an account of a camping holiday. Think about which you find most effective.

(a) I was watching television when the phone rang. My mother went to answer it. She came back and said, "It's for you." When I went to answer it I found out it was my friend who asked me if I wanted to go camping with them.

(b) The wind whistled around the tent and the rain hammered on the canvas. Shivering in my sleeping bag, I wondered why I had agreed to come.

(c) At last the day arrived. I checked to see that I had all my camping gear ready and waiting.

(d) My spirits rose as we left the town behind and sped towards the camping site in the mountains.

- Remember to include your thoughts and feelings – do not just say what happened,

- Choose words which indicate what you are feeling and how strong your feelings are.

- Look to see if there are places where you can include description. One way to do this is to use adjectives.

Language link

Synonyms

You may find that when you write on a particular topic you tend to use the same words repeatedly. English is full of words which have approximately the same meaning. These words are called synonyms. If you become more aware of them and their different shades of meaning you will be able to use a more varied and effective vocabulary.

SELF CHECK

What different shades of meaning do you see in these adjectives:

annoyed; angry; furious; irate
bright; shining; brilliant; gleaming; dazzling
brief; short; concise; limited

With some words you can find synonyms which have a stronger or weaker meaning.

Arrange the following words so that the 'weakest' is at the beginning and the 'strongest' at the end.

(a) agony; pain; twinge; torment

(b) marched; sauntered; strode; walked; shuffled

(c) looked; gazed; glimpsed; stared; glanced

Missing home

Being away from home, whether just for a holiday or more permanently, can make us miss it and imagine it very strongly. Here are two poems in which the poets give vivid pictures of the homes they miss, the first one India, the second one Trinidad.

Imagining India

Wide sandy roads with palm trees on either side
and bullocks, buffaloes and peacocks on them.

Some big brick houses
And other little mud ones.

At bazaars
People are buying
And selling
Saris, kurtas,
Herbs and spices.
The setting sun reflecting
on the cool water.

Geetanjali Mohini Guptara

ASSIGNMENT

Imagining India gives us a series of pictures of India. Choose two of the pictures, and write a few lines on each explaining what the words make you see.

BACK HOME

Back home
> *the sun does greet you with a smile*
> *creep up the bed clothes until*
> *you open your eye*
> *Bright and hot*
> *the sky blue and clear*
> *Every day does fill you with cheer*

Back home
> *is all type of mango*
> *banana, orange and plum*
> *growing in we garden*
> *ripening in the heat*
> *Any time you want you can*
> *pick some and eat*

Back home
> *the sea at we back door*
> *I could step out the house*
> *and run down to bathe*
> *listen to waves when I in bed*
> *They does soothe me good*
> *They does help me sleep*

Back home
> *But I not back home*
> *I here in England*
> *where the sun not so hot*
> *and the fruit not so ripe*
> *and the sea does chill your feet*

Back home
> *is just a sad-sweet memory*

Amryl Johnson

ASSIGNMENT

 Back Home uses pictures, repetition and contrast. Write a paragraph showing what picture of Trinidad the poet creates and how this contrasts with England. What feelings does the writer convey?

Guidelines *Writing about poetry*

- Read the poem through a couple of times. Try to hear it in your head as well as read it with your eyes.

- Underline or circle any words or phrases you find particularly striking. Do any of them appeal to your senses – what you can see, feel, hear etc.?

- Think about patterns in the poem – are there words which seem to go together? Are there words which break the pattern?

- What is the overall mood or feeling of the poem?

- What does the poem say to you? What does it make you think about?

Example *Back home*

> the sun does greet you with a smile
> creep up the bedclothes until
> you open your eye
> Bright and hot
> the sky blue and clear
> Every day does fill you with cheer

This verse could make you think of a place where the sun is always bright and the sky is always blue and clear. The words like 'bright and hot' and 'blue and clear' are simple but very expressive. They allow you feel the heat of the sun and see the cloudless sky.

Here are some more words you will find useful when discussing poetry and other writing. They refer to some of the techniques writers use to help create meaning and effect.

Alliteration

This is where the first letter of two or more words next or close to each other is repeated to give emphasis.

Example 'is just a sad-sweet memory'

Metaphor

This is where one thing is compared to something else but without using the words 'like' or 'as'.

Example 'the sun does greet you with a smile'

The sun is not literally smiling, and the poet could have said that it was as if the sun was smiling. What effect does she create by using this metaphor?

Rhythm

This is the pattern of beats in words. If you cannot read a poem aloud, try to hear it in your head. Much traditional poetry has regular rhythm; often in modern poetry the rhythm is freer and less structured. What do you think about the rhythm in these two poems?

- Write a poem of your own about a place you like. You could use the same structure as *Back Home* and begin every verse with the same words. You could base your poem on the same rhythm as well.

Foreign food

Eating meals in a different country or away from home can sometimes be difficult or a source of embarrassment.

This passage is adapted from *A Breath of French Air* and describes the Larkin family on holiday in France having their first meal at the hotel. The Larkin family consists of Pop Larkin; Ma Larkin; their eldest daughter Mariette who is married to Charley (or Mr Charlton); Montgomery; Primrose; Victoria; the twins.

Nearly an hour later, when Ma brought the children downstairs for dinner, closely followed by Charley and Mariette, Pop was already sitting moodily in a corner of the *salle à manger*.

Driven by ravenous hunger and thirst to the bar, Pop had found it furnished with a solitary stool, a yard of dusty counter, a dozing grey cat, and a vase of last year's heather. The stool had two legs instead of three and all about the place was that curious pungent odour that Ma had been so quick to notice earlier in the day: as if a drain had been left open or a gas-tap on.

In the *salle à manger*, in contrast to the silent half-darkness of the bar, a noisy, eager battle was being waged by seven or eight French families against the howl of wind and rain, the tossing lace curtains, and more particularly against what appeared to be dishes of large unpleasant pink spiders, in reality *langoustines*. A mad cracking of claws filled the air and one plump gentleman sat eating, wearing his cap, a large white one: as if for protection against something, perhaps flying claws or bread or rain.

Three feet from Pop's table a harassed French waitress with a marked limp and loose peroxide hair came to operate, every desperate two minutes or so, a large patent wooden-handled bread-slicer about the size of an old-fashioned sewing machine.

This instrument made crude groaning noises, like an old tram trying to start. Slices of bread, savagely chopped from yard-long loaves, flew about in all directions, dropping all over the place until harassed waiters and waitresses bore them off hurriedly to eager, waiting guests. These, Pop noticed, at once crammed them ravenously into their mouths and even gluttonously mopped their plates with them.

Presently the rest of the family arrived: Mariette immaculate and perfumed in a beautiful sleeveless low-cut dress of emerald green that made her shoulders and upper breast glow a warm olive colour, Ma in a mauve woollen dress and a royal blue jumper on top to keep out the cold. Ma had plenty of Chanel No. 5 on, still convinced that the hotel smelled not only of mice but a lot of other things besides.

As the family walked in all the French families suddenly stopped eating. They stopped ramming bread into their mouths like famished prisoners and gaped at the bare, astral shoulders of Mariette, Ma's great mauve and blue balloon of a body, and the retinue of children behind it.

Most of the older French women, Pop thought, seemed to be wearing discoloured woollen sacks. The younger ones, who were nearly all tallow-coloured, bruise-eyed and flat-chested, wore jeans. It was hard to tell any of them from boys and in consequence Pop felt more than usually proud of Mariette, who looked so fleshly, elegantly, and provocatively a girl.

Presently the waitress with the limp brought the menu and then with not a moment to spare hopped off to work the bread machine.

"Well, what's to eat, Charley-boy?" Pop said, rubbing his hands. "Something good, I hope, old man, I'm starving. By the way , Charley, what's "eat" in French?"

It was Pop's honest resolve to learn, if possible, a few new French words every day.

"*Manger*," Charley said. "Same word as the thing in the stable – manger."

Pop sat mute and astonished. *Manger* – a simple thing like that. Perfickly wonderful. Unbelievable. *Manger*. He sat back and prepared to listen to Charley reading out the menu with the awe he deserved.

"Well, to begin with there are *langoustines*. They're a kind of small lobster. Then there's *saucisson à la mode d'ici* – that's a sort of sausage they do here. Hot, I expect. Then *pigeons à la Gautier* – I expect that's pigeons in some sort of wine sauce. And afterwards fruit and cheese."

"Sounds jolly *bon*," Pop said.

Charley said he thought it ought to satisfy and Ma at once started remonstrating with Montgomery, Primrose, Victoria, and the twins about eating so much bread. She said they'd never want their dinners if they went on stuffing bread down. Pop too was stuffing down large quantities of bread, trying to stave off increasing stabs and rumbles of hunger.

The harassed waitress arrived a moment later to tell Charley, in French, that there were, after all, no langoustines.

"Sorry, no more *langoustines*, Mr Charlton said. "They've got *friture* instead."

"What's *friture*?"

"Fried sardines."

Ma choked; she felt she wanted to be suddenly and violently sick.

"Fresh ones, of course," Charley said. "Probably caught this afternoon."

Pop was still eating bread when the *friture* arrived.

"They're only tiddlers!" the twins said. "They're only tiddlers!"

"Sardines never grow any bigger," Charley said, "otherwise they wouldn't be sardines."

"About time they did then," Ma said, peering dubiously at piled scraps of fish, "that's all."

"*Bon appétit!*" Mr Charlton said, and proceeded enthusiastically to attack the *friture*.

Pop, turning to the attack too, found himself facing a large plateful of shrivelled dark brown objects which immediately fell to pieces at the touch of a fork. Scorched fragments of fish flew flakily about in all directions. The few crumbs that he was able to capture, impale on his fork and at last transfer to his mouth tasted, he thought, exactly like the unwanted scraps left over at the bottom of a bag of fish and chips.

"Shan't get very fat on these," Ma said.

In a low depressed voice Pop agreed. Ma's great bulk, which filled half the side of one length of the table, now and then quivered in irritation and presently she was eating the *friture* with her fingers, urging the children to do likewise.

The children, in silent despair, ate more bread.

After a short interval the *saucisson à la mode d'ici* arrived. This consisted of a strange object looking like a large pregnant sausage roll, rather scorched on top. Slight puffs of steam seemed to be issuing from the exhausts at either end.

Ma remarked that at least it was hot and Pop prepared to attack the object on his plate by cutting it directly through the middle.

To his complete dismay the force of the cut, meeting hard resistance from the surface of scorched crust, sent the two pieces hurtling in the air. Both fell with a low thud to the floor.

Weakly he started to eat more bread. He had, he thought, never eaten so much bread in his life.

"What do we have next?" the twins said. "What do we have next?"

"Pigeons," Pop said. The thought of stewed pigeons made his mouth water. In wine sauce too. "Pigeons."

"We want baked beans on toast!" the twins said. "And cocoa."

"Quiet!" Pop thundered. "I'll have order!"

A moment later a waitress, arriving with a fourth plate of bread, proceeded to announce to Mr Charlton a fresh and disturbing piece of news. There were, after all, no pigeons.

Pop felt too weak to utter any kind of exclamation about this second, deeper disappointment.

"There's rabbit," Charley told him, "instead."

Instantly Pop recoiled in pale, fastidious horror.

"Not after myxo!" he said. "No! Charley, I couldn't. I can't touch 'em after myxo!"

Myxomatosis, the scourge of the rabbit tribe, had affected Pop very deeply. To him the thought of eating rabbits was now as great a nausea as the thought of eating nightingales.

"Have an omelette," Charley said cheerfully.

"They don't suit him," Ma said. "They always give him heartburn."

"A steak then," Charley said. "With chips."

At this Pop cheered up a little, saying that a steak would suit him.

"Alors, *un filet biftek pour monsieur*," Charley said, "*avec pommes frites*."

"Biff-teck! Biff-teck!" the twins started shouting, punching each other, laughing loudly. "Biff-teck! Biff-you! Biff-you! Biff-teck!"

Pop was too weak to cry "Quiet!" this time.

Half an hour later he had masticated his way through a bloody piece of beef roughly the shape of a boot's sole, the same thickness, and about as interesting. He ate the chips that accompanied it down to the last frizzled crumb and even dipped his bread in the half-cold blood.

Ma said she hoped he felt better for it but Pop could hardly do more than nod.

"Don't even have ketchup," he said, as if this serious gastronomic omission were the last straw.

H. E. Bates, **A Breath of French Air**

ASSIGNMENT

1 What impression does the passage give of:

(a) the hotel;

(b) the French guests who are eating there;

(c) the waitress?

2 What does Pop think of the behaviour and appearance of the other guests?

3 What does Pop think of his own family's appearance and behaviour?

4 Compare the way Pop uses his bread at the end of the passage with what he thought of the French guests' behaviour at the beginning.

5 Write about a page showing how the writer creates comedy in this passage.

Guidelines *How comic effect is created*

- Look at the way the writer builds up our expectation of what will happen.

Example Pop becomes increasingly hungry.
     He is disappointed with every course.

- The language the writer uses adds to the comic effect. Look at the similes and the descriptive detail the writer uses.

Example 'a strange object looking like a large pregnant sausage roll'

- Comedy is often created through characters and the way the writer presents them.

Example Pop's attitude to the French language

- Imagine the Larkins having a meal at home. Write 350 to 500 words describing the occasion. Use the information you have gathered from the passage about their characters, the relationships between them and the way they talk.

- Imagine that you are a member of one of the French families having dinner that night at the hotel. Write about your impression of the Larkins and the way they behaved.

This passage is taken from *Vanity Fair*, a novel which was written in 1848. Rebecca Sharp is an orphan who is determined to marry a rich man. In this passage she is staying with the family of her great friend Amelia Sedley. Amelia's brother Joseph has just come home from his army posting in India and talks very enthusiastically about his time there.

A very stout, puffy man with several immense neckcloths that rose almost to his nose was reading the paper by the fire when the two girls entered, and bounced off his arm-chair, and blushed excessively, and hid his entire face almost in his neckcloths at this apparition.

"It's only your sister, Joseph," said Amelia, laughing and shaking the two fingers which he held out. "And this is my friend, Miss Sharp, whom you have heard me mention."

"No, never, upon my word," said the head under the neckcloth, shaking very much – "that is, yes – what abominably cold weather, Miss – ," and herewith he fell to poking the fire with all his might, although it was in the middle of June.

"He's very handsome," whispered Rebecca to Amelia, rather loud.

"Do you think so?" said the latter. "I'll tell him."

"Darling! not for worlds," said Miss Sharp, starting back as timid as a fawn.

The first move showed considerable skill. When she called Joseph a very handsome man, she knew that Amelia would tell her mother, who would probably tell Joseph, or who, at any rate, would be pleased by the compliment paid to her son. All mothers are. Perhaps, too, Joseph would overhear the compliment – Rebecca spoke loud enough – and he did hear, and (thinking in his heart that he was a very fine man) the praise thrilled through every fibre of his big body, and made it tingle with pleasure. Then, however, came a recoil.. "Is the girl making fun of me?" he thought. He conducted the young lady down to dinner in a dubious and agitated frame of mind. "Does she really think I am handsome?" thought he, "or is she only making game of me?"

Downstairs, then, they went, Joseph very red and blushing, Rebecca very modest, and holding her green eyes downwards. She was dressed in white, with bare shoulders as white as snow – the picture of youth and unprotected innocence. "I must be very quiet," thought Rebecca, "and very much interested about India."

Mrs Sedley had prepared a fine curry for her son, just as he liked it, and in the course of dinner a portion of this dish was offered to Rebecca. "What is it?" said she, turning an appealing look to Mr Joseph.

"Capital," said he. His mouth was full of it; his face quite red with the delightful exercise of gobbling. "Mother, it's as good as my own curries in India."

"Oh, I must try some, if it is an Indian dish," said Miss Rebecca. "I am sure everything must be good that comes from there."

"Give Miss Sharp some curry, my dear," said Mr Sedley, laughing.

Rebecca had never tasted the dish before.

"Do you find it as good as everything else from India?" said Mr Sedley.

"Oh, excellent!" said Rebecca, who was suffering tortures with the cayenne pepper.

"Try a chilli with it, Miss Sharp," said Joseph, really interested.

"A chilli," said Rebecca, gasping. "Oh yes!" She thought a chilli was something cool, as its name imported, and was served with some.

"How fresh and green they look!" she said, and put one into her mouth. It was hotter than the curry; flesh and blood could bear it no longer. She lay down her fork. "Water, for heaven's sake, water!" she cried.

Mr Sedley burst out laughing. The paternal laugh was echoed by Joseph, who thought the joke capital. The ladies only smiled a little. They thought poor Rebecca suffered too much. She would have liked to choke old Sedley, but she swallowed her mortification as well as she had the abominable curry before it and spoke with a comical, good-humoured air.

"You won't like everything from India now, Miss Sharp," said Mr Sedley; but later he said to his son, "Have a care, Joe; that girl is setting her cap at you."

W.M. Thackeray, **Vanity Fair**

ASSIGNMENT

Here are some of the words used in the passage in connection with Rebecca:

timid; innocence; modest; unprotected; poor Rebecca

1 What kind of person is suggested by these descriptions?

2 What is Rebecca really like?

3 Write about a page describing Rebecca's character and how she is presented. You could consider:

the strategies she uses to gain Joseph's interest;
the way she reacts after eating the chilli;
your own response to her character.

4 What impression does the passage give of Joseph?

5 What does Mr Sedley think of Rebecca?

6 Using the information you have gathered from the passage about Rebecca Sharp, the way she thinks and behaves and the way other people react to her, imagine her and Amelia at a very important ball where there are lots of eligible men. Rebecca has her eye on a man who is dancing with Amelia....write an account of what happens. (You could make Joseph a guest too, if you like.)

7 Describe what happens when you and your family or a group of friends go out for a meal. Try to show the difference in people's characters by the way you describe them and the way they talk and behave towards each other. Include some description and some conversation.

Guidelines   *Writing conversation*

• You must use inverted commas (" ") (sometimes called quotation marks or speech marks) to show the actual words used by a speaker. They are placed at the beginning and end of the words actually spoken. The words in inverted commas are referred to as 'direct speech'.

Example "He's very handsome," whispered Rebecca.

- Commas (,) are used to separate the words actually spoken from the rest of the sentence.

Example "Sardines never grow any bigger," Charley said, "otherwise they wouldn't be sardines."

- Direct speech begins with a capital letter even if it follows a comma.

Example Pop said, "Perfick. Just Perfick."

- When writing the words spoken all punctuation marks – the final full stop, the separating commas, question marks and exclamation marks – come inside the inverted commas.

Example "Oh, excellent!" said Rebecca.
"Do you really think so?" said the latter.

- If direct speech consists of more than one sentence broken up with a phrase of saying, like 'he said' or 'she yelled', use a full stop to show the end of the first sentence and begin the next sentence with a capital letter.

Example "Fresh ones, of course," said Charley. "Probably caught this afternoon."

- If direct speech consists of a series of sentences without interruptions, inverted commas come at the beginning and end of the whole speech.

Example "Well to begin with, there's a kind of small lobster. Then there's a sort of sausage they do here. Hot, I expect. Probably awfully good. Then pigeons in some sort of wine sauce. And afterwards fruit and cheese."

- Every time there is a new speaker, start a new line.

SELF CHECK

Write out the following sentences putting in the inverted commas, capital letters, exclamation marks, question marks and full stops where appropriate.

- (a) the train's late again grumbled the passenger
- (b) the train's late again grumbled the passenger and my feet are frozen
- (c) david said this time it's final
- (d) the shed's on fire yelled andy
- (e) geeta asked how much is this

Homophones

In the passage from *Vanity Fair* Rebecca was embarrassed because she confused the words 'chilli' and 'chilly'. English has lots of words that sound alike but have different meanings. These words are called 'homophones'. You should make sure you know the difference between the most commonly used ones.

stationery   stationary

(It might help you to think of the 'e' in 'stationEry' as standing for **Envelopes**.)

principal   principle

(It might help you to remember that 'princiPAL' refers to a person if you think of them being someone's **pal**.)

aloud	allowed
board	bored
formally	formerly
weather	whether
there	their
who's (who is)	whose

SELF CHECK

Choose the correct word for the following sentences:

(a) (Whose/who's) car was in front?
(b) I do not eat meat as a matter of (principal/principle.)
(c) Find out (weather/whether) the concert has been cancelled or not.

Leaving home

The following material deals with the subject of leaving home for the first time.

"I want to be on my own!" How many times have you said that? How many more times have you thought it? The need to be on your own can be very strong, especially when you are living at home. Even the best home can seem like a prison sometimes, and it is natural to long for a bit more freedom to do what you want to do.

Pete left home last year when he was 17. He was tired of all the rules and regulations: he couldn't bring friends back; he couldn't stay out all night; he couldn't have a motor bike; he couldn't smoke or get drunk. They didn't like any of his girlfriends (too old, too young, too clever, too good for him...!) or any of his friends, come to that. He couldn't have his posters up in his room. Every argument turned into a screaming match. Every weekend there was a row. It always ended up with "This is our house – you'll show some respect!" or "While you're under our roof you'll do as you're told!" Parents just never fight fair! Now Pete is on his own in a bedsit in Aberdeen and can do what he likes. He goes home twice a month and gets on better with his mum and dad. He feels he can be his own person and no longer challenges his parents. He doesn't need to. His mum and dad like the peace and quiet, and they enjoy having the house to themselves.

Most teenagers feel that leaving home is a good thing. They need to be independent and choose how they want to lead their own lives. Even if it is nice to get your meals cooked, your washing done and your room cleaned, home can be very restricting. Margaret left home six weeks ago and is struggling to live on her own. She left because she could not see eye to eye with her mother. Margaret's dad died last year and Margaret was the only daughter at home. When she and her mother disagreed over something, she found she could never really win. Even if she did win, the guilt she felt afterwards was unbearable. So she took her things and moved out. Some friends who

already lived in a flat let her sleep on their floor until she found a bedsit.

Is Margaret any happier? She says that although in some ways she is, she has had problems getting over the first few weeks on her own. It is not quite as easy as she thought it would be. Apart from being short of cash, she often feels very lonely. The hardest times are late at night and at weekends. Sundays are the worst. She often stays in bed just to kill the time. She does not go home because she still feels guilty. Her mother knows where she is, but still feels too hurt to come over and see her.

How would you cope with Sundays, if you lived on your own? What do your friends do – have you some who already live on their own? Loneliness is something most people do not talk about or admit to. It can be one of the biggest problems, especially when you first leave home. You may not believe it now, but you will miss your family. (So try to leave on good terms if possible.)

Carol Parsons and David Veal

ASSIGNMENT

1 Why did Pete leave home and what was the effect on him and his family?

2 Why did Margaret leave home and what was the effect on her and her family?

Place of your own

GOING SOLO

Pros	Cons
There'll be no-one to criticise you, you can live exactly as you please, and if you're fanatically tidy (or very untidy!), you can save an awful lot of arguments!	It can be quite miserable if you're ill or stuck with a quiet weekend - you'll need to put a lot more effort into organising a busy social life to avoid loneliness if you're the type who likes a lot of company.

You don't have to worry about a flatmate who leaves you in the lurch or who won't cough up their share of the rent.

Solo accommodation is harder to find, and more expensive.

When the bills roll in, they're all yours!

ACCOMMODATION TO LOOK FOR

Bedsit or 'studio' flat with self-contained facilities, although these can be pricey.

Your own room in a block of bedsit rooms where you share facilities with other residents.

Living as a lodger in someone's house, perhaps sharing their facilities and possibly sharing meals with the family – great if you've moved from home and aren't quite ready for total independence – although it's usually at the cost of your privacy.

SHARING WITH FRIENDS OR STRANGERS

Pros	Cons
Sharing can be great fun. Meeting friends of friends expands your social life, and if you're feeling lonely or depressed, someone will usually oblige with a chat or a shoulder to cry on.	Clashing personalities and lifestyles will inevitably lead to rows at some point, usually over petty things like someone forgetting to switch the immersion off, or not washing their dishes.

Shared accommodation is among the cheapest and easiest to find, because bills are split between you, easing financial pressure. Learning the 'give and take' attitude you need when living with others can make you far more tolerant and easy-going.

You can often feel as though your 'home' isn't your own, with other people's friends etc. always seeming to be there. There's also the lack of privacy to deal with.

Since no-one will want to do more than the minimum of housework, or clear up a mess that isn't their own, the place can often end up looking like a tip.

You'll probably be asked for a month's rent in advance, plus a deposit against damaged goods and/or property.

ACCOMMODATION TO LOOK FOR

'Person to share' small ads in local papers offering your own room in a shared house.

There'll sometimes be conditions, such a being a non-smoker, but try to choose people in a similar position to you (student/employed/same age/etc.). If you're in a group of friends who want to move in together, look for 'new lets' where you rent a whole house between you, either furnished or unfurnished.

WHERE TO LOOK

Estate Agencies often let out whole houses on behalf of the owners. They're sometimes a bit more expensive than homes advertised in the small ads, but you'll have a proper tenancy agreement and the house is normally in good condition.

Housing Associations are best for bed-sits and unfurnished flats, and the rents are usually very reasonable. Waiting lists can be long, though, and they'll normally only consider you if you're in steady employment.

Small ads offer everything from rooms, bedsits, lodgings and shared flats, all owned by private landlords, but you need to get in there fast, as there can be a high demand for private accommodation.

Council Housing tends to have huge waiting lists and you'll often only get quick accommodation if you have special needs (a single mother or completely homeless). You probably won't be able to sub let, and you must be prepared to live in an unpopular area, but the rent is reasonable and you'll have a proper tenancy agreement.

PITFALLS

Some landlords will try to charge extortionate rents for sub-standard accommodation. If you think yours is excessive, ask your Citizens' Advice Bureau for help in having the rent independently assessed. Insist on a rent book or a signed receipt as proof of your payments. If possible pay by cheque. Know your rights. Read tenancy agreements carefully before you sign – and make sure you have your own copy!

© D.C. Thomson & Co. Ltd.

ASSIGNMENT

Which of the options described in the article would you choose (or have you chosen) if you were looking for a place of your own? Think about your individual circumstances and your personality. Write 300 to 500 words explaining the reasons for your choice and referring to the information given in the passage.

When Ellen's parents have to move to another town they arrange for her to stay with the Barnetts so that she can finish at school. But she decides to move into a flat of her own.

"It's a lovely flat, Mrs Barnett, very modern and not a bit tatty. I think they must have had an interior designer in to do it up, but without destroying its character. Because that's what it's got – character," frantically recalling the more fanciful advertisements. "He's left the original rustic beams and installed a dormer window, which gives a panoramic view," probably of the gas works, she calculated. So far, all she had seen through the skylight was cloud speckled with bird droppings. "So there's a sense of uncluttered space in the main living area but a more intimate atmosphere has been achieved in the rest of the flat by imaginative use of limited space, combining a fully equipped kitchen within easy reach of the lounge," referring to a sink and ageing stove in a cubby next door, "and a stylish built-in bathroom with easy access. So there's no need to worry, everything's fine."

This was her place, she crooned as she looked round the empty room and paced out the uncluttered space of the main living area (fifteen feet). She frisked through her haversack for a tin of soup and exploring her environment in the mild hope of finding a tin-opener, came upon two drawers under the sink. Vigorous heaving at one shifted the unit an inch from the wall, but the drawer did not budge so she moved to the other and gave a massive pull. After picking herself from the floor and reassembling the drawer, she gathered up the contents: razor, nail clippers, matches, screwdriver, hammer and gimlet. She selected the last two and attacked the tin.

Demolition was coming on nicely, tomato soup squirting from perforations and the tin having a novel beaten up shape, when she became aware that the blows with the hammer did not coincide with the sound. Arrested in mid-swing, she listened. The noise continued. Ellen ran through a list of undesirable visitors: werewolves, vampires, ghouls, poltergeists. Then there was an interrogative cough at the door.

"We heard the banging," her landlord said.

"I'm only trying to open a tin."

He looked puzzled so she led him into the kitchen. "It's nearly finished," she told him.

"You're right there." His tone was respectful. Ellen had the impression that he was about to cross himself or doff his cap.

"You can buy proper little gadgets for that job, like this," he informed her and, fanning out the blades of his penknife, showed her an opener. "I'll give you a hand."

Which he nearly did. Blood gushed as, gripping the buckled cylinder, he hacked. "It's nothing," he assured her, sucking his palm. "Nice flavour of soup."

Ellen examined it. The colour prevented her determining whether it had received a transfusion. "Would you like some?" She ran to her haversack. "Found this in our garage," she explained as she tipped soup into the billy can.

The man's eyes searched the kitchen, slid unhindered along the bare windowsill, glided down the empty draining board, rattled against the reeded glass round the bath, then crawled over the six feet of fallow linoleum. "Well, no thank you, I'd rather not join you, just at the moment, if you don't mind," he gasped, then he backed out of the intimate atmosphere of the fully-equipped kitchen, skidded across the contemporary living area and made a lunge for the door.

June Oldham, **Moving in**

ASSIGNMENT

1 Make two lists, one of Ellen's room as she describes it and one as it really is. Use your lists to write a short description of the contrast.

2 What do you think the landlord thinks of Ellen?

3 How do you think Ellen will cope living by herself?

ASSIGNMENT

Your task is to script and record a radio programme called 'So you're going to leave home'. The programme is aimed at young people about to leave home for the first time and will last between five and ten minutes. It should make them aware of the pros and cons of living by themselves or with other people, of the financial implications, and of the practical and emotional issues involved.

1 Get into groups of four or five. Read through all the passages carefully and make notes on the points you will use. Group them under appropriate headings.

2 The programme will be introduced by one person who will also link all the items.

3 The programme should include interviews with people whose experience will be useful. You should choose who and how many to use. For example someone could be Pete or Margaret from the first passage and another could be someone who has shared with friends or strangers, as described in the second passage.

You could use a script layout like this:

Title of programme			
Speaker	Time	Sound effects (music, background noise etc.)	Words

 Write and practise the whole script before you tape it.

Language link

Prefixes

"tomato soup squirting through perforations" A perforation is a hole which has been made through something. The prefix *per* means 'through'. Like many prefixes it comes from Latin; learning the meanings of some of the common ones will help you to work out the meaning of unfamiliar words.

Prefix	Meaning	Examples
per	through	permanent, persuade
pre	before	predict, precede
contra	against	contradict, contrary
circum	round	circumference, circuit
con	with	contain, convene
post	after	postpone, posterity
sub	below	submarine, subway

The following three are from Greek

Prefix	Meaning	Examples
bio	life	biology, biography
auto	self	automatic, autobiography
hemi	half	hemisphere

SELF CHECK

Think of three words for each of the following prefixes:

arch	chief
super	above
pro	for, on behalf of

In this short story Eveline is about to leave home to marry Frank.

She sat at the window watching the evening invade the avenue. Her head was leaned against the window curtains, and in her nostrils was the odour of dusty cretonne. She was tired.

Few people passed. The man out of the last house passed on his way home; she heard his footsteps clacking along the concrete pavement and afterwards crunching on the cinder path before the new red houses. One time there used to be a field there in which they used to play every evening with other people's children. Then a man from Belfast bought the field and built houses in it – not like their little brown houses, but bright brick houses with shining roofs. The children of the avenue used to play together in that field – the Devines, the Waters, the Dunns, little Keogh the cripple, she and her brothers and sisters. Ernest, however, never played: he was too grown up. Her father used often to hunt them in out of the field with his blackthorn stick; but usually little Keogh used to keep nix and call out when he saw her father coming. Still they seemed to have been rather happy then. Her father was not so bad then; and besides, her mother was alive. That was a long time ago; she and her brothers and sisters were all grown up; her mother was dead. Tizzie Dunn was dead too, and the Waters had gone back to England. Everything changes. Now she was going to go away like the others, to leave her home.

Home! She looked round the room, reviewing all its familiar objects which she had dusted once a week for so many years,

wondering where on earth all the dust came from. Perhaps she would never see again those familiar objects from which she had never dreamed of being divided. And yet during all those years she had never found out the name of the priest whose yellowing photograph hung on the wall above the broken harmonium beside the coloured print of the promises made to Blessed Margaret Alacoque. He had been a school friend of her father. Whenever he showed the photograph to a visitor her father used to pass it with a casual word:

"He is in Melbourne now."

She had consented to go away, to leave her home. Was that wise? She tried to weigh each side of the question. In her home anyway she had shelter and food; she had those whom she had known all her life about her. Of course she had to work hard, both in the house and at business. What would they say of her in the Stores when they found out that she had run away with a fellow? That she was a fool, perhaps; and her place would be filled up by advertisement. Miss Gavan would be glad. She had always had an edge on her, especially whenever there were people listening.

"Miss Hill, don't you see these ladies are waiting?"

"Look lively, Miss Hill, please."

She would not cry many tears at leaving the Stores.

But in her new home, in a distant unknown country, it would not be like that. Then she would be married – she, Eveline. People would treat her with respect then. She would not be treated as her mother had been. Even now, though she was over nineteen, she sometimes felt herself in danger of her father's violence. She knew it was that that had given her the palpitations. When they were growing up he had never gone for her, like he used to go for Harry and Ernest, because she was a girl; but latterly he had begun to threaten her and say what he would do to her only for her dead mother's sake. And now she had nobody to protect her, Ernest was dead and Harry, who was in the church decorating business, was nearly always down somewhere in the country. Besides, the invariable squabble for money on Saturday nights had begun to weary her unspeakably. She always gave her entire wages – seven shillings – and Harry always sent up what he could, but the trouble was to get any money from her father. He said she used to squander the money, that she had no head, that he wasn't going to give her his hard-earned money to throw about the streets, and much more, for he was usually fairly bad on Saturday night. In the end he would give her the money and ask her had she any intention of buying Sunday's dinner. Then she had to rush out as quickly as she could and do her marketing, holding her black leather purse tightly in her hand as she elbowed her way through the crowds and returning home late under her load of provisions. She had hard work to keep the house together and to see that the two young children who had been left to her charge went to school regularly and got their meals regularly. It was hard work – a hard life – but now that she was about to leave it she did not find it a wholly undesirable life.

She was about to explore another life with Frank. Frank was very kind, manly, open-hearted. She was to go away with him by the night-boat to be his wife and to live with him in Buenos Aires, where he had a home waiting for her. How well she remembered the first time she had seen him; he was lodging in a house on the main road where she used to visit. It seemed a few weeks ago. He was standing at the gate, his peaked cap pushed back on his head and his hair tumbled forward over a face of bronze. Then they had come to know each other. He used to meet her outside the Stores every evening and see her home. He took her to see *The Bohemian Girl* and she felt elated as she sat in an unaccustomed part of the theatre with him. He was awfully fond of music and sang a little. People knew that they were courting, and, when he sang about the lass that loves a sailor, she always felt pleasantly confused. He used to call her Poppens out of fun. First of all it

had been an excitement for her to have a fellow and then she had
begun to like him. He had tales of distant countries. He had
started as a deck boy at a pound a month on a ship of the Allan
line going out to Canada. He told her the names of the ships he
had been on and the names of the different services. He had sailed
through the Straits of Magellan and he told her stories of the
terrible Patagonians. He had fallen on his feet in Buenos Aires, he
said, and had come over to the old country just for a holiday. Of
course, her father had found out the affair and had forbidden her
to have anything to say to him.

"I know these sailor chaps," he said.

One day he had quarrelled with Frank, and after that she had to
meet her lover secretly.

The evening deepened in the avenue. The white of two letters
in her lap grew indistinct. One was to Harry; the other was to her
father. Ernest had been her favourite, but she liked Harry too. Her
father was becoming old lately, she noticed; he would miss her.
Sometimes he could be very nice. Not long before, when she had
been laid up for a day, he had read her out a ghost story and made
toast for her at the fire. Another day, when their mother was alive,
they had all gone for a picnic to the Hill of Howth. She
remembered her father putting on her mother's bonnet to make the
children laugh.

Her time was running out, but she continued to sit by the
window, leaning her head against the window curtain, inhaling the
odour of dusty cretonne. Down far in the avenue she could hear a
street organ playing. She knew the air. Strange that it should come
that very night to remind her of the promise to her mother, her
promise to keep the home together as long as she could. She
remembered the last night of her mother's illness; she was again
in the close, dark room at the other side of the hall and outside she
heard a melancholy air of Italy. The organ-player had been
ordered to go away and given sixpence. She remembered her
father strutting back into the sick-room saying:

"Damned Italians! Coming over here!"

As she mused the pitiful vision of her mother's life laid its spell
on the very quick of her being – that life of commonplace
sacrifices closing in final craziness. She trembled as she heard
again her mother's voice saying constantly with foolish insistence:

"Derevaun Seraun! Derevaun Seraun!"

She stood up in a sudden impulse of terror. escape! She must escape! Frank would save her. He would give her life, perhaps love, too. But she wanted to live. Why should she be unhappy? She had a right to happiness. Frank would take her in her arms, fold her in his arms. He would save her.

She stood among the swaying crowd in the station at the North Wall. He held her hand and she knew that he was speaking to her, saying something about the passage over and over again. The station was full of soldiers with brown baggages. Through the wide doors of the sheds she caught a glimpse of the black mass of the boat, lying in beside the quay wall, with illumined portholes. She answered nothing. She felt her cheek pale and cold and, out of a maze of distress, she prayed to God to direct her, to show her what was her duty. The boat blew a long mournful whistle into the mist. If she went, tomorrow she would be on the sea with Frank, steaming towards Buenos Aires. Their passage had been booked. Could she still draw back after all he had done for her? Her distress awoke a nausea in her body and she kept moving her lips in silent fervent prayer.

A bell clanged upon her heart. She felt him seize her hand: "Come!"

All the seas of the world tumbled about her heart. He was drawing her into them: he would drown her. She gripped with both hands at the iron railing.

"Come!"

He rushed beyond the barrier and called to her to follow. He was shouted at to go on, but he still called to her. She set her white face to him, passive, like a helpless animal. Her eyes gave him no sign of love or farewell or recognition.

No! No! No! It was impossible. Her hands clutched the iron in frenzy. Amid the seas she sent a cry of anguish.

"Eveline! Evvy!"

James Joyce, **Dubliners**

ASSIGNMENT

1 Give some of the details in the story which help us to picture Eveline's home.

2 Describe Eveline's father, and her feelings towards him.

3 What would Eveline gain by going?

4 Why do you think that in the end she doesn't go? What do you think about her decision?

5 Write two paragraphs describing what Eveline's thoughts and actions might be in the next hour.

More suggestions for coursework

- You have been living away from home for a month. Write a letter to one of your friends or a member of your family describing your new surroundings and your new way of life.
- Write two contrasting descriptions (about a page each) in which you first describe your 'new life' in glowing terms for the benefit of friends at home, and then in a more realistic way!
- You can do this exercise in pairs, small groups or as a whole class. Each person prepares a description of a room, which is read to the class. The description should include details of the decoration (walls, furniture etc.) and also describe possessions which are in the room. Your partner or the rest of the group has to work out from the description and clues you have given what kind of person the room belongs to.

QUIZ

Try this quiz to see if you are ready to live independently! ... For each question circle the letter which seems the most applicable and find out how you score.

1 When you get your weekly/monthly/termly money do you:

(a) go out and buy something new to wear, or a CD, or something else for yourself?

(b) work out how much you will need for rent, food, fares, bills before you spend anything?

(c) give back money you've borrowed from friends?

2 When the bills arrive do you:

(a) put them in a drawer and forget about them until the final demand?

(b) ask your parents to pay them?

(c) pay them with the money you've put aside for this purpose?

3 One evening all the lights go out. Do you:

(a) grope your way to the phone by torchlight and phone an electrician?

(b) ask a neighbour what you should do?

(c) mend the fuse?

4 You are planning a party for Saturday night. Do you:

(a) tell your neighbours and say they are welcome to drop in?

(b) borrow the best sound system you can and clear a bit of space?

(c) make sure anything breakable or likely to be damaged is locked away?

5 Your landlord receives complaints about the party and says you must leave by the end of the week. Do you:

(a) apologise, say it won't happen again and ask him to change his mind?

(b) consult your tenancy agreement or the Citizens' Advice Bureau to find out what you should do?

(c) leave. You hate rows.

Score

1 a) **1**	b) **3**	c) **2**
2 a) **2**	b) **1**	c) **3**
3 a) **1**	b) **2**	c) **3**
4 a) **3**	b) **1**	c) **2**
5 a) **2**	b) **3**	c) **1**

Add up your score

5-8 Are you sure you are ready for this? Be prepared for some difficult times – but you can always learn from your mistakes!

9-12 You're fairly on the ball, and should take the ups and downs in your stride.

13-15 You're ready to take this step. Remember to keep asking for advice and information so that you make the right decisions.

Running away

Every year hundreds of people disappear from home with no warning.

This is a scene from a film called *Runners* in which an eleven year old schoolgirl, Rachel, disappears on a lonely country road. Her father, Tom, is convinced she's alive and two years later finds her in London. She agrees to meet him.

EXTERIOR. LONG SHOPPING ARCADE. DAY.

TOM   (smiling) You're late.

RACHEL. I know. I couldn't help it. I came as quick as I could.

She glances back towards the entrance she's just come from.

TOM   (following her look) Does anybody know you're here?

RACHEL. No. I don't think so.

TOM   (looking down at the paper bag he's holding). I brought you
           some doughnuts. (nervous laugh) The first of many
           celebrations, so we can make pigs of ourselves.

RACHEL. Thanks. (She takes one and bites into it; it's gone in a second,
           the jam all over her lips. Slight smile.) I still like these.

Tom is glancing down at her bare arms, as she reaches for the
doughnut – and then as she's eating it, sees flashes of her arms through
the cardigan. Tom is looking for any trace of needle marks.

TOM   You want to take your cardigan off.

RACHEL. No, it's OK. (Jam on her lips) It's not hot.

TOM   (touching her hair, glancing at her arms. She looks at him
           doing this). Just reminding myself what you look like.
           (Touching her hair, running his fingers through it.) I thought
           you might have purple patches in your hair, or have it done up
           in spikes. (Smiles.) You know, a bald hole here.(Touching the
           back of her head.)

RACHEL. No, I've never had it like that.

TOM.   You've had your ears pierced.

RACHEL. Yes, that was a long time ago.

Stephen Poliakoff, **Runners**

ASSIGNMENT

1 Imagine you are Tom in *Runners*. Write about your thoughts and feelings after your meeting with Rachel.

2 Imagine you are Rachel in *Runners*. Write about your thoughts and feelings after your meeting with Tom.

Use the information you get from the extract and include any other ideas you have about Tom and Rachel and the situation. You could think of a reason for Rachel's leaving home if you like.

Many publications carry details of missing persons like the ones below.

Have you seen these people?

Sarah Cole, 17, has been missing from her home in Rochdale since May 9th. She drove to school in her father's car that day and crashed it near the school. By the time her parents arrived she had disappeared and hasn't been seen since. She is thought to be in London and may be begging in the West End. Sarah is five foot six and has blonde shoulder length hair, blue eyes and a faint scar above her left eyebrow. Her parents cannot explain her disappearance. 'We just want to know she is alive and well,' Sarah's mother says. Her message to Sarah is, 'Just get in touch.'

Mark Conway, 21, disappeared three years ago when he left his home in Ipswich to visit his girlfriend. He never arrived, and his car was found abandoned. His parents have growing fears for his safety. His father says, 'We just want to know that Mark is all right. There is no pressure on him to do anything he doesn't want to do.' Mark is five foot ten with red curly hair and freckles.

(Both the examples of missing persons advertisements above are ficticious.)

ASSIGNMENT

1 Write an account of a day in the life of either Sarah or Mark. You will need to decide what might have happened to them and why they disappeared. Use the information in the *Have you seen these people?* column as a basis and build your story around that. Try to include thoughts and feelings as well as things happening.

---

2 Do this exercise in pairs or threes. Interview the parents of Sarah or Mark about why they think their daughter or son disappeared. You could write up an account of the interviews afterwards.

More suggestions for coursework

- Choose three members of a family and describe each person's thoughts and feelings about the disappearance of one of the family.
- Imagine that someone who has run away suddenly turns up at home. Describe what happens. You could write this as a story or a play.

Helping the homeless

SHELTER is the National Campaign for Homeless People. Shelter believes that a decent affordable home should be available to everybody as a basic human right.

Homelessness is one of Britain's most pressing social problems, but all too often it is reduced to just numbers – how many people, how many new homes are needed, how much will it all cost? The numbers are important. But they're not as important as the people behind the statistics.

This report highlights the human cost for the thousands of homeless people who will today wake up in temporary accommodation or on the streets. Despite the popular stereotype of these people as being wise to the system, shouting for their rights, the reality is that most homeless people suffer in silence. People like Meena Roberts, repossessed after the family business failed, who says her husband to this day can't talk about living in bed and breakfast accommodation. He feels that by losing their home he let them down. People like Jenny Logan, who describes living in temporary accommodation as 'being dumped and forgotten'.

The message from these stories is that homelessness can, and does, happen to anyone. And the nightmare of homelessness doesn't end when someone finds temporary accommodation – for many, the problems get worse. Insecurity, squalor, disruption of jobs and education – enduring these can be as bad as the initial trauma of homelessness itself.

The people in this report have stopped suffering in silence to speak out about the personal misery of homelessness and the difference a personal home can make. And they're not alone. Perhaps it is the realisation that it can happen to anyone that is making a growing number of people speak out against homelessness. More people than ever are supporting Shelter's work financially, and we desperately need that money to run our services. But we also need your voice. We need you to speak out against homelessness wherever you can – to your local politicians, to your local paper, in your school or college, in your church. Tell them what you've read in this report. Tell them that the provision of at least 100,000 affordable rented homes has to be a priority.

Please add your voice and your support to Shelter's campaign – only if we all speak out can we give a voice and hope to all those, who, tonight, will go to sleep without a home to call their own.

Chris Holmes
Director of Shelter

ASSIGNMENT

1 What are the main points the Director of Shelter makes about the kind of people who become homeless?

2 Why does he not use lots of statistics in his message?

3 What are the two main kinds of help that he asks for?

I never thought it would happen to us....

When their house was repossessed after their business failed, Mr and Mrs Roberts and their two young children had to spend six months in a bed and breakfast hotel in Bristol.

Meena Roberts: "We bought our house when we were both working. Soon after I was laid off from my job and our income halved. Interest rates began to soar and in December 1991, when I was expecting my first daughter, we received a possession order. We had no option but to let everything go and move into bed and breakfast.

The B&B had 51 rooms, all full of families and we all had to share one kitchen which was often dirty. The only place to keep food was in our room. Hygiene was terrible. Plates and cutlery were washed in the same sink as hands and clothes. We had our room fumigated because we were all coming up with rashes and headlice. Food poisoning was a big problem. One resident died and was carted out in front of all the children.

Living in bed and breakfast affected my family in many ways. To this day my husband can't talk about being there. He feels that by losing the house he let us down. My son's experience in bed and breakfast made him aggressive and he now finds it very difficult to make friends.

When we came to this house my husband painted it straight away and tried to pretend bed and breakfast had never happened. But I kind of gave up. I'd used up so much energy trying to maintain a facade of being OK I felt completely drained. I think if I had been there for another three months I would have had a complete breakdown.

I feel like I'm different from everyone else.....

Ellie and her mother Barbara were made homeless after a rent dispute. They currently live in temporary council property surrounded by derelict houses in Welwyn Garden City. Ellie has been homeless for two years and, when interviewed, had not been to school for over six weeks.

Ellie: I was the first child born in a bed and breakfast hotel in St Albans and became homeless again when I was eight. The worst thing about being homeless is that you can't do anything about it. When we had to leave our home I lost all my toys. I used to cry every night.

We stayed with friends and then we lived in two other places before we came here. In this house I feel like I'm different from everyone else. They've all got their nice houses.

When we moved here I couldn't get to school because it was too far away by bus. I've been doing my lessons at home for the last six weeks. We don't have a telephone. We're completely cut off.

Sometimes I feel very sorry for my mother. Moving all the time is very tiring and has made her bad tempered. Her rheumatism has got worse as well because it's damp here. When she shouts at me it makes me feel even more upset. She never used to be like that.

This house isn't cosy. I don't like touching the walls and I hate the furniture. I feel like I'm surrounded by spiders. The earwigs and woodlice come out from under the floor.

Living here I don't have anyone home for tea. I've been so scared of not knowing where I might go next. Sometimes I just want to scream and yell and jump in the air.

Everyone just walked on by.....

Sean was brought up in care until he was sixteen. He spent nearly three years sleeping rough in Edinburgh, London and Liverpool. He now lives in a hostel in Liverpool.

Sean: I was moved around from children's home to children's home – seven in all, and was separated from my sister when I was ten. At fourteen I was abused by a care worker and spent six weeks in hospital, before being sent back to the same children's home.

I was finally expelled from care for defending a boy who was being assaulted by a member of staff. Overnight I was moved into a bedsit with my friend Miff. We had to share a kitchen and lounge with two 35 year olds who threatened us with violence. We turned to the streets because we thought it would be safer.

The streets of Edinburgh were very violent and I was introduced to a lot of crime. I was always on the move for fear of being beaten up by passers-by and because of the cold. People didn't want to see the homeless on their doorstep.

The drug scene on the street is big and it's very easy to get sucked into it. If you don't have willpower you're dead. Nine of my friends died on the streets. My friend Miff lay dead for three days in a public place with a needle in his arm. Everyone just walked by.

In July 1989 I went to London after two and a half years of living rough in Edinburgh. I wanted to try and find a flat but could never raise enough money for a deposit.

The lowest points were during the bad winters when it dropped to less than -5 degrees. My health was badly affected and I now have chronic bronchitis and a heart murmur.

Things got better when I moved into a cottage on the Scottish Borders with my girlfriend and took a pre-nursing course. But when our relationship broke down I packed my bags and came to Liverpool. I was back where I started.

I've spent the last two years living in hostels. People who live here have no respect for themselves or the place. There's a lot of vandalism, the walls are covered in graffiti, the rooms stink and drug taking is rife.

I'm desperate to get out of the hostel. Housing is being built for the students in Liverpool but the homeless are completely overlooked. Society has turned its back on the problem because it's too scared to face it.

ASSIGNMENT

1 For which of the three people whose stories are told do you personally feel most sympathy?

2 Write about a page, making reference to all the stories in your answer.

Example Although Meena had a very distressing time in temporary accommodation, it was for only six months. Ellie and Sean, on the other hand.......

3 Why do you think these particular examples, Meena, Ellie and Sean, have been chosen as part of Shelter's publicity material? (Think about the people who are likely to be particularly influenced by each story.)

4 Although their situations are different, the three people have had similar experiences. What similarities do you find in the three accounts?

In 1994 365 000 individuals were accepted as homeless by councils in England.

Shelter estimates that there are up to 8600 people sleeping rough in England.

Around 60% of rough sleepers are found outside of London.

At the end of 1994 there were 47 760 families living in temporary accommodation in England.

The Nightline telephone service offers emergency assistance every night of the year. In 1993/4 it answered 24 805 calls and found emergency accommodation for 3559 people. £792 keeps Nightline running for one night.

Shelter 1995

ON THE STREETS

How many times can you cross Dean Street in the course of a day?
The streets of Soho sound and smell of action, glamour, success,
excitement. The cabs, the bikers, the lorries they never let you through.
You're walking about, at 18, in the ashes of a lifetime and you can't
cross the street.
And they don't care. They pass you by.

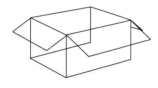

You and your mates, living in a box.
Living in a cardboard box.
Living in cardboard boxes can't really be a good idea otherwise more
people would do it.
"No problem, you'd prefer a cardboard box to a 3-bedroomed semi, we
can arrange that, Sir."
Estate agents don't often say that, do they?
And people walk past you and think, "Homelessness, it's bad, but it's
there, "instead of thinking, "It's there, and it's bad."

You still can't get across Dean Street. The traffic, the movement.
If you die sleeping on the streets you die of natural causes.
How can the way you live be thought to be unnatural but your death
natural?

Tony has spent several years on the streets. He has noticed the difference.
"Different now. Different. All kids now. Children sleeping on the streets.
When I was a nipper we'd heard about the stuff happening in
Victorian times.
Not now. Couldn't believe it. Begging. Nippers begging.

Begging. You know how to do it. "Homeless, Hungry, Help Me" cards
everywhere.
But that doesn't hide the pain, the suffering, the awfulness of sleeping
on the streets.
The dreadful feeling of not being as good as the people walking by.
The terrifying feeling of another, yet another night hiding in a corner
hoping you won't be noticed, hoping you don't matter but praying
you do.

Anonymous

ASSIGNMENT

1 Talk about the poem in pairs or small groups. What different methods does the poet use to get his message across? Which parts of the poem do you find most effective?

2 Discuss what you think and feel when you pass someone like the poet or the people he describes.

3 In pairs, role play what happens when you and your friend disagree about whether you should give money to someone begging.

ASSIGNMENT

Your college is deciding what charities it should support this year and is asking people who support particular charities to make a presentation to the charity committee in support of their claim. The presentation should consist of a short talk (three minutes) and a one-page handout. You decide to put forward Shelter.

1 Using the information given in all the above passages and the poem, write the speech you will give. (Remember the audience will be a college group, so think of ways to gain their interest and involvement.)

2 In pairs or small groups, listen to each other's speeches and give the speaker some constructive feedback about the content and delivery.

3 Design the handout. (You may want to refer to the guidelines for writing a leaflet given in chapter one.)

Spelling check

Confusions

'365,000 individuals were accepted as homeless'

'accept' and 'except' are sometimes confused.

accept = to take or receive

Example I **accepted** the invitation to the party.

except = not including
Example Everyone **except** James was present.

Other words which are often confused are: 'effect', 'affect'
effect = a result or change
Example The **effect** of the decision was felt immediately.
        The language has a sad effect.

affect = to cause a change in
Example I was not affected by the bus strike because I walk to work.

SELF CHECK

Use accept or except in these sentences

(a) Jenny was told that no more excuses for being late would be........
(b) When it started to rain heavily, everyone ran for cover .... one man.

Use affect or effect in these sentences

(a) The sound ....were the best thing about the film.
(b) He seemed quite un............ed by the news.

Same place, different time

Here are three descriptions of places in London. The first was written in 1802, the second in 1852 and the third in 1994.

Passage A

Composed upon Westminster Bridge , September 3, 1802

Earth has not anything to show more fair:
Dull would he be of soul who could pass by
A sight so touching in its majesty:
This city now doth like a garment wear
The beauty of the morning; silent, bare,
Ships, towers, domes, theatres, and temples lie
Open unto the fields, and to the sky;
All bright and glittering in the smokeless air.
Never did sun more beautifully steep
In his first splendour valley, rock or hill;
Ne'er saw I, never felt, a calm so deep!
The river glideth at his own sweet will:
Dear God! the very houses seem asleep;
And all that mighty heart is lying still.

William Wordsworth

ASSIGNMENT

1 In your own words describe the scene in the poem. You could think about what time of day it is, and the view the poet sees from the bridge.

2 What feelings does the scene inspire in the poet?

3 Pick out some words or phrases that you think help to create the atmosphere of the poem.

Passage B

This extract from *Bleak House* is about Jo, a young boy who lives on the streets of London and makes a living by sweeping away the dirt from the place where people cross the road. He stays in a street called Tom-all-alone's which is full of slum property.

Jo sweeps his crossing all day long. He sums up his mental condition, when asked a question, by replying that he "don't know nothink". He knows that it's hard to keep the mud off the crossing in dirty weather, and harder still to live by doing it.

Jo lives – that is to say, Jo has not yet died – in a ruinous place, known to the like of him by the name of Tom-all-alone's. It is a black, dilapidated street avoided by all decent people; where the crazy houses were seized upon, when their decay was far advanced, by some bold vagrants, who, after establishing their own possession, took to letting them out in lodgings. Now, these tumbling tenements contain, by night, a swarm of misery. As, on the human wretch, vermin parasites appear, so, these ruined shelters have bred a crowd of foul existence that crawls in and out of gaps in walls and boards and coils itself to sleep in maggot numbers where the rain drips in.

Twice, lately, there has been a crash and a cloud of dust in Tom-all-alone's; and each time, a house has fallen. These accidents have made a paragraph in the newspapers, and have filled a bed or two in the nearest hospital. The gaps remain, and there are not unpopular lodgings among the rubbish. As several more houses are nearly ready to go, the next crash in Tom-all-alone's may be expected to be a good one.

Charles Dickens, **Bleak House**

ASSIGNMENT

1 What impression does the writer give of Jo's life?

2 In your own words describe what Tom-all-alone's is like.

3 Pick out some words and phrases which help to create the atmosphere of the description.

Passage C

This extract from *Ashes By Now* by Mark Timlin gives a modern point of view.

When I told the driver where we were headed, he wasn't happy. He hummed and hawed, and eventually demanded a tenner out front, in case I did a runner. I paid him without argument otherwise I knew he'd just turf me out of the car, and that would be that.

I didn't blame him for not wanting to go. If I'd been a cab driver I wouldn't have wanted to take a fare to the Lion Estate either. It was a sink. A black hole where the local council dropped all the tenants it didn't want to know about: the thieves, junkies, arsonists, non-payers of rent, bad neighbours. It was a no-go area for postmen, milkmen, doctors, dustmen, meter readers, bailiffs, everyone. The fire service only went in with police protection, and ambulances had stopped entering the estate after three false alarms in as many days ended up with three ambulances being stripped of all drugs, medication and saleable parts. And Canvey House: that was the worst part of a lousy place. The water-stained concrete that it was built of was scarred with smoke, bullet holes, the lot. Inside it was infested with every bug and insect known to man, and probably a few that weren't. A perpetual rain of garbage, old TV sets and furniture poured off the building, day and night, because the tenants couldn't be bothered to take their junk downstairs by more conventional means.

The cab driver dropped me off at the outskirts of the estate. He point-blank refused to drive into the maze of narrow turnings that covered it. I didn't blame him. Cab hijacking by joy riders was one of the new games on the estate. And his Volvo wasn't in bad nick.

Mark Timlin, **Ashes By Now**

ASSIGNMENT

1 What impression of the estate does the writer create? Write a short response referring to words and phrases in the passage.

2 Make a list of all the words and expressions that a reader from an earlier century would not understand. In pairs, take it in turns to be the modern reader and the one from an earlier time and explain to each other the meaning of each expression.

ASSIGNMENT

1 Copy out and fill in the chart with words and phrases taken from passages B and C which describe:

a) the streets and houses;
b) the people.

A couple have been done for you.

	Passage B	Passage C
streets/houses	ruined shelters	no-go area
people	swarm of misery	thieves

2 What do you think is the attitude of each writer to the place and people he describes?

3 Choose the word or phrase which refers to the language and style of each passage, and write it under the appropriate heading of passage B or C.

slang; poetic phrases; imagery; short sentences; colloquial; mainly long sentences

Passage B	Passage C

More suggestions for coursework

- Write two descriptions, about a page each, of places you know well, or if you prefer, places you imagine. One description should be a place you like, which makes you feel good, and the other a place which you dislike. Try to make your feelings clear by the words and phrases you use to describe the place.
- Write two descriptions of the same seaside scene, one in summer and one in winter.
- Write a description of the living room the morning after a party.

Out of place

Here is a passage about someone who feels out of place. *Sumitra's Story* is about a young Asian girl whose parents were expelled from Uganda and brought Sumitra and her sisters to England. She becomes torn between her parents' way of life and the new one she experiences.

The festival of Diwali came and went. New clothes were bought and gifts of money exchanged. They all went to the temple and to

the dances. Girls were chaperoned by their mothers or married sisters to dances which were held once a week. Sumitra and Sandya took their places in the inner ring while the boys formed an outer circle. The musicians sat down on the floor – as the drums began to beat Sumitra always felt the rhythm obliterating her thoughts. The dancers held sticks which they clicked as they passed each other. As the pace quickened, as the sitar and tabla chased each other in a wild, controlled frenzy, their feet moved faster, the sticks tapped louder.

An Indian photographer often came to the temple. He specialised in the old style of picture and would wax ecstatic about his skill. "Anyone can draw English photo," he pointed out sarcastically. "Just say cheeses, or watching birdies, mister smile, finish. One, two days later mister coming for picture. Picture ready. Picture of mister saying cheeses. No skill, no class." he paused, then continued, "I study," and on the word study his voice broke and squeaked in emphasis, "I study subject, add sceneries. You saying what you want, flower, clouds, hands, I balance and paint." So the Patels had photographs of themselves taken. Mai and Bap issued magically from the clouds like science fiction characters. The four sisters appeared to stand in the palm of a gigantic hand. Sumitra had one taken on her own, emanating from the centre of a lotus blossom. The photographs were painted with delicate tints, made into cards, and sent as greetings and mementoes to friends.

Yet they found that despite these colourful interludes, it was very hard to adjust to their new life. Bap hated his job and could not reconcile himself to the fact that he had no home of his own. He was used to dispensing hospitality, not receiving it. Mai was cowed and ill, and spent most of his time in bed. As the months went by Sumitra found that she was helping more and more in the home. As soon as she pushed open the door after school, she heard Motiben calling, "Come, girl, you must grind the mustard seed!" or "The house needs cleaning!" or "Iron your father's shirt!"

Because of this she could not begin her homework until late at night, after she settled Ela and Bimla in bed. Within ten minutes she was nodding over her books red-eyed and exhausted. She couldn't concentrate at school and, although she now understood perfectly what the teacher was saying, could not remember a word.

Mr Jones called her into his study. "We are very pleased with the way you have settled in, and some of your work this term has been very good. But many of your teachers complain that your homework is never complete and that you appear withdrawn in class. Is anything the matter?"

Sumitra studied the carpet. It was duty grey, slightly muddied from the tramping of wet boots. "I'm sorry, Mr Jones," she said. "I just have to help a lot at home. I don't seem to have much time to study."

"Shall I go and see your parents?" he asked. "After all, I imagine that one of the reasons they came to England was so that you could have a good education."

Sumitra twisted her hair round her finger, making patterns on the carpet with her shoe at the same time. It was obvious put like that. But to her family school was something that finished at 4.30. Her allegiance then was to them. When Hilary went home it was to a clean house and a hot meal. She did her homework in her bedroom and then went downstairs to watch television. Girls and women in the Indian community were expected to clean and cook. Meals could take up to three hours to prepare. Hilary's mother bought bread from the baker, but chapattis and pooris had to be freshly prepared for each meal.

She sighed. She felt as if she were a bridge between two countries, two banks that would never meet, two cultures that could never merge. She was like a bridge and everyone was walking over her, from one land to another, like tourists visiting a foreign country but not fully comprehending the strange customs they observed.

Rukshana Smith, **Sumitra's story**

ASSIGNMENT

1 What are the main features of the dances at the temple?

2 Describe the way the photographer takes his pictures. Why is he proud of them?

3 What sentence tells you that Sumitra and her family enjoyed the dances and being photographed?

4 What tensions does Sumitra experience? Describe the way her homelife conflicts with her school life.

5 Write a paragraph expressing Sumitra's feelings. Use the passage but put your ideas in your own words.

6 Write a story or description based on the idea of feeling out of place. It could be to do with feeling out of place in the same way as Sumitra, or it could be feeling out of place among friends, or in a family, or at work.

More suggestions for coursework

- Choose a festival or holiday which you and your family celebrate. Write a description of what happens. You could include details of any traditions you have for that day (such as when you open presents, or if you visit anyone) and any special food that is eaten or clothes that are worn. Write about 300 to 500 words.
- Write about somebody who envies the home life of a friend.

END-OF-CHAPTER ASSIGNMENT

 Write about some of the difficulties and pleasures associated with living in an environment which is new or which you have not chosen. Refer to four or five of the extracts in this chapter in your answer.

SUMMARY

In this section you have covered the following aspects of GCSE requirements.

SPEAKING AND LISTENING

group discussion
role play
making an appeal
radio programme

READING

travel writing
tourist information
travel brochure
poetry written since 1900
poetry written before 1900
non-European poetry written since 1900
prose written since 1900
prose written before 1900
magazine article
short story written since 1900
publicity material
screenplay

WRITING

factual description
formal letter
informal letter
imaginative account
personal writing
poetry
conversation/dialogue
radio script
opinion
description

LANGUAGE STUDY

commas
synonyms
rhyme

rhythm
alliteration
metaphor
adjectives
inverted commas
homophones
prefixes
easily confused words
language change

REVISION AND FURTHER ASSIGNMENTS

1 Write out the following sentences inserting commas.

(a) We had only fifteen minutes to pack up the tent the groundsheet the sleeping bags the stove.

(b) Rob Charles the footballer having retired from the game began a new career as a sports presenter.

(c) Eric however in spite of everyone's advice put all his money into stocks shares risky schemes.

2 Write sentences of your own listing the contents of a drawer or handbag.

3 Give a few synonyms for each of these words, then use each appropriately in a sentence:

(a) something you sit on;
(b) angry;
(c) good;
(d) nice.

4 Make each of these nouns into an adjective:

(a) winter;
(b) noise;
(c) poison.

5 Check your understanding of the rules for using inverted commas and punctuating direct speech by writing conversations based on the following:

(a) A parent telling a child to tidy up its bedroom.

(b) Janet asking her friend if she saw the film on television last night. Janet enjoyed the film but missed the end because she had to answer the phone.

(c) Farrukh asking his friend which pair of trainers he should buy.

6 Choose the correct word in the following sentences:

(a) The van backed into the stationery/stationary car.
(b) The principal/principle of the college presented the awards.
(c) Sunil quickly became used to his new roll/role as supervisor.

7 What figure of speech is being used here? "I'm over the moon about it!"

Explain the literal meaning of the words. What is the effect of using this figure of speech?

8 What is the meaning of the prefix in these words:

(a) autograph;
(b) subsidence?

9 Use the following topics as a starting point for writing. Where there are no specific instructions use the titles as the basis of a story, or personal writing, or an article, or an argument/discussion, or a script etc.

10 You have bought a piece of sports or electrical equipment which has turned out to be faulty. Write the letter you send to the shop or manufacturer.

11 Write a letter to your local newspaper complaining about an increase in bus fares.

12 My home town. (You could write some contrasting descriptions such as your town as it would appear in a tourist guide, as seen from the point of view of a child, as seen by a visitor from another country.)

13 A place you would like to visit or re-visit.

14 A guide to spending a holiday in a place you know well. (Who is the guide for – students? families? Use headings such as accommodation; things to do; where to eat.)

15 Away from home.

16 Running away.

17 The beach.

DIFFERENT VOICES

Autobiography

An autobiography is someone's life story, written by that person. If you are going to write about your life you have to make some decisions about where to start. Many writers begin in their childhood and describe the people and places which were important. In these three extracts the writers focus on early memories.

Weighing the half-pounds of flour, excluding the scoop, and depositing them dust-free into the thin paper sacks held a simple kind of adventure for me. I developed an eye for measuring how full a silver-looking ladle of flour, mash, meal, sugar or corn had to be to push the scale indicator over to eight ounces or one pound. When I was absolutely accurate our appreciative customers used to admire: "Sister Henderson sure got some smart grandchildrens." If I was off in the Store's favour, the eagle-eyed women would say, "Put some more in that sack, child. Don't you try to make your profit offa me."

Then I would quietly but persistently punish myself. For every bad judgement, the fine was no silver-wrapped Kisses, the sweet chocolate drops that I loved more than anything in the world, except Bailey. And maybe canned pineapples. My obsession with pineapples nearly drove me mad. I dreamt of the days when I would be grown and able to buy a whole carton for myself alone.

Although the syrupy golden rings sat in their exotic cans on our shelves year round, we only tasted them during Christmas. Momma used the juice to make almost-black fruit cakes. Then she lined heavy soot-encrusted iron skillets with the pineapple rings for rich upside-down cakes. Bailey and I received one slice each, and I carried mine around for hours, shredding off the fruit until nothing was left except the perfume on my fingers. I'd like to think that my desire for pineapples was so sacred that I wouldn't allow myself to steal a can (which was possible) and eat it alone out in the garden, but I'm certain that I must have weighed the possibility of the scent exposing me and didn't have the nerve to attempt it.

Maya Angelou, **I know why the caged bird sings**

ASSIGNMENT

1 Describe what the writer enjoyed about working in the store.

2 Pick out the words and phrases which express her love of pineapples.

3 What do you learn from the extract about the writer's character?

Walk into the morning disorder of this room (the scullery) and all the garden was laid out dripping on the table. Chopped carrots like copper pennies, radishes and chives, potatoes dipped and stripped clean from their coats of mud, the snapping of tight pea-pods, and the tearing of glutinous beans from their nests of wool.

Large meals were prepared in this room, cauldrons of stew for the insatiate hunger of eight. Stews of all that grew on these rich banks, flavoured with sage, coloured with Oxo, and laced with a few bones of lamb. There was, it is true, little meat at those times; sometimes a pound of bare ribs for boiling, or an occasional rabbit dumped at the door by a neighbour. But there was green food of great weight in season, and lentils and bread for ballast. Eight to ten loaves came to the door every day, and they never grew dry. We tore them to pieces with their crusts still warm, and their monotony was brightened by the objects we found in them – string, nails, paper, and once a mouse; for those were days of happy-go-lucky baking. The lentils were cooked in a great pot which also heated the water for the Saturday-night baths. Our small wood-fire could heat sufficient water to fill one bath only, and this we shared in turn. Being the youngest but one, my water was always the dirtiest but one, and the implications of this privilege remain with me to this day.

Laurie Lee, **Cider with Rosie**

ASSIGNMENT

1 Describe the scullery in your own words.

2 What do you learn about the family and their way of life? What feelings does the writer convey about his childhood?

Raghunathpur was a typical Indian village: a rustic, ancient backwater of dusty, uneven streets and crumbling old houses made up of mud-bricks covered in masks of cement. It boasted no great achievements or personalities. All that existed was a hard-working community who expected or desired little from life other than a healthy existence and a proud family. It was very rural and so, inevitably, it was also very poor. I spent the first years of my life in that archaic Bengali village. The three of us – my mother, my sister and I – lived in the two-roomed house of my fathers' parents, and the rooms were both very small – so tiny that a double bed could barely be fitted in. Still, we knew nothing of any other way of life and lived there quite contentedly.

The smell of the Indian countryside was clear-cut and distinct. It was the pleasant, burning odour of the dust-laden air. That smell was an aromatic photograph which was able to bring back the true feeling and atmosphere of India. It was as manifest as the soft-blue, cloud-free sky. We lived in an area of the village known as "Nandura" and it was a short walk down the dust-sedimented lane lined with sun-baked houses with exteriors that from a distance looked like leopard skins thanks to the presence of round, dark cow-pats lining the sand-coloured walls, cooking solid in the scorching heat of the day. The lukewarm wind blew dust into our faces from time to time and large, loose swarms of mosquitoes flew around in their irregular formations.

Subhajit Sarkar, **Earliest memories**

ASSIGNMENT

1 What impression have you gained of the village?

2 Find words and phrases which appeal to the senses. Choose one you find effective and write a sentence explaining why.

123

More suggestions for coursework

- Write about your early memories. You can focus on a place, as in the passages you have read, or you can explore other ideas. Jot down as many headings as you like – you could, for example, think about family and friends (your first best friend, a brother or sister being born) or first times (the first time you went to school, the first time you got into trouble). Choose three memories and develop them into a piece of writing of about 300 to 500 words.

Stealing memories

Autobiographies usually contain descriptions of incidents which were significant in the writer's life. In these passages the writers describe what happened when they stole something.

*Nature

One summer evening (led by her)* I found
A little boat tied to a willow tree
Within a rocky cave, its usual home.
Straight I unloosed her chain, and stepping in
Pushed from the shore. It was an act of stealth
And troubled pleasure, nor without the voice
Of mountain echoes did my boat move on;
Leaving behind her still, on either side,
Small circles glittering idly in the moon,
Until they melted all into one track
Of sparkling light. But now, like one who rows,
Proud of his skill, to reach a certain point
With an unswerving line, I fixed my view
Upon the summit of a craggy ridge,
The horizon's utmost boundary; for above
Was nothing but the stars and the grey sky.

She was an elfin pinnace; lustily
I dipped my oars into the silent lake,
And, as I rose upon the stroke, my boat
Went heaving through the water like a swan;
When, from behind that craggy steep till then
The horizon's bound, a huge peak, black and huge,
As if with voluntary power instinct
Upreared its head. I struck and struck again,
And growing still in stature the grim shape
Towered up between me and the stars, and still,
For so it seemed, with purpose of its own
And measured motion like a living thing,
Strode after me. With trembling oars I turned,
And through the silent water stole my way
Back to the covert of the willow tree;
There in her mooring-place I left my bark,
And through the meadows homeward went, in grave
And serious mood; but after I had seen
That spectacle, for many days, my brain
Worked with a dim and undetermined sense
Of unknown modes of being; o'er my thoughts
There hung a darkness, call it solitude
Or blank desertion. No familiar shapes
Remained, no pleasant images of trees,
Of sea or sky, no colours of green fields;
But huge and mighty forms, that do not live
Like living men, moved slowly through the mind
By day, and were a trouble to my dreams.

William Wordsworth

ASSIGNMENT

1 What can you find out about the setting of this incident? Make notes on the time of day, the time of year and the natural surroundings.

2 What were the boy's feelings as he took the boat?

3 As he rowed, he fixed his eyes on a ridge in the distance, then became frightened. What was it that frightened him?

4 Talk about the effect this incident had on the boy.

The thing that sticks in my mind most from when I was very young is the first time I stole something; I was about two years old at the time. My mother and I were visiting friends who had some older children who had practically every toy under the sun because they had rich relatives who spoilt them. Anyway, even at such an early age I wondered why they could have so many lovely toys when all I had was a few cars, a teddy bear and a bedraggled old doll. So I decided that I would have some of their toys. I remember picking out the things that would not be missed, and I stuffed them behind the pillow in my pram which was very easy to climb into. When it was time to go home, my mum told me to get into the pram, but I refused. So I walked home. When we got home I started taking the toys out. My mum was very angry and brought me back with the toys. I had to say sorry, and I remember feeling very resentful because I thought it was just not fair – they had everything they wanted, and I didn't.

Anna Leitrim, **Me and my history**

ASSIGNMENT

1 Why did the writer steal the toys?

2 Afterwards, what did she feel about what she had done?

STEALING

The most unusual thing I ever stole? A snowman.
Midnight. He looked magnificent; a tall, white mute
beneath the winter moon. I wanted him, a mate
with a mind as cold as the slice of ice
within my own brain. I started with the head.

Better off dead than giving in, not taking
what you want. He weighed a ton; his torso,
frozen stiff, hugged to my chest, a fierce chill
piercing my gut. Part of the thrill was knowing
that children would cry in the morning. Life's tough.

Sometimes I steal things I don't need. I joy-ride cars
to nowhere, break into houses just to have a look.
I'm a mucky ghost, leave a mess, maybe pinch a camera.
I watch my gloved hand twisting the doorknob.
A stranger's bedroom. Mirrors. I sigh like this – Aah.

It took some time. Reassembled in the yard,
he didn't look the same. I took a run
and booted him. Again. Again. My breath ripped out
in rags. It seems daft now. Then I was standing
alone amongst lumps of snow, sick of the world.

Boredom. Mostly I'm so bored I could eat myself.
One time, I stole a guitar and thought I might
learn to play. I nicked a bust of Shakespeare once,
flogged it, but the snowman was strangest.
You don't understand a word I'm saying, do you?

Carol Ann Duffy

ASSIGNMENT

1 What impression have you gained of the character the poet presents? Find examples of behaviour and attitude to illustrate your points.

2 Why was the snowman particularly appealing?

3 Discuss with a partner or in your group if you think the character is a man or a woman. Then find out what other groups thought and compare your responses.

ASSIGNMENT

Write a brief description of each of the characters in the three passages you have read. Say what you think about them and the incidents they describe. Write about 300 to 500 words.

More suggestions for coursework

- Choose an incident which has had a lasting effect on you. Describe it as clearly and vividly as you can, and make clear why it was important.
- Write a story about someone who commits a crime. Try not to give an account of a film you've seen or of something from television, but create your own character and situation. Before you begin drafting make notes on:

  character;

  motivation;

  setting.

  You could plan a longer piece of work, and write the first chapter.

Life stories

Sometimes people use their own experiences and turn them into a story. The stories are written as if they are autobiographies using 'I' but in fact the characters are invented or fictional. The following extracts are the beginnings of novels that are fictional autobiographies.

It was like this. I had been thrown out of my parental home because Sanji and I had been caught having a 'love you, love me' session, in the back of his car after the party, that evening. A so-called friend of the family just happened to be driving through the deserted, off-street car-park somewhere in West London, when he spotted me, or my long curly hair rather, jostling about like some sycamore tree in a hurricane. Oh dear, what a nightmare that was! And what a pity for him that we hadn't being doing anything extremely naughty for all our clothes were in their rightful place, including my new beige sandals. Unfortunately, Kumar-Uncle had been watching one too many documentaries on teenagers, and therefore decided to do some hands-on censoring.

Kumar-Uncle tapped on the window and attempted to line his bifocal lenses with the glass. In doing that, he found it hard to move the rest of his head, thus limiting his view. He was most frustrated. Releasing his face, he called my name, and groped at the door handle.

"Oh, blast! it's Kumar-Uncle!" I cried, dismantling my arms from Sanji.

As I rolled down the window, Sanji couldn't bear the shame of facing this man. He glanced away as Kumar-Uncle's angry expression came into sight and smiled innocently to show that no misadventure had occurred.

"Oh, hello Kumar-Uncle! What are you doing here?"

"I should ask you the same thing, young lady!" shouted Kumar-Uncle, in his deep Delhi born and bred accent. "What business do you have in the car of this young man? Particularly on the back seat?"

My face was overcome with innocence as my mind searched for a viable reason, other than the truth. I sighed, deciding not to insult Kumar-Uncle's intelligence.

"Sanjay and I wanted to be alone."

"Alone?" Kumar-Uncle screamed. "Your parents will come to hear of this, Anupa, I am warning you now! No respectable girl should be out so late at night and especially in the company of a young man...!"

Angela Jariwala, **Pardesi**

ASSIGNMENT

1 How would you describe the tone of the passage? Choose some words from the following to help you explain:

formal	informal	straightforward	direct
friendly	grand	polite	restrained
morbid	humorous	comic	dignified
self-conscious	ironic	casual	

2 What do you learn from the passage about Anupa and her family?

3 How does the writer make you want to read on? (You could think about the questions you might ask about what is going to happen next.)

humorous

When 'humour' is turned into an adjective the 'u' before the 'r' is dropped.

Example I like people who have a sense of humour.
Although he sounded stern there was a humorous twinkle in his eye.

This is the beginning of *Jane Eyre*, written by Charlotte Brontë in 1847.

There was no possibility of taking a walk that day. We had been wandering, indeed, in the leafless shrubbery an hour in the morning; but since dinner the cold winter wind had brought with it clouds so sombre, and a rain so penetrating, that further outdoor exercise was now out of the question.

I was glad of it; I never liked long walks, especially on chilly afternoons: dreadful to me was the coming home in the raw twilight, with nipped fingers and toes, and a heart saddened by the chidings of Bessie, the nurse, and humbled by the consciousness of my physical inferiority to Eliza, John, and Georgiana Reed.

The said Eliza, John and Georgiana were now clustered round their mama in the drawing-room: she lay reclined on a sofa by the fireside, and with her darlings about her (for the time neither quarrelling nor crying) looked perfectly happy. Me, she had dispensed from joining the group, saying, "She regretted to be under the necessity of keeping me at a distance, but that until she heard from Bessie, and could discover by her own observation that I was endeavouring to acquire a more sociable and childlike disposition, a more attractive and sprightly manner – something, lighter, franker, more natural as it were – she really must exclude me from privileges intended only for contented, happy little children."

"What does Bessie say I have done?" I asked.

"Jane, I don't like cavillers or questioners; besides, there is something truly forbidding in a child taking up her elders in that manner. Be seated somewhere; and until you can speak pleasantly, remain silent."

A small breakfast-room adjoined the drawing-room. I slipped in there. it contained a bookcase; I soon possessed myself of a volume, taking care that it should be one stored with pictures. I mounted into the window-seat: gathering up my feet, I sat cross-legged, and, having drawn the red curtain nearly closed, I was shrined in double retirement.

ASSIGNMENT

1 Decide whether the following statements are true or false.

Statement	True	False
Jane enjoys long walks		
Jane is physically strong		
Jane feels she is as strong as her cousins		
Jane is frequently told off by Bessie		
Jane is made to feel part of the family group		
Jane would like to be part of the family group		
Jane's aunt doesn't like her		
Jane's aunt wishes she were more like the other children		
Jane accepts criticism without question		
Jane has a sense of justice		
Jane's aunt thinks that children should always be pleasant and contented		
Jane envies her cousins		
Jane is scornful about her cousins		
Jane likes being by herself		
Jane likes using her imagination		
Jane seems a solitary person		

2 Use your answers to write a description of Jane's character and situation.

3 Using the information in the passage as a basis, either write about a day in Jane's life, or describe a typical mealtime.

In this extract the writer imagines that she and her friends are the Brontë sisters. There were three Brontë sisters, Charlotte, Emily and Anne, and a brother Branwell. She sees their lives as full of wild passion and deep emotions, and very different from her home, and the dull suburban existence she leads. She sees herself as Charlotte, her friend Damaris as Emily and her friend Anne as Anne.

Reader, I was born in Kingston Hospital (alight at Norbiton) and brought up in Worcester Park. It follows that well into adolescence my close friends – equally disadvantaged – and I were never without the bitter taste of not having been one of the Brontë sisters. Our temperaments seemed to dictate it: some terrible failure of astral conjunctions must have occurred to put us down in Kingston in the 1950s rather than Yorkshire in the 1840s.

Of the three of us Damaris was the Emily figure, the intellectual giant, so to speak. I think of Emily as wasted with moral intensity, capable alike of breaking glass with the sheer energy of her genius, or tossing off a verse on mortality with one hand and humping whole wheat bread around the kitchen with the other. Damaris is the sort of person who feels pangs of loss when a leaf falls, and who spends long hours seeing the skull beneath the skin.

Reader, I was Charlotte. That is, several inches shorter than Damaris, my body hardly robust enough to support the Gothic passions that frequently wracked it, given to performing sado-masochistic historical dramas in front of the dressing-table mirror. Picture me trembling with technicoloured tragic imaginings in my boxy bedroom with the candlewick bedspread, the current fantasy of voluptuous cruelty among royal persons slowly giving way to the bay window with the Terylene net curtains, and through it to row upon row of other bay windows and other Terylene curtains.

Anne was Anne. She had no specific creative thrust. She had the same effect on people as a dose of Valium or *The Sound of Music*. At the age of nine or ten she had a painting in a local authority exhibition, but she was burnt-out at twelve and, quite frankly, the most we hoped for Anne was a husband from the professional classes.

Ursula Bentley, **The Natural Order**

ASSIGNMENT

1 How would you describe the tone of the passage? Use the list in given in the assignment for the first passage to help you explain. Why do you think the writer uses this sort of tone?

2 What impression have you gained of the three friends in the passage? Choose some of the following words to help you explain. Write them in the appropriate column and use them to help you write your answer.

content	dissatisfied	mocking
uncertain	imaginative	clever
unconventional	angry	rebellious
creative	dull	literary
ordinary	conventional	confident
sensitive		
Writer (Charlotte Brontë)	Damaris (Emily Brontë)	Anne (Anne Brontë)

More suggestions for coursework

- Write the scene which might occur when Kumar-Uncle speaks to Anupa's parents. Make up their characters. You could write the scene as a playscript if you wish.

- Write a story or a description based on someone feeling left out.

- Choose somebody you admire, or see as a role model (someone whose life or behaviour gives you something to base your own behaviour on). It could be a personality from sport or entertainment, or somebody you know, or a character in a book or film, or a historical figure. Give a short talk to your group briefly describing the person and explaining why you admire him or her.

• In this task you will be writing in the first person (I), but not about yourself! Work in pairs. You are going to interview your partner about his or her life, and find out the kinds of incidents, experiences and reflections which might be included in a life story. You will then use the ideas you have collected to write the opening page of the autobiography. So, for example, if an important element in your partner's life is that he always looked up to his older brother, you might decide to begin: "I always admired my older brother, ever since the time when..."

Guidelines

Interviewing

• Decide what the interview is for. What kind of information do you want to get? Is it just facts, or do you want to hear some opinions and ideas as well? Do you want stories, examples, anecdotes?

• Decide the kinds of questions you will ask. The right kind of question will help you to find out what you want to know. If you want your interviewee to talk easily you need to ask the kind of question which will encourage a full response. You will find these question types useful:

   (a) *Open questions*. Start with "Tell me about:" or "What were your feelings about?"
   (b) *Prompts*. Use phrases like "So what happened then?"
   (c) *Hypothetical*. These ask "What if?" So you might ask "What if you could do it again?"

• Take notes during the interview, or tape-record it to listen to later. If you take notes, try not to be so absorbed in writing that you lose eye contact with your partner.

• Before you finish the interview check that you have got all the information you want. Also check that you have understood what has been said. You could say something like "So the most important thing that happened to you was..."

• Select from your information the ideas you will use for your opening page. Plan and draft three paragraphs. Try to write an opening line which catches the reader's attention.

• When you have written your final version, you could read or show it to your partner.

Same but different

Sometimes the same subject can be treated in very different ways, according to the writer's purpose. Here are three different accounts of a sixteenth century sea battle in which Sir Richard Grenville, captain of The Revenge, fought with the Spanish.

In 1591, when a squadron of queen's ships under the command of Lord Thomas Howard was sent to the Azores to look out for the homeward-bound treasure fleet of Spain, Grenville, as Vice-admiral, or second in command, was appointed to the Revenge, a ship of 500 tons and 250 men. As a defence against this or any other squadron the king of Spain fitted out a powerful fleet of ships of war, and despatched it to the Azores. The Earl of Cumberland, however, then on the coast of Portugal, sent off a pinnace to warn Howard of the impending danger. Howard, then lying at anchor on the north side of Flores, had scarcely heard the news before the Spanish fleet was in sight. It is said to have numbered 53 sails all told. Of English ships there were in all 16, but half the men were down with fever or scurvy. Howard determined at once that he was in no condition to fight a force so superior and set out to sea. Grenville, not knowing or not believing the news which the pinnace had just brought, was convinced that the ships coming round the western point were the long waited-for treasure ships, and therefore refused to follow Howard. Such seems to have been the opinion of Monson, a contemporary seaman. On the other hand, Raleigh, writing, it must be remembered, as a cousin and dear friend, has stated that Grenville was delayed in getting his sick men brought on board from the shore. But the other ships had also to get their sick men on board, and sickly as the Revenge was, she was no worse off than the others. It is quite certain, however, that by some cause the Revenge was delayed, and before she could move the Spanish fleet had cut her off from the admiral and the rest of the squadron. Grenville might still have got clear but he was not a seaman, nor had he much experience of the requirements of actual war. Acting from what is difficult to describe otherwise than as a false notion of honour, scornfully and passionately, with angry voice and gesture, he expressed his determination to pass through the Spanish fleet. In attempting to do so she was overpowered after a long and desperate resistance. The Revenge was captured, and Grenville, mortally wounded, was taken on board the Spanish admiral's ship where he died a few days afterwards.

His chivalrous courage has been very generally held to atone for the fatal error. It is therefore necessary to point out that, in the opinion of contemporaries well qualified to judge, the loss of his ship, of his men, and of his own life was caused by Grenville's violent and obstinate temper, and a flagrant disobedience to the orders of his commanding officer.

Dictionary of National Biography

ASSIGNMENT

Make a list of all the facts that are reported and a list of all the opinions that are given. Remember opinions can be indicated by the kinds of words and descriptions used. They do not necessarily have to include phrases like "I think" or "It is my opinion that".

Grenville, Sir Richard (b. June 15 1542 – d. September 1591), colourful and daring English naval commander who fought heroically, against overwhelming odds, in a celebrated encounter with a Spanish fleet off Flores island in the Azores.

In 1591 he was made second in command (under Lord Thomas Howard) of a squadron of about 15 vessels sent to intercept a Spanish treasure fleet off the Azores. When 53 Spanish vessels approached to protect their treasure ships, the English retreated, but Grenville was delayed and cut off. Undaunted, he attempted to run his ship, the Revenge, through the Spanish line. After 15 hours of hand-to-hand combat against 15 Spanish galleons and a force of 5000 men, the Revenge with her 190 man crew was captured. (Sept. 9/10 1591) A few days later the wounded Grenville died on board the Spanish flagship.

Encyclopaedia Britannica

ASSIGNMENT

 Make a list of all the facts reported in the passage and a list of all the opinions that are given.

ASSIGNMENT

"Both these accounts are very biased in their attitude to Grenville". Write about a page in response to this statement, basing your answer on your findings in the previous assignments.

THE REVENGE

At Flores in the Azores Sir Richard Grenville lay,
And a pinnace, like a fluttered bird, came flying from far away:
"Spanish ships of war! we have sighted fifty three!"
Then sware Lord Thomas Howard: "Fore God I am no coward;
But I cannot meet them here, for my ships are out of gear,
And half my men are sick. I must fly, but follow quick.
We are six ships of the line; can we fight with fifty three?"

Then spake Sir Richard Grenville: I know you are no coward;
You fly then for a moment to fight with them again.
But I've ninety men and more that are lying sick ashore.
I should count myself the coward if I left them, my Lord Howard,
To these Inquisition dogs and the devildoms of Spain.

Sir Richard spoke and he laughed, and we roared a hurrah, and so
The little Revenge ran on sheer into the heart of the foe,
With her hundred fighters on deck, and her ninety sick below;
For half their fleet to the right and half to the left were seen,
And the little revenge ran on through the long sea-lane between.

Thousands of their soldiers looked down from their decks and laughed,
Thousands of their seamen made mock at the mad little craft
Running on and on, till delayed
By their mountain-like San Philip that, of fifteen hundred tons,
And up-shadowing high above us with her yawning tiers of guns,
Took the breath from our sails, and we stayed.

And the sun went down, and the stars came out far over the
summer sea,
But never a moment ceased the fight of the one and the fifty three.
Ship after ship, the whole night long, their high-built galleons came,
Ship after ship, the whole night long, with her battle-thunder
and flame;
Ship after ship, the whole night long, drew back with her dead and
her shame;
For some were sunk and many were shattered, and so could fight us
no more –
God of battles, was ever a battle like this in the world before?

For he said, "Fight on! fight on!"
Though his vessel was all but a wreck;

And it chanced that, when half of the short summer night was gone,
With a grisly wound to be dressed he had of Grenville left the deck,
But a bullet struck him that was dressing it suddenly dead,
And himself he was wounded again in the side and the head,
And he said, "Fight on! Fight on!"

And we had not fought them in vain,
But in perilous plight were we
Seeing forty of our poor hundred were slain,
And half the rest of us maimed for life
In the crash of the cannonades and the desperate strife;
And the sick men down in the hold were most of them stark and cold,
And the pikes were all broken or bent, and the powder was all of
it spent;
And the masts and the rigging were lying over the side;
But Sir Richard cried in his English pride,
"We have fought such a fight for a day and a night,
As may never be fought again!
We have won great glory, my men!

And a day less or more
At sea or ashore,
We die – does it matter when?
Sink me the ship, Master Gunner – sink her, split her in twain!
Fall into the hands of God, not into the hands of Spain!"

And the gunner said, "Ay, ay" but the seamen made reply:
"We have children, we have wives,
And the Lord hath spared our lives.
We will make the Spanish promise, if we yield, to let us go;
We shall live to fight again and to strike another blow."
And the lion there lay dying, and they yielded to the foe.

And the stately Spanish men to their flagship bore him then,
Where they laid him by the mast, old Sir Richard caught at last,
And they praised him to his face with their courtly foreign grace;
But he rose upon their decks, and he cried:
"I have fought for Queen and Faith like a valiant man and true;
I have only done my duty as a man is bound to do;
With a joyful spirit I Sir Richard Grenville die!"
And he fell upon their decks, and he died.

Alfred Lord Tennyson

ASSIGNMENT

What impression of Grenville do you get from the poem? Do you think the poet entirely approves of him, or entirely disapproves? Write a short response (about half a page) giving your opinion.

More suggestions for coursework

- Imagine that you are one of the men on board The Revenge. Write your account of what happened, making your thoughts and feelings clear.
- Write two descriptions of a park where Sunday football is played, one from the point of view of a supporter, and one from the point of view of a neighbour whose house overlooks the pitch.

Grammar box

Verbs

roared, fight, cried, sink, strike – all these words are verbs from the poem. You can see how these verbs help to create a sense of action.

A verb is a doing word. Every verb in English has several tenses which tell you the time when the action occurred. You have to be careful when you use different tenses because the form of the word changes.

Example   He sings in the chorus every night
He sang in the chorus last week.
He had sung in the chorus previously.

I do the paper round every morning.
I did the paper round last week.
It was a long time since I had done the paper round.

SELF CHECK

1 Make up sentences of your own like the ones above using different tenses of buy; bring; speak; steal.
2 Here are some verbs to describe different ways of sitting. Use them in a paragraph describing people in your common room or coffee bar.

perch   lounge   sprawl   loll   recline

139

3 Arrange these verbs in order of strength, beginning with the weakest.

march	saunter	stride	stroll	ramble
yell	whimper	shout	call	squeal

ie and ei

'and they yielded to the foe'.

There is a simple rule which tells you if a word should be spelt with 'ie' or 'ei'. If the sound of the word is 'ee', then the rule is **'i' comes before 'e', except after 'c'.**

Example   field, niece, believe (sounds 'ee'; so the 'i' comes before the 'e') ceiling, deceive, receive (sounds 'ee', but it comes after 'c')

but   weird, beige, height, leisure (no 'ee' sound)

Exception   seize

There is another group of words which breaks the 'i before e' rule.

conscience   ancient   deficient   efficient   sufficient

You could remember these by their pronunciation: they all have the sound 'sh'.

SELF CHECK

Complete the following:

1 I was dec...ed into bel...ing my n..ce.
2 My n..ghbour will be ..ghteen tomorrow.
3 The counterf..t money was s..zed in the f..ld.
4 Th..r golden retr..ver is an effic..nt guard dog.

Something to say

People make their voices heard when they feel strongly about an issue. Sometimes they just want to express their thoughts and feelings; sometimes they want to persuade others to take action, or give money, or buy their product.

The following material shows different responses to the issue of legalising cannabis.

Elaine Walsh, 18, a student from Birmingham, feels that legalising cannabis would lead to major problems.

"It's not that I'm a total prude, but the more accessible cannabis is, the more people are going to use it – and we don't know enough about the effects of long-term use. We'll be creating new problems. Cannabis is dangerous – it is partly depressant and can have an hallucinogenic effect, and taking it changes your personality. The Government already spends a fortune discouraging drink-driving and smoking. Cannabis may have therapeutic benefits for certain conditions, but that doesn't warrant total legislation. And how should we define 'therapeutic use'? Would it be available on prescription or over the counter? I think we'd have all sorts of people creating ailments that require it as a treatment. Thirty years ago we though smoking tobacco was therapeutic and now we know that it kills.

I think the allure would be transferred to harder drugs if cannabis was legalised. Kids would look to something else for excitement – things that are more harmful. The pushers would sell more amphetamines and LSD than ever.

People argue that without cannabis, the police would have more time and money to spend on hard drug traffickers. It's a good point, but I still don't think it's reason enough to go to the extreme of legalising another drug. But maybe penalties for possession of small amounts of cannabis could be relaxed and on-the-spot fines introduced which would act as a deterrent.

I'm not trying to take away the rights of individuals – I think making cannabis a symbol of freedom of expression is unhelpful as it diverts you from the real issue. Even though a lot of people take cannabis, it doesn't mean that legislation is the way forward. I've tried it and don't particularly like it but, even if I'm in a minority, we have to think in terms of public health and whether legalising another drug will help the population as a whole. If you're under the influence of any drug, you are experiencing a narrower view of life.

Let's give people more self-worth, more jobs and a better lifestyle rather than promoting drugs as a way of having a better time.

"Yes, cannabis should be legalised. Absolutely. In fact, I think they should teach you to skin up in school."

(Caitlin Moran, Naked City)

"People should be allowed to take acceptable risks with their own lives providing they are not harming anyone else. Cannabis does not make people alcoholics, criminals or social deviants – it's time we faced up to that."

(Mike Goodman, director of Release, a national drugs and legal advice service)

"Like all drugs, cannabis damages adolescents much more than adults – emotionally and socially. The people arguing for legislation are only considering their individual indulgence."

(Peter Stoker, drug prevention consultant with Positive Prevention Plus)

"It's crazy that it's all right for kids to go into a pub and drink half a dozen pints in one night and stagger home, but it isn't all right for someone to sit and have a joint. Marijuana is not a violent drug. It makes everybody happy."

(Robin Campbell, UB40)

"I've been smoking cannabis for six years and I'm a sane and healthy person. Lots of people think like me – and I'm not just talking about my age group. I know friends' parents, doctors and lawyers who feel the same. I object to there being restrictions. We could make the legal age 17, for example. People say legalising dope would turn everyone into hardened drug addicts, but only a tiny percentage of people who smoke cannabis go on to harder stuff like heroin. There's no proven link. The only reason the two drugs are associated is because they're both illegal. The real danger as the law stands is that people who buy dope from dealers are often introduced to harder drugs. If dope was freely available over the counter, people wouldn't come into contact with dodgy dealers.

Decriminalisation would be a good start. We could operate a system like Amsterdam's where you go to a cafe for a smoke. The law there hasn't been changed, but the police don't prosecute any more. But making it available on prescription alone would be wrong. It should be as readily available as cigarettes."

Cannabis – the facts

The Government has toughened its stance on cannabis and the Home Secretary recently put forward a proposal to increase the maximum fine for possession of cannabis from £500 to £2500.

A growing number of police at all levels are calling for decriminalisation of cannabis possession to enable them to spend more time and money on higher grade drug dealers. of the 37 444 cases of cannabis possession in 1992, 22 113 were dealt with by cautions.

Cannabis was actually available on prescription in the UK until 1971.

What the British Medical Association says

Studies by the British Medical Association (BMA) have found that cannabis use can suppress the immune system, impair fertility, result in chronic respiratory disease and increase the risk of lung cancer. Five out of eight studies show short-term memory loss to be a persistent side-effect of cannabis use. The BMA also believes that cannabis impairs the performance of people doing skilled tasks, such as driving. But they conclude that even chronic use is unlikely to lead to a deterioration in personality or an increase in aggressive behaviour. There are no known deaths as a direct result of smoking cannabis and there is no evidence to suggest that it is more harmful than tobacco or alcohol.

A recent survey by the BMA revealed that 74 per cent of 290 GPs and hospital doctors approved of cannabis use for 'proven therapeutic reasons'.

"19" magazine

Language link

chronic

'chronic' respiratory disease is a disease which develops slowly, over a long period of time.

It comes from the root chronos which means 'time'.

How does this help you understand the meaning of:
chronology;
chronicle?

Look up the exact meaning of these words in a dictionary. Find two more words which are formed from the same root.

ASSIGNMENT

Discuss the facts and opinions given in all these passages with your group. Make notes under headings 'For' and 'Against'. Use the information in the passages and your own thoughts and ideas. Then prepare for a debate on the topic: Cannabis should be legalised.

Write your points on prompt cards, or prepare brief notes. Remember that whatever kind of speech or talk you are giving you should not read it, but should use reminders such as cards or notes so that you can maintain contact with your audience.

Guidelines   *Having a debate*

- Choose a chairperson, two people to speak for the motion and two people to speak against it.

- In a debate people speak in a particular order. Remember that a debate is more formal than a discussion, and certain rules have to be observed.

- The chairperson should open the debate by stating what the motion is and introducing the speakers. Make clear which side they are speaking on.
- The speaker proposing the motion (in this case, the one arguing that cannabis should be legalised) speaks first. Your speech should be about four minutes.
- The speaker opposing the motion (in this case, the one arguing that cannabis shouldn't be legalised) speaks next. Your speech should be between two and four minutes.
- The second speaker proposing the motion goes next. Your speech should be a little shorter, say two or three minutes. Try to answer some of the points the opposer made.
- The second speaker opposing the motion then speaks. Your speech should be about two or three minutes. Try to answer some of the points the proposer made.
- When all the main speakers have delivered their speeches it's the turn of the audience:

  (a) The chairperson asks for people to speak, and controls the discussion. It's your job to see that everyone who wants to speak has a chance to do so.

  (b) Do not let people get into private or prolonged arguments.

  (c) Everyone who wants to speak has to have your permission.
- The first speaker for the motion sums up the main points for that side. Try to answer points the audience made in its discussion.
- The first speaker against the motion sums up the main points for that side. Try to answer points the audience made.
- The chairperson asks the audience to vote, then announces how many are in favour, how many against, and how many abstentions (people who decided not to vote for or against).
- Sometimes in debates a vote is taken before the debate, when people vote according to what they think about the topic, then another vote is taken after the debate when people vote according to how persuasive the speakers have been.

2 Write 300 to 500 words on the topic: Should cannabis be legalised? giving both sides of the argument.

Guidelines *Discussion essay*

- In a discussion essay you are asked to give both sides of the case, not just argue for one or the other.

- Using the material given, your own ideas and other people's, prepare the points for and against. You might find it helpful to draw up two columns:

  For legalising cannabis   Against legalising cannabis

- Go back to each point in turn and think about how you can expand it. Can you give a reason for the point, or an example which illustrates it?

- Use your list as a basis for your first draft. Organise your points. Group together similar ideas for your paragraphs.

- Introductory paragraph. Make clear what the essay is about, and give some indication of how you will approach it. You may be able to think of a dramatic first sentence which catches the reader's attention straight away.

- In paragraph two you should begin your argument in favour of the topic. So here you make your first point in favour of legalising cannabis. Do not forget to give examples or illustrations.

- In paragraphs three and four start each new paragraph with a main point which adds to the argument. Remember phrases like 'Another reason for' . Simple words like 'also' can help to make individual points clear.

- In paragraphs five and six you give the other point of view, taking your ideas from the list 'against legalising cannabis'. Make it clear that you are now presenting the argument for the other side. You might use phrases like 'on the other hand' and words like 'although'.
  (h) In the final paragraph you sum up and make your own views clear.

- Check through your draft and check that your ideas and expression are clear before writing your final version. Look at the guidelines for writing an argument essay.

3 Take it in turns in your group to finish the following sentences:
   What really makes me mad is.....
   If I had my way I'd.......

Explain your reasons as fully as you can. If you have time you could take one of the subjects you spoke about and write an essay on it.

Running a campaign

There have been a number of campaigns aimed at stopping drug abuse. Read the following newspaper article which gives the background of a particular campaign, and study the advertisement.

The 'Madchester' music scene of the late 1980s gave Manchester an unparalleled reputation for exciting night life.

With its plethora of successful dance clubs, the city was also the ideal place for a rapid growth in ecstasy use. It soon had first hand experience of the drug's potentially horrific consequences.

In 1989, 16-year-old Clare Leighton died after taking a tablet of ecstasy at the Hacienda night club. By the end of 1991, six of Britain's 13 ecstasy deaths were from the North-West.

Manchester city council was in a tricky situation: it wanted to promote its vibrant youth culture, crucial to the local economy, but did not want to be accused of having blood on its hands.

After discussion with Lifeline, a drugs agency, it developed the most progressive strategy in Britain for tackling ecstasy use in night clubs.

The safer dancing campaign introduced a 'ravers' code of conduct which venues would have to follow to get their entertainment licences.

Medical evidence put some of the drug deaths down to overheating, and clubs were told they had to provide adequate ventilation, free cold water and 'chill out' areas where dancers could cool down. Door staff also received medical training.

An extra problem was how to get through to the drug users. Lifeline realised ravers would not be keen to visit a place considered to be a hangout for heroin users.

The solution was to distribute a comic featuring an invented character, Peanut Pete, who has become a credible figure for clubbers. He comes with no moral baggage, he rarely says no to drugs, and shows the good as well as the bad effects of taking them.

The Safer Dancing campaign has been criticised by some for being too liberal, but others say it is the only way to reduce the risk of ecstasy deaths. A council spokesman said: "Thousands of people come into Manchester and make the private decision to take drugs. We try to make them take those drugs as safely as possible. If we shut down all the clubs where people take drugs, they would go elsewhere and there would be more problems."

Lifeline worker Alan Houghton said there have been many occasions when the Safer Dancing campaign has saved lives. "We have been able to defuse potential dangers for individuals because we have known what to look for."

Alex Bellos, The Guardian

ASSIGNMENT

1 Why was there a lot of ecstasy use in Manchester?

2 What was the tricky situation the council found itself in?

3 What was the name of the campaign it devised?

4 Describe what the campaign involved and why it was progressive.

5 What replies were given to people who criticised it?

6 Why do you think Peanut Pete was a successful part of the campaign?

7 You have been asked to present the outline of a campaign for educating a younger age group in some aspect of health care or social behaviour. You could choose dental care, for example, or an issue like dropping litter or road safety. Part of the campaign will be a cartoon character.

(a) Make notes under the following headings:

Aim of campaign: To..........

Description of target age group:

Main points to get across:

Main methods:

Description of cartoon character (including name):

Example of kind of thing character will say/do:

Sample cartoon frame

(b) Now use your notes to make a short presentation of your campaign to the rest of your group.

Explain the topic you chose, and why, and give an outline of the methods you will use. In particular, give a clear idea of your cartoon character and the effect you hope it will have.

audience (parents)

What do you say when their best friend offers them drugs?

shock contrast – a friend is known and trusted

attacks stereotype of dealer

language is informal and direct

Many of the teenagers who've tried drugs have tried them because they were offered by a friend.

Not, as you might think, by a seedy-looking dealer loitering on a street corner.

The problem with drugs isn't just that people sell them to children, which is bad enough, but that some children want to try them.

In other words, you're not going to be able to stop your child being exposed to drugs, but you can influence how they'll react.

For a start you need to understand why your child might take the drug that's being offered to them.

If friends of theirs have already taken drugs, they could be under enormous pressure to do the same.

They may feel left out if they don't.

Being part of a group is very important to them. (Remember what it was like for you at that age.)

Try and help them see that standing up for themselves, not following everyone else, will earn them respect within that group.

Ask them for their opinions.

Find out why they think their friends would want to try drugs. Get them to tell you if they know anyone who's refused a drug when it was offered. Give their answers proper consideration.

What you learn from your child can only be useful to you both.

You'll find it much easier to influence their attitude to drugs, if you understand what they know first.

It's often said the more you treat a child like a responsible person, the more likely they are to act like one.

But whatever they say, try and keep calm. Some of the things they say may make you fear for their safety or make you angry.

Threatening behaviour may make you feel better, but it won't help your child.

There is no magic formula. Every child is different, as is every parent and every family. The best way will always be to talk positively.

If you need more information to help you do this, there is a leaflet you can send off for by filling in the coupon below. (It's also available from most public libraries and doctors' surgeries, or by phoning free on 0800 555 777.)

If you handle the situation properly, your child will have a real friend who can always be relied on to help – you.

offers advice

Please send me a copy of "Drugs & Solvents - you & your child".

Name _____
(BLOCK CAPITALS PLEASE)

Address _____

Postcode _____

Send to: Drugs & Solvents, FREEPOST (BS4335), Bristol BS1 3YX. You can also phone free for your copy on 0800 555 777.　　　SEB1

If you don't talk to your child about drugs, someone else will.

slogan gives dramatic warning

picture is of ordinary-looking young people (anyone's son or daughter)

ASSIGNMENT

1 What methods does this advertisement use to gain parents'
interest and confidence? You could consider:

> the language;
> the layout;
> the main ideas about drugs;
> the attitude to children.

There are some notes on the advert to help you start thinking.

Guidelines *Analysing advertisements*

- Look at the advertisement and decide who is advertising. For
example, sometimes it will be a company advertising a product
or service, sometimes it will be a pressure group persuading
you to adopt their point of view. Can you think of any others?
- Decide who the advertisement is aimed at. Try to be as precise
as you can about the type of person it is addressing – think
about age, sex, background.
- What is the point of the advert? Does it want you to buy
something, give money, join a group, change your behaviour?
Find examples of advertisements which illustrate these
messages, and any others you can think of.
- How does the advert try to persuade you? Look at the use of language
and the use of pictures. Are there any words designed to arouse a
particular response? What about the tone? Is there a slogan or a caption?
- Think about the words you use to express your ideas. Here are
some suggestions.

Instead of saying:	You could say:
puts over	conveys, communicates, suggests
good	appealing, effective, convincing
buyer	audience, market

More suggestions for coursework

- In pairs, role play the conversation between a parent and child
where the parent follows the advice in the advertisement.
- Write a story set in a club or disco, or if you prefer, write a description.
- Design and write an advertisement for one of the following: a
package holiday; a charity; a brand of trainers.
- Write about the following advertisement describing how it tries to
persuade its audience. Use the guidelines and your work on the
previous advertisement to help you.

The versatile HP LaserJet 4 Plus.
Saves money. Saves paper. Saves wildlife.

The HP LaserJet 4 Plus.
So versatile you have all these ways
to save money, time and even wildlife.

If the HP LaserJet 4 set the industry standard for quality printing, the HP LaserJet 4 Plus takes that concept into a whole new dimension.

Add on all the accessories and you have a faster, more efficient printer that saves you time, your company money and helps endangered wildlife as well. Because, for every machine sold, with our duplex tray, we'll make a contribution of US$20 to the World Wide Fund For Nature.

HP LaserJet 4 Plus

SAVE
You'll save at least half the paper you normally use because, with a duplex tray attached, the HP LaserJet 4 Plus prints on both sides of the paper.

Which automatically saves you money both on paper and on postage because you send less.

You'll also save on space because you have less paper to file.

SAVE
With the optional Flash SIMM module installed in your HP LaserJet 4 Plus, you can store formats for all your company's forms. That means you can make big savings in many areas.

You'll save on print costs because you won't need to have forms printed in advance.

You'll save on paper because you won't need to throw away old forms just because a detail is changed.

You'll save time because you won't have to fill in forms on a typewriter.

You'll save on space because you won't have to have piles of different forms waiting to be filled out.

And because the formats for your forms are stored on the Flash SIMM module rather than in your PC, you save time on the network by reducing traffic and cutting the time it takes to download information.

SAVE
Use our optional 500 sheet feeder and you save time because you don't have to keep running to the printer to fill it up with paper. This is particularly labour-saving with long print jobs.

SAVE
For the really big jobs, the optional envelope feeder and 1000 sheet output stacker for the HP LaserJet 4 Plus save you even more time.

And if each of these accessories didn't make your job easier in their own right, you can save even

more time by using them all at the same time.

SAVE
With the HP LaserJet 4 Plus you save more than just time or money. You will also help save the wildlife on this planet because we will give a donation of US$20 when you buy our versatile printer together with the duplex tray.

So don't waste any more time. If your company buys an HP LaserJet 4 Plus with a duplex tray, just add the serial number of the printer and the duplex tray when they arrive to the coupon below, and send it back to us.

But you'll have to hurry. This offer ends on the 28th of April 1995.

And if you don't need to save time, money and effort, you must have an HP LaserJet 4 Plus already.

There can't be any other reason.

If you purchase an HP LaserJet 4 Plus or 4M Plus printer plus a duplex tray, just fill in this coupon and send it off. Within 28 days you should receive a confirmation that the World Wide Fund For Nature has received a donation of US$20. If you have any queries about the offer, please write to the address given on the coupon. Please complete in capitals using ink or ball-point pen:

NAME: (MR/MRS/MS) _____ JOB TITLE: _____

COMPANY NAME: _____ ADDRESS: _____

POSTCODE: _____ COUNTRY: _____

TELEPHONE NUMBER: _____ TYPE OF BUSINESS: _____

HP LASERJET 4 Plus/4M Plus PRINTER SERIAL NUMBER: _____

HP DUPLEX TRAY SERIAL NUMBER: _____ **DATE OF PURCHASE:** _____

Please send your completed application form to: World Wide Fund For Nature Donation, Hewlett-Packard Ltd, FREEPOST LON258, PO BOX 4712, LONDON SW8 1BR.

All applications must be received by **28/4/95.**

TERMS AND CONDITIONS: 1. This offer is open to all residents of the UK except for employees and their families of Hewlett-Packard Limited, their agencies or any other company directly associated with the administration of this offer. 2. All application instructions form part of the terms and conditions of this offer. 3. All applications must be received by 28/4/95. Responsibility cannot be accepted for any applications lost, damaged or delayed in transit to the offer address. Proof of posting will not be accepted as proof of delivery. Illegible, incomplete or altered applications will be deemed invalid as will those without the revelant serial numbers. 4. Please complete the application form in ink or ball-point pen and print your name and address clearly. 5. Please allow 28 days from receipt of application to receive a confirmation that the WWF has received a donation of US$20. 6. No cash alternative will be offered to yourself in lieu of the offer advertised. 7. Only correct serial numbers of both the HP LaserJet 4 Plus or 4M Plus together with the serial number of the duplex unit will be deemed as valid proof of purchase in this promotion. 8. The WWF will receive a donation from Hewlett-Packard of US$20 from each application. 9. The offer close by date is 28/4/95. **THE PROMOTER: Hewlett-Packard Ltd, Amen Corner, Cain Road, Bracknell, Berkshire RG12 1HN.**

- Prepare a short talk (3 to 5 minutes) on a topic which interests you or that you feel strongly about. The aim of your talk is to communicate your interest to your audience, or to persuade them to agree with your point of view. Take it in turns to give your talk to the group. After each talk have a couple of minutes for questions and comments.

Keeping a diary

Most diaries are written for the writer's own private and personal reasons. They are used for a variety of purposes, such as to keep a record of events, or to describe thoughts and feelings. Sometimes people's private diaries or journals are published after their death, sometimes actually in their lifetime. Here are some different examples.

These are brief extracts from the diaries of Samuel Pepys who lived in the seventeenth century and kept a diary over about ten years.

March 12 1662
At office from morning till night, putting of papers in order, so that I may have my office in an orderly condition. I took much pains in sorting and folding of papers.

March 13
All day either at the office or at home, busy about business till late at night. And I find great pleasure in it, and a growing content.

March 26
Up early. At noon came my good guests. I had a pretty dinner for them – a brace of stewed carps, six roasted chickens, and salmon hot, for the first course. And we were very merry all the afternoon, talking and singing. In the evening they went with great pleasure away, and I with great content, and my wife, walked half an hour in the garden, and so home to supper and to bed.

January 6 1663
Somewhat vexed at my wife's neglect in leaving her scarf and waistcoat in the coach today, though I confess she did give them to me to look after – yet it was her fault not to see that I did take them out of the coach.

January 12 1663

So home, and find my wife's new gown come home and she mightily pleased with it. But I appeared very angry that there were no more things got ready for tomorrow's feast, and in that passion sat up long and went discontented to bed.

January 13 1663

So my poor wife rose by 5 o'clock in the morning and went to market and bought fowl and many other things for dinner – with which I was highly pleased.

Samuel Pepys

ASSIGNMENT

From the extracts you have read, what impression have you gained of Samuel Pepys? Make notes, then write a paragraph commenting on his personality and way of life.

This is an extract from a diary written by a young girl in Yugoslavia in 1992. She calls her diary Mimmy.

Saturday 2 May 1992

Dear Mimmy,

Today was truly, absolutely the worst day ever in Sarajevo. The shooting started around noon. Mummy and I moved into the hall. Daddy was in his office, under our flat, at the time. We told him on the interphone to run quickly to the downstairs lobby where we'd meet him. We brought Cicko (Zlata's canary) with us. The gunfire was getting worse, and we couldn't get over the wall to the Bonbars, so we ran down to our own cellar.

   The cellar is ugly, dark, smelly. We listened to the pounding shells, the shooting, the thundering noise overhead. We even heard planes. At one moment I realised that this awful cellar was the only place that could save our lives. We heard glass shattering in our street. Horrible. I put my fingers in my ears to block out the terrible sounds. I was worried about Cicko. We had left him behind in the lobby. Would he catch cold there? Would something hit him? I was terribly hungry and thirsty. We had left our half-cooked lunch in the kitchen.

Thursday 7 May 1992

Dear Mimmy

I was almost positive the war would stop, but today...Today a shell fell on the park in front of my house, the park where I used to play with my girlfriends. A lot of people were hurt. Selma lost a kidney. AND NINA IS DEAD. A piece of shrapnel lodged in her brain and she died. She was such a sweet, nice little girl. We went to kindergarten together, and we used to play together in the park. Is it possible I'll never see Nina again? Nina, an innocent eleven-year-old girl – the victim of a stupid war.

Zlata Filipovic, **Zlata's Diary**

ASSIGNMENT

What comments and details in Zlata's diary do you find particularly effective? How is reading it different from reading an account in, say, a newspaper? Write a paragraph giving your views.

This diary entry is part of a book written in the form of a long letter to the writer's daughter.

Summer 1955

We arrived on the beach really early and bagged a good spot while Dada unloaded in the car park. Then we got a couple more deck chairs from the man and set up our patch. Mama made a bit of a tent for Claire with towels across the deckchairs, in case she wanted a sleep, and then we all changed into our costumes in the Ladies. We were starving by then so Dada got a tray of tea from the beach cafe, and the man remembered us from last year.

It was an absolutely glorious day. The sun shone and shone. We swam and played with Claire and had a game of cricket with the family next to us.

About seven, Mama said we'd have to think of moving soon. It was still really hot and we didn't want to go. Just then Dada came back from the car park. He'd been talking to a family who had a tent in the back of their van. They were staying the night, sleeping in the car park.

Dada looked at Mama and Auntie.

"Shall we stay? Shall we stay the night?"

At first the ladies weren't sure ... Where would we sleep? ... In the end they said yes. Madness but yes ... We flattened out all the seats in the car to make a big bed for Auntie and Mama and Claire. Dada would sleep in a deck chair and Gabe and I on a pile of towels with a rug.

At eight, Dada went for fish and chips and got the cafe to fill up our thermoses and the other family got a fire going so we all sat round together and chatted and sang songs, till we went to sleep.

Pauline Collins, **Letters to Louise**

ASSIGNMENT

1 In the diary entry Pauline Collins says it was "an absolutely glorious day". Make a list of all the things that made the day so enjoyable.

2 What impression does the diary entry give of her family and their way of life? Make notes of all the points you find and use them to write a couple of paragraphs giving your impression.

ASSIGNMENT

1 Which diary extract did you find most interesting? Write about a page, giving your reasons.

2 Which character from the diaries would you most like to meet? Write about a page, giving your reasons.

3 Write a series of diary entries (about three) which give an idea of what's going on in your life at the time of writing. Include your thoughts and comments as well as a record of events that happen. Remember that although it will be read by an audience it is a personal and reflective piece of writing, so you can use notes, lists and abbreviations.

More suggestions for coursework

- Make up a character and a situation, and tell the story through a series of diary entries.
- Take one of the following situations and write two diary entries, one for each person. Write 300 to 500 words in all. Try to bring out their contrasting thoughts and feelings.
- A parent and child argue about the child's decision to drop out of a course of study.
- Friend A tells friend B about his/her plans to marry someone B can't stand.

Keeping in touch

Although it may be true to say that fewer personal letters are written now than in previous years, they are still an important means of communication. Personal letters can include thank you letters, invitations, chatty letters from friends and family. They can give you a way of communicating important thoughts and feelings about different matters which is very different from communicating them by phone.

Here are two letters written to parents.

This is part of the last letter written by Wilfred Owen, a poet who fought in the first world war, to his mother. He was killed four days afterwards. The war ended a week later.

Thursday 31 October 1918.

Dearest Mother

So thick is the smoke in this cellar I can hardly see by a candle twelve inches away. Splashing my hand, an old soldier with a walrus moustache peels and drops potatoes into the pot. By him Keyes, my cook, chops wood; another feeds the smoke with the damp wood.

It is a great life. I am more oblivious than yourself, dear mother, of the ghastly glimmerings of the guns outside, and the hollow crashing of the shells.

There is no danger down here, or if any, it will be well over before you read these lines.

I hope you are as warm as I am; as serene in your room as I am here.

Wilfred   Owen

ASSIGNMENT

1 What impression does Wilfred Owen give of the atmosphere in the cellar, and of his state of mind? Write a short paragraph on this.

2 Imagine you are the person receiving this letter. Write about 200 words describing your thoughts and feelings as you read.

The writer left this letter for her father to find when he came home from holiday.

Dear Ba

Thank you for the postcard which you sent me. I hope you had a good holiday.

Before you went away you remember we had a few discussions about the future and you gave me a choice of staying with you on your own terms or going for good. At the time it seemed to me it would be best for both of us if I stayed, but during the last month I have thought about it a lot and it now seems that it would be better for me to go so that you can be freer and not have the constant worry of supporting me.

I have left you a copy of the letter I have written to Mr Kelly and you will see that I have got things sorted out for myself. At the moment I don't want to give you my address because I want you to have time to get used to things.

I am all right so please don't worry or do anything silly like go to the police or anything. I will be in touch with you regularly by post to let you know how I am getting on. I have told Ma of my decision and I shall continue to write to her as usual. Perhaps in a few months we could see each other again. I have left the £20 (for emergencies) with this note. Thank you for leaving it with me. I have also left the key. Don't bother to find me because I have not told anyone my address.

I hope you will write and let me know how you are. It would be nice if we could stay friends. I do hope that you see why I have done what seems to be something dramatic, but what in fact was the only way I could see of making life better for both of us.

Shreela Ghosh, **Transforming moments**

ASSIGNMENT

What impression does the letter give you of the relationship between the writer and her father? Write a couple of paragraphs explaining your ideas.

ASSIGNMENT

1 Both the letters in the extracts above are written for very different purposes. Write a couple of sentences describing the purpose of each letter.

2 Sometimes there is a choice to be made between writing and phoning. In your group or with a friend discuss the advantages and disadvantages of writing or phoning in the following situations. Remember to think about the purpose of the letter, the circumstances, and the person receiving it as well as the person writing.

(a) You are away from home at college or university.

(b) Your son or daughter is studying away from home.

(c) Your best friend is abroad for a year.

(d) You would like to get in touch with an old school friend you haven't seen for years.

(e) You want to apologise for upsetting someone.

(f) You have decided to make a significant change in a relationship (leave home; break up with someone; make something permanent.)

3 Choose one of the above situations, or another one if you prefer; and

(a) role play the telephone call;

(b) write the appropriate letter.

Punctuation mark

Semi-colon

"I hope you are as warm as I am; as serene in your room as I am here".

A semi-colon shows a pause that is longer than a comma. It is used to break up a sentence – but unlike a comma, it can be used to join two complete sentences together. You should use it when you want a pause in what you are saying but feel a full stop and a new sentence would be too abrupt.

Example The night was drawing in; she drew the curtains.

Semi-colons can also be used to separate items in a complicated list.

Example Sonya gave her reasons for refusing to go. It was too far away; she had too much to do; she wouldn't enjoy it anyway.

The semi-colon can also be used to show how statements are balanced against each other.

161

> *Example* Old Trafford is a football stadium; Headingley is a cricket
> ground.
>
> ---
>
> **SELF CHECK**
>
> Use the following notes to write a series of sentences. Use a semi-colon where appropriate.
> Family visiting relatives – haven't seen them for a long time – not everyone looking forward to visit – heavy traffic on motorway – delayed in jam – arrive late – persuaded to stay night.

Literary letters

Sometimes letters are used in fiction, interspersed with the narrative. Some books are made up entirely of letters the characters write to each other.

October 7th

Dear Vera

I'm so sorry not to have corresponded before now, and to get you into a tizz. I am absolutely fine, thank you, so there is no cause for concern. I do hope you are more organised with the builders now. Personally I always pay that little bit extra and get a reputable firm. It saves time and money in the long run.

To be quite frank, I didn't write at first because of my annoyance over Audrey Roscoe. I bet I know what she said about me, and it has very little basis in truth. Clive was very drunk at the time, and didn't know what he was doing, and anyway I was on holiday. But I don't know why I'm bothering to go into it. It's all in the past and that sort of woman isn't worth the paper and ink.

Anyway, that isn't the main reason why I didn't write, only the first reason, which I soon got over, and am completely over now. In fact if you see her again, do please give her my kindest regards, and tell her I hope her son is better now. He went to prison you know – did she tell you? I think that's why she moved so far away.

I can't write much more just now, because Bill is coming over to take me out to a dinner dance. Life has been so hectic since he has been paying his attentions, and I must say it has perked me up no end. He is a widower, and an old friend of Clive's and mine. His wife died very slowly and painfully last year, and I have never seen a man so devoted. Actually he was at Lesley's wedding. You may remember him. I'm sure you'd like him very much.

Actually, most Sundays we go out for a run in his car, and I've been thinking of suggesting that we drive over to see you. It's just a suggestion of course, and I quite understand if you're too busy. Bill says he knows an exquisite French restaurant quite near Little Potterton – he knows the owners very well – and says he would be delighted to take us both there for Sunday lunch. Would you enjoy that? Life can be so lonely on your own, I know. Anyway, I'll leave it with you and wait until you get in touch, but the first and third Sundays in November would be fine with us.

Do take care of your asthma. There's nothing worse than a nasty chest.

Fondest wishes,

Irene

ASSIGNMENT

1 What does the first paragraph tell you about Irene's attitude to Vera?

2 Irene gives the impression she doesn't care about the incident with Audrey Roscoe. Do you think she does still care? Jot down your thoughts and discuss them in your group.

3 What impression does Irene give of her relationship with Bill? What do you think about the way she suggests their visit?

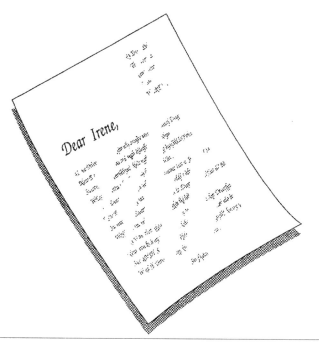

October 20th

Dear Irene

How pleasant to hear from you at last. I am so glad you haven't allowed your new 'interest' to completely take over your life. I always think people live to regret abandoning old friends when new ones appear – particularly as one can never be certain how long these things will last. I do indeed remember 'Bill' from the reception. He was the one who dropped the Salmon Mousse all down his front, wasn't he? I remember he swore rather loudly – I assumed because his suit was hired. How nice that he has a car to take you around in. You know, you really should have learned to drive, there is no substitute for independent wheels.

Do by all means come over and see me one Sunday, though I can't recommend the restaurant you mention. However, if you would like to sample some dishes at my humble abode, I'd be delighted. It would have to be the 3rd Sunday as the first is the Blood Donors Remembrance Service, and I always do the flowers.

Best wishes

Vera

PS. My chest is much better. Mabel Thrush knitted me a thermal boob tube.

Irene Spencer and Vera Small, **Ladies of letters**

ASSIGNMENT

1 What feelings does Vera convey in the first three lines?

2 What does she seem to think about Bill?

3 What do you think about the way she responds to Irene's suggestion?

ASSIGNMENT

1 Write a couple of paragraphs describing the relationship between the two women.

2 Imagine the occasion when Irene and Bill go to visit Vera, as arranged. Write the next exchange of letters between them.

More suggestions for coursework

Choose one of the following pairs of characters and write the letters they might send to each other (write a letter from one and a reply from the other).

Someone in prison and a relative or friend outside;

Someone trying to decide whether or not to take a job overseas and a friend who will miss him/her;

Someone describing a very grand occasion, like a ball, to a friend who is resentful at not having been there.

Hearing one person

Sometimes a story, play or poem will unfold one person's thoughts as you read or listen. This type of form is called a monologue. As you read these passages, think about the characters that have been created, the kind of people they are and the situations they are in.

HER DANCING DAYS

Those old tunes take me back. I used to go
to dances every Saturday. Of course
I wasn't never going to give it up,
and nor was Lily Cannon, but we did.
We wasn't taught, we just picked up the steps.
In Summer there was dances in Brent Park;
they called them 'flannel dances': out of doors.
The men could wear grey flannels, not the girls.
I used to make my dresses, buy the stuff
up Cricklewood, and sew them in a day.
I liked the winter-evening dances best,
and used to dance with Horace – he was tall,
and we danced well together – Percival –
he was a butler, rather serious –
Jack Roach, Jack Young, and I forget who else;
but there was one I used to like, and then
one Saturday he wasn't there, and I
was heartbroke. Then he wrote.
I was to meet him at the Bald Faced Stag
one Sunday afternoon. We'd never met
by day. I didn't like the looks of him,
And Horace was engaged. Then, at a fair
with Lil, she was all out for a good time,
we met these two. One of them wore a cap.
I don't like caps. "I'll have him then," said Lil;
all four slid down the helter-skelter, then
the heel came off me shoe; I had to hop;
he fixed it for me. Later, we arranged
to meet again next evening at the Hyde.
    Lily come round, and sat down by the fire
to knit. "I'm going out," I said. "You're not,
it's raining." But I was. I had to go.
We didn't know each other's names,
or where we worked, or anything.
And there he waited for me, in the wet,
and fifty years began.
    I said I'd never give up dancing, and
he said the same of football, but we did;
and Lily gave up dancing too, quite soon.
    We was both seventeen.

Anna Adams

ASSIGNMENT

1 In pairs, write down all you learn about the poet and:
the part dancing played in her life;
the young men she met;
the places they used to go;
her friend Lily;
how she met her husband.

2 Look carefully at the last four lines. What feeling is being expressed, do you think?

3 Write about the woman in the poem in any way you like - you could describe one of the Saturday night dances, or write a conversation between herself and Lily, for example. Use the information in the poem and add ideas of your own, based on it.

In this monologue seventy-five year old Doris, who lives alone, has fallen and broken her hip while trying to dust. Zulema is her home help; the Social Services would like her to go into a home. The extract is from a television play A cream cracker under the settee first broadcast by the BBC.

Shan't let on I was dusting.

She shoves the duster down the side of the chair.

Dusting is forbidden.

She looks down at the wedding photo on the floor.

Cracked the photo. We're cracked, Wilfred.

Pause

The gate's open again. I thought it had blown shut, only now it's blown open. Bang bang bang all morning, it'll be bang bang bang all afternoon.

Dogs coming in, all sorts. You see Zulema should have closed that, only she didn't.

Pause

The sneck's loose, that's the root cause of it. It's wanted doing for years. I kept saying to Wilfred, "When are you going to get round to that gate?" But oh no. It was always the same refrain. "Don't worry, Mother. I've got it on my list." I never saw no list. He had no list. I was the one with the list. He'd no system at all, Wilfred. "When I get a minute, Doris." Well, he's got a minute now, bless him.

Pause

Feels funny this leg. Not there.

Pause

Some leaves coming down now. I could do with trees if they didn't have leaves, going up and down the path. Zulema won't touch them. Says if I want leaves swept I've to contact the Parks Department.

I wouldn't care if they were my leaves. They're not my leaves. They're next-door's leaves. We don't have any leaves. I know that for a fact. We've only got the one little bush and it's an evergreen, so I'm certain they're not my leaves. Only other folks won't know that. They see the bush and they see the path and they think, "Them's her leaves." Well, they're not.

I ought to put a note on the gate. "Not my leaves." Not my leg either, the way it feels. Gone to sleep.

Pause

I didn't even want the bush, to be quite honest. We debated it for long enough. I said, "Dad. Is it a bush that will make a mess?" He said, "Doris, rest assured. This type of bush is very easy to follow," and he fetches out the catalogue. "This labour-saving variety is much favoured by the retired people." "Anyway," he says, "the garden is my department." Garden! It's only the size of a tablecloth. I said, "Given a choice, Wilfred, I'd have preferred concrete." He said, "Doris. Concrete has no character " I said, "Never mind character, Wilfred, where does hygiene come on the agenda?" With concrete you can feel easy in your mind. But no. He had to have his little garden even if it was only a bush. Well, he's got his little garden now. Only I bet that's covered in leaves. Graves, gardens, everything's to follow.

'I'll make a move in a minute. See if I can't put the kettle on. Come on leg. Wake up.

Go to black

Come up on Doris sitting on the floor with her back to the wall. The edge of a tiled fireplace also in shot.

Fancy, there's a cream cracker under the settee. How long has that been there? I can't think when I last had cream crackers. She's not half done this place, Zulema.

I'm going to save that cream cracker and show it to her the next time she starts going on about Stafford House. I'll say, "Don't Stafford House me, lady. This cream cracker was under the settee. I've only got to show this cream cracker to the Director of Social Services and you'll be on the carpet. Same as the cream cracker. I'll be in Stafford House, Zulema, but you'll be in the Unemployment Exchange.

Alan Bennett, **A cream cracker under the settee**

ASSIGNMENT

1 In pairs, write down all you learn about Doris and:
    her memories of Wilfred;
    her attitude to Zulema;
    her ideas about cleanliness and order.

2 Imagine a conversation that might have taken place between Doris and Wilfred. Build your ideas around what you have learnt about them from the passage.

More suggestions for coursework

Write a monologue expressing the thoughts and feelings of one of the following:
    a shop assistant two days before Christmas;
    someone at a wedding;
    someone looking forward to a party.

Says who

There are many different types of English, many varieties of style and tone. Sometimes language demonstrates someone's own particular culture, and uses its own particular types of expression. Sometimes we use words and expressions which are especially associated with particular jobs, or used by particular groups of people. Read the following passage.

Even my own cousin Ben was there – riding away, in the ringing of bicycle bells down the road.

They can't keep doing that. They'll see!

I only want to be with Nat, Aldo, Jimmy and Ben. It's no fair reason they don't want to be with me. Anybody could go off their head for that. Anybody! A girl can not, not let boys get away with it all the time.

Bother! I have to walk back home, alone.

I know total-total that if I had my own bike, the Wheels-and-brakes Boys wouldn't treat me like that. I'd just ride away with them, wouldn't I?

Over and over I told my mum I wanted a bike. Over and over she looked at me as if I was crazy. "Becky, d'you think you're a boy? Eh? D'you think you're a boy? In any case, where's the money to come from? Eh?"

Of course I know I'm not a boy. Of course I know I'm not crazy. Of course I know all that's no reason why I can't have a bike. No reason! As soon as I get indoors I'll just have to ask again – ask Mum once more.

At home, indoors, I didn't ask my mum.

It was evening time, but sunshine was still big patches in yards and on housetops. My two younger brothers, Lenny and Vin, played marbles in the road. Mum was taking measurements of a boy I knew, for his new trousers and shirt. Mum made clothes for people. Meggie, my sister two years younger than me, was helping Mum on the verandah. Nobody would be pleased with me not helping. I began to help.

Granny-Liz would always stop fanning herself to drink up a glass of iced water. I gave my granny a glass of iced water, there in her rocking-chair. I looked in the kitchen to find shelled coconut pieces to cut into small cubes for the fowls' morning feed. But Granny-Liz had done it. I came and started tidying up bits and pieces of cut-off material around my Mum on the floor. My sister got nasty, saying she was already helping Mum. Not a single good thing was happening for me.

With me even being all so thoughtful of Granny's need of a cool drink, she started up some botheration against me.

Listen to Granny-Liz: "Becky, with you moving about me here on the verandah, I hope you don't have any centipedes or scorpions in a jam jar in your pocket."

"No, mam," I said sighing, trying to be calm. "Granny-Liz," I went on, "you forgot. My centipede and scorpion died." All the same, storm broke against me.

"Becky," my Mum said. "You know I don't like you wandering off after dinner. Haven't I told you I don't want you keeping company with those awful riding-about bicycle boys? Eh?"

"Yes, mam."

"Those boys are a menace. Riding bicycles on sidewalks and narrow paths together, ringing bicycle bells and braking at people's feet like wild bulls charging anybody, they're heading for trouble."

"They're the Wheels-and brakes-Boys, mam."

"The what."

"The Wheels-and-brakes Boys."

"Oh! Given themselves a name as well, have they? Well, Becky, answer this. How d'you always manage to look like you've just escaped from a hair-pulling battle? Eh? And don't I tell you not to break the back down and wear your canvas shoes like slippers? Don't you ever hear what I say?"

"Yes, mam."

"D'you want to end up a field-labourer? Like where your father used to be overseer?"

"No, mam."

"Well, Becky, will you please go off and do your homework?"

Everybody did everything to stop me. I was allowed no chance whatsoever. No chance to talk to Mum about the bike I dream of day and night! And I knew exactly the bike I wanted. I wanted a bike like Ben's bike. Oh, I wished I still had my scorpion on a string to run up and down somebody's back!"

James Berry, **Becky and the wheels-and-brakes boys**

ASSIGNMENT

1 What impression have you gained of Becky's character and personality?

2 What have you learnt about Becky's family and their way of life (the story is set in the West Indies)?

3 Write a few lines describing the effect of the language in the story.

Read the following two versions of the same story.

SNOW-WHITE AND THE SEVEN DWARFS

Once upon a time there was a Queen who had a baby daughter. Her daughter's skin was as white as snow. Her cheeks were ruby red and her hair as black as ebony. The Queen called her Snow-White. Sadly, she died soon after Snow-White was born and her husband the King married again. The new Queen was very beautiful and very proud of her beauty. She could not bear to think that any woman might be more beautiful. She had a magic mirror on the wall. Every day she would gaze at herself in the mirror and ask "Mirror, mirror on the wall, Who is the fairest of them all?"

The mirror always told the Queen that she was the most beautiful woman in the land.

One day, however, the mirror had a different reply. It told the Queen that although she was beautiful, there was a woman even more lovely. That woman was Snow-White, who was growing into a beautiful young girl. This so angered the Queen that she told a huntsman to take Snow-White into the forest and kill her.

The huntsman had to obey, but when Snow-White begged him to spare her life, he took pity on her and left her in the forest, alive.

Snow-White wandered through the forest, terrified. She had no idea where to go or what would become of her. She came upon a cottage by the side of a mountain. She knocked but there was no reply, so she let herself in. She lay on a bed and fell asleep.

Now the cottage belonged to seven dwarfs who worked in the mountains digging for gold. When they came home and found Snow-White asleep they said, "What a beautiful child!"

When she woke and told them her sad story they took pity on her. They said, "If you look after us, keep our house clean and tidy, cook and wash and mend for us, you can live here with us and we will take care of you and protect you from harm."

"Oh, you are so kind!" said Snow-White. She was very happy living with the dwarfs.

ASSIGNMENT

In your group, discuss the way the story is told. What do you notice about the language?

MS SNOW WHITE WINS CASE IN HIGH COURT

Justice Goodbye outlined the circumstances under which the case came before her. Ms White had been abandoned in the heart of the forest, when she was seven years old by an agent acting on behalf of her stepmother, who wished to get rid of her. She pointed out that it was open to bring an action for cruelty on foot of this. Ms White, after wandering round for some considerable time, had then stumbled on a small house. Exhausted, she had lain down to sleep. Upon waking, she was confronted by seven men, who were returning home from work as gold-diggers. Justice Goodbye made the point that Ms White was in no fit mental or physical condition, by virtue of her age and circumstances, to make any decision which could amount under any circumstances to mean "the right to choose" in the legal sense of the word. Consequently, everything which took place following the initial encounter was tainted.

Messrs Dopey, Sneezy, Happy, Grumpy, Doc, Sleepy and Bashful proceeded to enter into a contract with Ms White, who was still exhausted, and in any event, of an age not legally held to be old enough to enter into a contract. Effectively under duress, Ms White agreed - following various promptings from the seven men - to look after the house while they were out gold-digging. She also agreed to cook and wash for all seven, to make all the beds, to sew and knit and generally look after their welfare. Ms Justice Goodbye said that the contract, apart from its earlier mentioned failings, was derelict further in so far as there was no limit to the contractual obligations entered upon by Ms White. In return for agreeing to those conditions, Ms White was allowed to sleep in the house, and also have enough food to eat. The contract was, in the words of Justice Goodbye, "a travesty of natural justice". She also said that Ms White must have been "the handiest slave these seven men would ever have the good fortune to encounter."

Clodagh Corcoran, **Sweeping Beauties**

ASSIGNMENT

1 Talk about the way the story is told. What do you notice about the language?

2 Make a list of all the words and phrases which are to do with the law.

ASSIGNMENT

Write a short description of how the use of language in the second version of the Snow White story changes the whole meaning of the original fairy tale.

More suggestions for coursework

- Choose two activities which are very familiar to you - a sport, perhaps, or listening to music. Make a list of words and phrases which are used when discussing the activity. For each subject, write a short guide to help someone new to the subject understand the meaning of the phrases and the way they are used. You could use a framework like this:

Expression What it means   When you would use it   Example

- In pairs, take it in turns to describe a recent evening out. Now imagine that you have been asked to give an account of the same evening as evidence in a court case. Describe the same events again, but in a way more appropriate to the new situation.
- Discuss the way you used language in each situation.
- Write out each account.
- Choose a familiar story like Goldilocks or Cinderella. Write an account for a newspaper reporting on the events in the story. Specify the type of newspaper you are writing for.

Language link

New expressions

One of the ways we get variety in language is through new words and phrases which come into use. Sometimes they are expressions which at first are used by only a few people, such as groups with particular interests, or of a particular age group, then they become more widespread as they are found to be effective expressions.

Explain the meaning of the following words and phrases. You could either write a short explanation, or take it in turns to explain the meaning to your partner or group. Give one or two examples of how the phrase might be used.

	Meaning	Examples
Internet		
Fax		
Designer label		
Lager lout		
Bimbo		
Toyboy		
Cardboard city		
Care in the community		

END-OF-CHAPTER ASSIGNMENT

Your college is having a 'Department link' day for students and staff to find out what kind of work goes on in all areas of study. Your group has been asked to give a short presentation on the work you have done in English this term. Part of the presentation must be material and extracts from this chapter. Write a report to your tutor recommending three or four passages you think should be included. Make clear your response to the extracts you choose and your reasons for choosing them.

SUMMARY

In this section you have covered the following aspects of GCSE requirements.

SPEAKING AND LISTENING

pair/group discussion
giving a talk
interviewing
debating
role play
presenting a campaign
discussion of language

READING

prose written since 1900
non-European prose written since 1900
poetry written before 1900
poetry written since 1900
non-literary accounts
magazine article
newspaper article
advertisements
diaries
letters
television script

WRITING

comprehension
personal account
autobiography
about poetry
narrative
discussion essay
about advertisements
designing a campaign
designing advertisements
diary entries
letters
about language

LANGUAGE STUDY

vocabulary building
spelling groups
verbs
semi-colons
varieties of language
language change

REVISION AND FURTHER ASSIGNMENTS

1 Fill in the correct form of the verb in the following sentences.

(a) Vicky was pleased she had been (choose) for the team.
(b) This time next week you will have (forget) the whole thing.
(c) The box was (break) beyond repair.
(d) Shala and I (was/were) going to the shops.
(e) Who (was/were) you with at the cinema?
(f) She asked who had (speak).

2 Make verbs from the following words.

education	description	success	moisture
provision	solution	large	friend

Make up sentences using each one.

3 Complete the gaps in the words with 'ie' or 'ei'.

(a) It was a wonderful v..w from the top of the hill.
(b) The c..ling was painted white.
(c) The principal congratulated the students on th..r ach..vements.

4 Arrange these verbs in order of strength, then use each in a sentence.

mention   hint   suggest   announce

5 Write sentences from the following notes, using semi-colons where appropriate.

(a) shut in – two doors – tried one – locked – tried other – locked as well

(b) concert cancelled – lead singer sore throat

(c) two friends with different tastes in holidays – one likes sun and sea – the other likes exploring cities

Use the following topics as a starting point for writing. Where there are no specific instructions you could use them as the basis of a story, or personal writing, or argument or discussion, or a playscript.....

A chapter from your autobiography.

Feeling guilty.

Getting into trouble.

Choose a character you find interesting from a book, or from film or television, and

(1) write an interview with the person;

(2) write an exchange of letters between you.

How women and men are portrayed in television advertisements.

Advertisements I dislike.

The needle of death.

What I'd tell my children about drugs.

GENERATION GAMES

The age of innocence?

Sometimes people talk about when they were young as if everything about being a child in the past was wonderful; at other times you hear people say that children of today are the lucky ones. See what you think after reading this passage.

Some of us cling to a belief that in the past, children grew up in simplicity and innocence. The myth of the golden age of childhood is a potent one. Somewhere in our minds there is fixed the idea of the 'perfect childhood' – a cross between Peter Pan and Wind in the Willows: a world where children had adventures, played out in the street, had innocent friendships and fun: where they had their tea by five and were in bed by seven.

Today, it all seems much more complicated. Pop culture now embraces school children of nine and ten, who are drawn into the imagery flaunted by fashionable groups. It is common for children as young as ten and eleven to have 'boyfriends' and 'girlfriends'. Open the pages of any teenage magazine and you get a dismaying picture of children under intense pressure, caught up in a school life where fancying a boy or a girl is taken to the point of obsession. Children's parties now demand a diet of pop music; even the Brownies have their own discos. It's all a far cry from Enid Blyton and the Famous Five.

Do children really grow up more quickly today than ever before? How real was all that childhood innocence? Most of our cherished convictions turn out to have been illusory. In fact, the pressures on children to achieve adulthood have, in some ways, never been more relaxed.

Worried by spots and obsessed by stars our children do not, now, lead pit ponies through coal shafts or sip gin (lovingly ladled out to them by their mothers) in public houses. And yet, only two generations ago, the working class family depended for its survival on all members working. Children were expected to start full-time work from the age of 13. As late as the 1920s, boys were recruited for factory work, engineering and mining while one in four of all teenage girls were in residential domestic service. At the age of 12, many boys and girls were allowed to work half-time, provided they had passed the 'Labour Exam' (a basic competence test) or attended school 300 times over the previous 5 years. Even before full-time work,

most children worked for their parents from a very early age. Children worked alongside their mothers making artificial flowers or wire brushes, arduous, low-paid jobs which were necessary to make ends meet. Children were also expected to help with domestic chores and child minding. In large families, the eldest daughter acted as 'little mother' to the younger children, helping to dress and feed them. Frances Sherlock remembers growing up in Chester in the 1920s as the eldest daughter in a family of 12.

"Every other year as I grew up my mother had a baby, which meant that, being the eldest, I had lots of chores to do and four kids to look after. I had napkins to wash, messages to run. I had to find anything I could to keep the fire going — old shoes, anything that would burn....and I don't ever remember having a chair: mother and father had a chair but we just stood round the table. Everything was hard work then."

Attitudes were harder too. In the poorest inner city areas, at the turn of the century, as many as half of all babies died before their first birthday. Of those who did survive, one in four died before they reached the age of five. Poverty and over-crowding made many parents harsh disciplinarians. Most families were 'father-centred' rather than 'child-centred' and indulgence towards children was limited. The father would have the warmest seat by the fire, the best piece of meat, the first tomato, the best butter, with margarine for the rest of the family.

Few expect their young children to work, either at home or in a factory. They contribute little to the economic well-being of the family. They are freer than they have ever been before simply to be children. We see them as the centre of the family, around which the rest of life revolves: we protect them from responsibilities which were forced on earlier generations. For today's affluent children there is all the time in the world. The golden age of childhood should be here and now. And yet, it is not.

Time and leisure, heaped on our children in abundance, have their own disadvantages. They create a vacuum which children are slowly losing the ability to fill for themselves. Ready-made entertainment – theme parks, leisure centres, videos, television – spring up to plug the gap. But they can destroy a child's ability to make a rich inner life for himself from his imagination. As a child, like past generations, I played unsupervised in the street and the park. But who would think it safe to let children play like this today? Theme parks may amuse and entertain the young, but people must drive them there in their cars, we must watch and supervise them all the time and sit through a traffic jam to drive them home again. Then there is television. If a child wants entertainment, television will always provide a stimulus. But what sort of stimulus? When BBC television began broadcasting in the 1950s, children's programmes came to an end at six o'clock. Then there was an hour's 'closedown' before adult television resumed, so that parents could put their children to bed. Today, children's television has virtually ceased to exist. What do our children watch now? Soap

operas whose plots are composed of violence and greed.

When children of large families were compelled to share rooms with siblings, there was always a companion at hand. There was security, conversation and someone to play with. Free from the pressures of overcrowding we think it natural today that children should demand their own room. From there, it is a small step to turning the child's room into a replica of adult space, fitting it out with television, video, cassette and Walkman. There, surrounded by various forms of instant entertainment, the child sits alone, planning the purchase of his next electronic gadget.

Diptheria, child labour, grinding poverty are well lost. One can only pity the cruelly short, disease-ridden lives of those early children. But I think our generation has failed its children too. We have given them the world, but we have also taken a world away. We have not made them happier. As the distinguished child psychologist, Bruno Bettelheim, put it: "Objectively speaking, it may seem that much less is asked of the modern child compared to times past, but frequently children end up deeply dissatisfied with themselves and the world, without quite knowing why, which makes such feelings more disconcerting."

(Adapted from LEAG examination paper)

ASSIGNMENT

1 Look at all the points the passage makes about the advantages and disadvantages of being a child today rather than in the past. Make headings for four columns.

Today		Past	
Good	**Bad**	**Good**	**Bad**

Make notes from the passage under each heading.

2 Using your notes as a basis, write an article for a magazine on the advantages and disadvantages of being a child today rather than in the past. The magazine is one aimed at parents of young and teenage children. Use the ideas in the passage and also include any of your own. End the article with a sentence giving the readers something to think about - perhaps use a rhetorical question.

3 Imagine that you are a child living a hundred years ago. Using the ideas from the passage and any others of your own write a diary extract describing a day in your life, or if you prefer, write a story or playscript about it.

(Adapted from LEAG examination paper)

Rhetorical question

A rhetorical question is one which is asked for effect rather than for an answer or information.

Example: "How many more times do I have to stress the importance of getting your work in on time?"

The speaker doesn't really expect to be told the likely number of times - the question is being asked in order to make a point.

'Rhetoric' is the art of using language effectively, often to persuade or influence.

SELF CHECK

Make a list of rhetorical questions which are often used in everyday situations.

More suggestions for coursework

- Interview an adult who had a very different childhood from your own. It could be that it was in a different country or part of the country, or just that the way of life was very different at that time. Write up the results of the interview. You could keep it in question and answer format:

  Me: "What did you do for entertainment?"
  Kashif: "Well, we used to..."

  or write it up as an article.

- In the passage you have just read the writer refers to books about childhood like the ones written by Enid Blyton. Think about the ideas of childhood and children conveyed in those books, or in any books or magazines you used to read. Write a few paragraphs describing this fictional picture, then a few paragraphs comparing it to the reality you experienced!

- Children's games

  (a) In your group, discuss the games you played as children. You could use these prompts to help you think about them:

  ball games
  team games
  dressing up /role playing
  chants/rhymes
  boys' games/girls' games
  competitive/non-competitive

(b) Make notes as a record of your discussion.

(c) Ask an older person, a parent for example, what games they played. Use the prompts to help them remember.

(d) Find out from someone much younger what kind of games they play now. If you have younger friends or relatives you might be able to make notes from your observation.

(e) Write up the results of your discussions. You could write a description of the way games have changed, or you could discuss any differences you have found between the games boys play and the games girls play.

Write a story or a description in which a children's playground features.

Punctuation mark

Colon

'We see them as the centre of the family, around which the rest of life revolves: we protect them from responsibilities which were forced on earlier generations.'

The colon is used to indicate a pause in the sentence. It suggests a close connection between both parts of the sentence.

Often it introduces an explanation or development of the first part of the sentence, as in the example from the passage.

It is used most commonly to introduce a list or a series of items.

Example The jacket is available in a choice of colours: green, navy blue, brown and grey.

It can be used to balance or contrast two ideas in a sentence, like the semi-colon, but stronger.

Example It started with love and affection: it finished with bitterness and recrimination.

SELF CHECK

Using the colon, write a sentence to say that sausages, beans, chips, burgers and salads are available from the canteen.

Using the colon, write a sentence to express that red is a colour suggesting fire and yellow is a colour suggesting optimism.

Gangs and territories

In this extract from *Paddy Clarke Ha Ha Ha* Roddy Doyle describes some of the adventures Paddy and his friends got up to in the imaginary Barrytown in Ireland.

Martin and them built huts. We did too, from the stuff we got off the building sites – it was one of the first things we did when the summer was coming – but theirs were better, miles better than our ones. There was a field behind the newest of our type of houses – not the one behind the shops - and that was where most of the huts got built. It was full of hills like dunes, only made of muck instead of sand. It used to be a part of a farm but that was years before. The wreck of the farmhouse was at the edge of the field. The walls weren't bricks; they were made of light brown mud full of gravel and bigger stones. They were dead easy to demolish. I found a piece of cup in the nettles against the wall. I took it home and I washed it. I showed it to my da and he said it was probably worth a fortune but he wouldn't buy it off me. He told me to put it in a safe place. It had flowers on it, two full ones and a half one. I lost it.

The field looked like they had started to get it ready for building on but they'd stopped. There was a wide trench, wider than a lane, down the middle and other trenches grown over. Some

of the fields hadn't been touched. Da said that the building had been stopped because they'd had to wait till the mains pipes were down and finished, with water in them.

I ran through the untouched part of the field – for no reason, just running – and the grass was great, up to way over my knees. I had to lift my legs out of it, like in water. It was the type of grass that could cut you sometimes. It had tops like wheat. I brought loads of it home to my ma once but she said you couldn't make bread out of it. I said she could but she said you couldn't, it was a pity. My feet made swoosh noises going through the grass and then there was another noise, one in front of me. And the grass moved. I stopped, and a long bird flew out of the grass. And stayed low, flew out in front of me. I could feel its wings beating. It was a pheasant. I turned back.

Kevin's brother built his huts in the hills. They dug long holes; they got lends of their da's spades. Terence Long had his own one; he got it for his birthday. They divided the hole into segments, rooms. They covered the hole with planks. They sometimes got hay out of Donnelly's farm. That was the basement.

When I came out of a hut my hair was full of clay and muck. I could make my hair stand up.

Roddy Doyle, **Paddy Clarke Ha Ha Ha**

ASSIGNMENT

1 The story sounds as if it is being written by Paddy Clarke, who is about ten years old. How does the writer give this impression? Make notes from the passage, then write about a page. Give examples from the passage to illustrate your points.

2 Some of the language in the extract is the kind we use when speaking rather than when we are writing formally. Find some examples of this kind of colloquial language. Write a few sentences explaining how it makes the passage effective.

The following passage is taken from *Cat's Eye* by Margaret Atwood.

We've forgotten the time, it's getting dark. We run along the street that leads to the wooden footbridge. Even Grace runs, lumpily, calling, "Wait up!" For once she is the one left behind.

Cordelia reaches the hill first and runs down it. She tries to slide but the snow is too soft, not icy enough, and there are cinders and pieces of gravel in it. She falls down and rolls. We think she's done it on purpose, the way she made the snow angel. we rush down upon her, exhilarated, breathless, laughing, just as she's picking herself up.

We stop laughing, because now we can see that her fall was an accident, she didn't do it on purpose. She likes everything she does to be done on purpose.

Carol says, "Did you hurt yourself?" Her voice is quavery, she's frightened, already she can tell that this is serious. Cordelia doesn't answer. Her face is hard again, her eyes baleful.

Grace moves so that she's beside Cordelia, slightly behind her. From there she smiles at me, her tight smile.

Cordelia says, to me, "Were you laughing?" I think she means, was I laughing at her because she fell down.

"No," I say.

"She was," says Grace neutrally. Carol shifts to the side of the path, away from me.

"I'm going to give you one more chance," says Cordelia. "Were you laughing?"

"Yes," I say, "but..."

"Just yes or no," says Cordelia.

I say nothing. Cordelia glances over at Grace, as if looking for approval. She sighs an exaggerated sigh, like a grown-up's. "Lying again," she says. "What are we going to do with you?"

We seem to have been standing there for a long time. It's colder now. Cordelia reaches out and pulls off my knitted hat. She marches the rest of the way down the hill and onto the bridge and hesitates for a moment. Then she walks over to the railing and throws my hat down into the ravine. Then the white oval of her face turns up towards me. "Come here, " she says.

I walk down to where Cordelia stands by the railing, the snow not crunching but giving way under my feet like cotton-wool packing. It sounds like a cavity being filled, in a tooth, inside my head. Usually I'm afraid to go so near the edge of the bridge, but this time I'm not. I don't feel anything as positive as fear.

"There's your stupid hat, " says Cordelia; and there it is, far down, still blue against the white snow, even in the dimming light. "Why don't you go down and get it?"

I look at her. She wants me to go down into the ravine where the bad men are, where we're never supposed to go. It occurs to me that I may not. What will she do then?

I can see this idea gathering in Cordelia as well. Maybe she's gone too far, hit, finally, some core of resistance in me. If I refuse to do what she says this time, who knows where my defiance will end? The two others have come down the hill and are watching, safely in the middle of the bridge.

"Go on then, " she says, more gently, as if she's encouraging me, not ordering. "Then you'll be forgiven."

I don't want to go down there. It's forbidden and dangerous; also it's dark and the hillside will be slippery. I might have trouble climbing up again. But there is my hat. If I go home without it, I'll have to explain, I'll have to tell. And if I refuse to go, what will Cordelia do next? She might get angry, she might never speak to me again. She might push me off the bridge. She's never done anything like that before, never hit or pinched, but now that she's thrown my hat over there's no telling what she might do.

I walk along to the edge of the bridge. "When you've got to it, count to a hundred," says Cordelia. "Before coming up." She doesn't sound angry any more. She sounds like someone giving instructions for a game.

I start down the steep hillside, holding onto branches and tree trunks. The path isn't even a real path, it's just a place worn by whoever goes up and down here: boys, men. Not girls.

When I'm among the bare trees at the bottom I look up. The bridge railings are silhouetted against the sky. I can see the dark outlines of three heads, watching me.

My blue hat is out on the ice of the creek. I stand in the snow, looking at it. Cordelia is right, it's a stupid hat. I look at it and feel resentment, because this stupid-looking hat is mine, and deserving of ridicule. I don't want to wear it ever again.

I can hear water running somewhere, down under the ice.

Margaret Atwood, **Cat's Eye**

ASSIGNMENT

1 What have you gathered about Cordelia's character and personality from reading the extract? Go through the passage carefully and make notes on:

what she does;

what she says;

how her behaviour, thoughts and feelings are described;

what the other characters say to her;

what the other characters think of her.

Use your notes as the basis of a written answer (about a page).

2 Describe the feelings of the girl telling the story. Go through the passage carefully and make notes on:

what she does;

what she says;

what she thinks and feels.

Use your notes as the basis of a written answer (about a page).

This is taken from a radio programme about a group of girls living in East London. This part of the interview was taped in the youth centre they go to.

"I'm Cathy, I'm 16 years old. I'm part of the group. My sister Denise, she's 18 years old, going on for 19, there's Dionne, she's 14, Eileen's 12, Anna's 18, Janet's 15. We're known as the Brick Lane Girls but we don't think that we're the Brick Lane Girls but they just like calling us that because we all live in that area."

"If there was no centre I wouldn't have nowhere to go cos there's no other clubs, well there is other clubs round here, boys' clubs, strictly Asian clubs, Somalian clubs, em, clubs that I don't like to go up into and er there's nowhere else for us to go. So it's really important to us."

"Well since we live in Brick Lane, it's mostly an Asian area, there's hardly any girls out on the street, it's all boys, and my mum gets really protective and thinks, she, she really wonders what I do on the street because there are so many boys and she thinks it's unsafe for me, but since I've lived here 14 years I know everyone in the area. I know all the places round here but my mum just doesn't get it. She thinks we're stupid to get into trouble but we don't. Not all the time anyway."

"All right it's a bad area but it's nothing compared to other areas. Even though I used to hang in Peckham like with my other mates from South London like I still wouldn't feel safe to walk down the streets down there because you know for a fact you're gonna get jumped, someone's gonna get your trainers off you, your earrings, even your rings."

"Me, Janet and was it Cathy, I think, was coming from my house and these girls were getting like kind of mouthy and Janet and Cathy they didn't want to stand there and take it so what happened was we run up to get Denise and the others and we chased them and we em it just like we rushed them and we got caught by the police. (laughter) The police separates the blacks from whites and they didn't know what Janet was so they just put her up against their ice cream van (lots of laughter) The fight was mainly with me and I got done for robbery and assault and – what's that thing called, Denise? – not GBH – ABH – but, but they kept me in there from - what time did I get arrested, about 3? From 3 o'clock till half eleven that night, right, and em like I had to get a solicitor right and then like she said to me like she wanted to know the truth from me but the police over-exaggerated like they said (laughs) they said that that I gave her a busted nose and swollen face.(Voice: She had a busted nose) Yeah but it weren't all that bad how they explained it."

"We do feel safe in a group because if anyone starts with any of us we'll stick up for them as well. Because if you're friends and you stick with a group you stick together."

Radio 4

ASSIGNMENT

1 This passage gives a record of the words actually spoken in the interview. Make a list of all the words and phrases which tell you this. (Look for the phrases and little expressions we all use when we are speaking but do not use in writing.)

2 Choose a few lines and turn them into written comments which give information on what Cathy says and does.

3 Using your list and your new version as a basis, write an account of what you think are some of the main differences between spoken and written English.

Grammar box

Adverbs

"Go on," she says, more gently.

'Gently' is an adverb. Adverbs add to the meaning of a verb, making it more precise. They can also add to the meanings of adjectives and other adverbs.

They generally answer questions like when? where? how?

They are usually formed from the corresponding adjective by adding 'ly'.

Example gentle - gently

SELF CHECK

Write a couple of sentences about each of the following situations, using some of the adverbs from the list.

Someone in the library looking up references and making notes.
Someone waiting for exam results to arrive.
Being in the garden on a hot day.
Thinking you hear footsteps outside.

cautiously	fearfully	vaguely
carefully	anxiously	warily
lazily	impatiently	attentively
methodically	apprehensively	eventually
slowly	distinctly	painstakingly

Comparison of adverbs

Adverbs are compared in the same way as adjectives (see chapter two). Usually you add 'more' and 'most' to the word.

Example

loudly	quickly
more loudly	more quickly
most loudly	most quickly

Exceptions

badly	much	well
worse	more	better
worse	most	best

Check the meanings of any words you are unsure of in a dictionary

---

SELF CHECK

Complete the chart:

carefully	slowly	far

More suggestions for coursework

- Write a story or description of what happens when some members of a group of friends gang up against one of their number.
- Write a story or description in which the idea of territory plays an important part.

Fathers and sons

The following material presents different experiences of the relationships between fathers and sons.

SO LONG DAD

Home again.
The streets are not much cleaner.
The quaint old south-side scenery
Is quaint no more,
Just older than before.
Go up the stairs and down the hallway
To my daddy's door.

Your son is home, dad, he's found a girl.
She's the greatest girl in all the world.
I think you'll like her, dad, I hope you do -
But if you don't that's all right too.

What's new?
Do you still work at the drugstore,
Is that true?
Still polishing the same floor?
I miss my good old dad.
My, but I'm glad to see you!
Home again.

No, I won't be staying here, dad.

Come and see us, poppa, when you can.
There'll always be a place for my old man.
Just drop by when it's convenient to.
(Be sure and call before you do.)

So long dad
So long dad

Randy Newman

ASSIGNMENT

1 What is the situation described in the song?

2 How would you describe the speaker's attitude to his father? (Think carefully about tone here.) Write a couple of paragraphs describing it.

3 Write about a side describing what the father's thoughts and feelings might be when his son left.

Language link

Tone

When we speak we express our feelings and attitudes with the words we use and how we say them. Usually we judge whether someone is serious or joking or excited by their tone of voice. When we write we communicate attitudes and feelings in the same way, through the words we use and how we arrange them. Although the words are not spoken, they can be 'heard' in the mind of the reader.

When you write it is important to choose the appropriate tone, or register. Register is the word used to indicate the form of language appropriate for a particular situation. For example, you would use slang or local dialect talking to a friend and legal terms when drawing up a contract.

SELF CHECK

- Look at the different registers you might use greeting different people. What might you say and how might you say it to: a good friend; a casual acquaintance; a child; a shop assistant; someone interviewing you for a job.
- "Still doing the same job?" Try saying this sentence in the following tones: interested; uninterested; patronising; eager.

This extract is taken from *Father and Son* in which Edmund Gosse describes what it was like being brought up as a member of the Plymouth Brethren, a very strict religious sect. Here he describes a couple of incidents which change his attitude to his father.

It was about the date of my sixth birthday that I did something very naughty, some act of direct disobedience, for which my Father, after a solemn sermon, chastised me, sacrificially, by giving me several cuts with a cane. This action was justified, as everything he did was justified, by reference to Scripture – "Spare the rod and spoil the child". I suppose there are some children, of a sullen and lymphatic temperament, who are smartened up and made more wide-awake by a whipping. It is largely a matter of convention, the exercise being endured (I am told) with pride by the infants of our aristocracy, but not tolerated by the lower classes. I am afraid that I proved my inherent vulgarity by being made, not contrite or humble, but furiously angry by this caning. I cannot account for the flame of rage which it awakened in my bosom. My dear, excellent father had beaten me, not very severely, without ill-temper, and with the most genuine desire to improve me. But he was not well-advised; there are some natures which are not improved by being humiliated. I have to confess with shame that I went about the house for some days with a murderous hatred of my father locked within my bosom. He did not suspect that the chastisement had not been wholly efficacious, and he bore me no malice; so that after a while, I forgot and thus forgave him. But I do not regard physical punishment as a wise element in the education of proud and sensitive children.

My theological misdeeds culminated, however, in an act so puerile and preposterous that I should not venture to record it if it did not throw some glimmering of light on the subject which I have proposed to myself in writing these pages. My mind continued to dwell on the mysterious question of prayer. It puzzled me greatly to know why, if we were God's children, and if he was watching over us by night and day, we might not supplicate for toys and sweets and smart clothes as well as for the conversion of the heathen. Just at this juncture, we had a special service at the Room, at which our attention was particularly drawn to the subject of idolatry, which was severely censured. I cross-examined my father very closely as to the nature of this sin, and pinned him down to the categorical statement that idolatry consisted in praying to anyone or anything but God himself. Wood and stone, in the words of the hymn, were peculiarly liable to be bowed down to by the heathen in their blindness. I pressed my father further on this subject, and he assured me that God would be very angry, and would signify His anger, if anyone, in a Christian country, bowed down to wood and stone. I cannot recall why I was so pertinacious on this subject, but I remember that my father became a little restive under my cross-examination. I determined, however, to test the matter for myself, and one morning, when both my parents were safely out of the house, I prepared for the great act of heresy. I was in the morning-room on the ground floor, where, with much labour, I hoisted a small chair on to the table close to the window. My heart was now beating as if it would leap out of my side, but I pursued my experiment. I knelt down on the carpet in front of the table and looking up I said my daily prayer in a loud voice, only substituting the address "O Chair!" for the habitual one. Having carried this act of idolatry safely through, I waited to see what would happen. It was a fine day, and I gazed up at the slip of white sky above the houses opposite, and expected something to appear in it. God would certainly exhibit his anger in some terrible form, and would chastise my impious and wilful action. I was very much alarmed, but still more excited; I breathed the high, sharp air of defiance. But nothing happened; there was not a cloud in the sky, not an unusual sound in the street. Presently I was quite sure that nothing would happen. I had committed idolatry, flagrantly and deliberately, and God did not care.

The result of this ridiculous act was not to make me question the existence and power of God; those were forces which I did not dream of ignoring. But what it did was to lessen still further my confidence in my father's knowledge of the Divine mind. My father had said, positively, that if I worshipped a thing made of wood, God would manifest his anger. I had then worshipped a chair, made (or partly made) of wood, and God had made no sign whatever. My father, therefore, was not really acquainted with the Divine practice in cases of idolatry.

Edmund Gosse, **Father and Son**

ASSIGNMENT

1 Choose one sentence from each of the following groups of sentences which you think best reflects what happens in the passage at that point. It might be a good idea to do this exercise by yourself then compare answers with your partner or in your group. Be ready to refer to the passage to explain your choice.

(a) Edmund's father caned him severely because he had been disobedient.

(b) When Edmund had been disobedient his father gave him a serious talk then caned him.

(c) Edmund's father caned him to prove he wasn't aristocratic.

(a) Edmund felt smarter and more awake as a result.

(b) Edmund was angry with his father for ever after that incident.

(c) Edmund was furious with his father for a short time but then forgave him.

(a) Edmund questioned his father closely about the meaning of 'idolatry'.

(b) Edmund asked his father if it was all right to worship a chair.

(a) Edmund prayed to a chair to test his father's teaching.

(b) Edmund prayed to a chair for toys and sweets.

(a) When Edmund prayed to the chair a sign appeared in the sky.

(b) When Edmund prayed to the chair nothing happened.

(a) This incident made Edmund question the existence of God.

(b) This incident made Edmund question his father's knowledge and power.

2 Write a short play or a story in which a young person goes against the beliefs of his or her parents. (The beliefs might be religious, political, moral etc.)

Language link

Exact meanings

You may have found some of the vocabulary in this extract difficult. Column A lists some of the difficult words in the passage. Their meanings as they are used in the passage are listed in column B. Match the words with their meanings.

A	B
chastised	outrageously
lymphatic	childish
inherent	an opinion opposed to the usual belief
contrite	spite
efficacious	sluggish
malice	irreverent
theological	natural
censured	remorseful
puerile	effective
idolatry	unyielding
pertinacious	to do with the divine
heresy	condemned
impious	worship of an image
flagrantly	punished

The sins of the fathers

This short story describes a boy's relationship with this father, focusing on a time when they each did something wrong.

Even at night, when he was lying on his bed of plaited coconut leaf, he could hear the wind, loud as in the daytime. It came wet and chilly off the sea, blew through the holes in the patched wooden walls of the tiny hut where he lived with his mother and father. When rain fell he had to shift in his bed to avoid the spray which flew through the eastern wall of the hut. "I got to fix up this house," his father always used to say, but it was never done.

He could hear the wind in the canefields now, howling faintly, swishing along the cane-leaves and the arrows, and above it all he could hear the sound of the kites. There was the loud pervading roar of the big singing-angels, the whine of the little ones swaying at the end of their thread, the flapping sound of the brown paper bulls on the kites with single roundheads. It was like this day and night, when the kite-season came. When the Easter winds began to blow the kites went up, and from then until long past Easter there would be kites in the sky, newer ones, different ones, for it was very seldom that a kite could survive the length of the Easter season. Very few flyers could preserve their kite that long. No champion could hold his title that long, though some had come fairly close. Then there were the numerous mishaps that befell the kites; the electric wires, depending on where one was flying his kite, the trees, the sea, the wind itself. Kites came and went, but the kite-flying went on until, sometime around the end of April, they would all be gone.

He had never had a kite. His father had never given him one, and none of the boys made kites for free. They would want six cents at least, and he never had any money. Then there was the matter of string. It was the real problem; string was expensive, his father would never give him a ball of twine. He never asked his father for a kite and twine; he had heard his mother asking in vain for too many other more important things. But he had to get a kite that year, and he knew how.

He had tried chasing the kites when they broke their string, but he was no fast runner. Besides, from the time a kite broke, the alarm would be given, and so many boys would give chase that no individual could benefit from the chase; the string would have to be divided among too many.

But he dreaded the thought of putting his idea in practice. he knew that boys had been beaten by the kiteflyers already, for trying the same thing. Not even the owner of the kite could object if his kite broke and you chased it, and claimed it as your own. It was always a matter of Finders, Keepers, then. But it was something quite different to take a kite from the air. Everyone knew it was unfair simply because a flyer had no chance to save his kite; no skill in the world could stop it from coming down.

But he had long since considered the possibilities of being caught, and mapped out his plan of escape. It should be fairly easy, he knew, but he still wasn't sure if he wanted to do it. And he would have to go somewhere else to fly the kite, so it wouldn't be recognised. It wouldn't be much fun flying the kite, with strange boys from another district, though. They wouldn't be friendly. They would bob your cord if you went a little way away to fix your kite, you had to watch them all the time.

He lay awake thinking and listening to the kites, and around six o'clock he heard his father stir in the coconut fibre bed behind the little drape, where he slept with his mother. His father coughed and pushed aside the curtain and came out. He crossed to the door and unlatched it, letting the cold light in, and he hawked and spat and held his chest for a long time, bending his head. Then he wiped his mouth and looked at his hand for a moment, stepped away from the door and moved out of the range of the boy's vision. He lay pretending to be asleep and heard his father sharpening his cutlass on the hearthstone. The bed made a noise and then his mother came through the curtain and went to make the coffee for his father, and the boy continued to lie there until he smelt the coffee.

He got up and went to the hearth where the clay pot was still steaming; took down a cup and dipped it full. He put in a spoonful of brown sugar and turned, sipping it, to look at his father and mother. She was standing by the door and he was sitting on the step outside, sipping from his calabash. His fishing ropes were draped around his shoulder, and his net and crocus bags were in the yard, close by his feet.

"Is Good Friday," his mother said. "You ain't have to go out today. It ain't seem right to me."

"What you want me to do, go to church?" his father said. He put down the calabash on the step and walked away, out of the enclosure of plaited coconut leaf that formed the paling. He grew smaller as he walked down the long beach in the widening daylight, and the wind flapped the ends of his shirt.

"He is a very sick man," his mother said, as if talking to herself. "I don't like him alone out there in that condition. Why you don't go out and help your father, boy? You big enough, and you know jest as much 'bout it as he. You jest good for nothing, won't hear nothin' I say at all. You want he to dead?"

He stopped drinking and stared at her.

"Good Friday," she said. "Easter Day two days off. And nothing at all. It going be jest like any other day."

When she started to talk like that, he knew that he should get out of the house, else she would spend the whole day grumbling and shouting at him.

"I going get some water," he said, and slipped outside. He took up the overturned bucket in the yard and moved away, headed for the standpipe a short distance away. As he walked he looked up at the kites speckling the sky, hundreds and hundreds of them, he thought, and all those colours, scattered out up there, like confetti.

Later in the day, he crouched in the canefields and looked up at the kites. He had a spool of his father's fishing line, which he knew must be returned to his box before he missed it. He had tied a stone about the size of his fist to the end of the fishing line. There was a stiff piece of wire through the hole in the spool, so that it could spin freely.

Most of the kites were high, and there strings swayed, following their movements. There were no sharp tugs on their lines; they would be ties out, he knew, with nobody holding onto their string, and perhaps nobody watching the one that he was after. It was a big singing-angel with a short tail; when the wind increased it looped and swung in a wide area of sky. He could see its swizzle, two bits of glass and razor glinted on the end of its tail. As he watched, it came up roaring out of a dive, climbed high in the sky, moved sideways and hooked itself across the string of a kite even larger than itself. Its head came down and it was pulled into a dive by the pressure on its tail. The heavy cloth raked its length along the tightened string and the bigger kite snapped away, suddenly silent, and went nodding and drifting away in the distance. Already he could hear the faint shouts, "Kite popped!" and he saw the boys running, shouting and pointing. The wind was hard and the kite was taking long to fall and he was glad because he knew it would keep some of them occupied for a while. But he thought of all this within a second, because the swizzle-tailed kite was close to the tops of the canes, now recovering from its dive, and he jumped up and threw with all his might before it could rise. The spool jerked in his hand and the stone curved and fell, dragging the fishing line across the string. He hauled swiftly, feeling the strong pull as the kite struggled to rise, and hauled until it crashed into the canes. Then he ran forward, grabbed its string and tugged. Somewhere across the canefields, the string broke and he pulled swiftly, wrapping it around his hand as he ran stumbling through the cane clutching the kite. From afar, over the other side of the gully, boys were shouting angrily. He ran with all his might, out of the canes and over some rocks, down to the beach, to the cave he had chosen for its hiding-place.

He came home happy, sure that he had not been seen. But he had scarcely gone inside the house when he heard the voices outside, and the knock on the door.

"What wunna want?" his mother said.

"We come for we kite. Trevor have we kite. He thief it and run with it."

"I ain't know, I ain't seen him with no kite. I ain't think he would do that. Trevor!" she called. "These three boys out here say that you have them kite. That is true?"

Trevor looked up from where he was sitting on his bed. "What kite? I ain't know nothing 'bout no kite."

His mother came close and looked at him. He knew that she knew he was lying, and he looked away from her face. She stood over him, arms akimbo.

"Where the kite, Trevor? Where you put it?"

"I ain't see no kite," he said. "Them can't say they see me with no kite."

"We see him, " one of the boys shouted from outside. "We was looking at the kite through my father spying glass, and we see him close up when he was running out of the canes."

His mother shook her head slowly, and turned to the window. "I can't control him," she said. "He won't hear to me at all. You have to wait till his father come home this evening. Don't worry, he going have to give yuh back."

"Huh! All right. I coming back this evening, and if I don't get it he better watch how he walking 'bout outside here. We bound to catch he sometime." And the boys went away,

When his father came in from the sea that evening he heard the story and he didn't waste any time. "Boy, go and get that kite from wherever you hiding it," he said, and Trevor knew better than to argue. He went down to the cave on the beach and brought it back to the house. Then his father flogged him with his heavy canvas belt.

"I beating you because you know better than that," he said. "I ain't raising you up to be no thief. And you no right telling yuh mother lies either. If you did want a kite as bad as that I woulda help get one for yuh. You didn't have to do that at all."

And the next day his father gave him ten cents and he went at Boysie's shop and bought a beautiful round-kite. His father gave him part of an old fishnet and he unravelled it to make his twine, and he spent the whole of Easter Sunday flying his kite, except when he went home for the midday meal.

It was a special meal after all; his mother had cooked a turkey that his father brought home the night before. The three of them sat in the house and ate, enjoying it, knowing that a long time would pass before such a treat would come their way again. His belly was full when he returned to the gully to let his kite out again, and he flew it there until the evening. Then, not wanting to risk leaving it out for the night, he hauled it in and headed for home.

When he came into the yard he stopped in surprise. There was a policeman standing there, and for a minute he thought that the boys had sent him to recover their kite. But there were two other men, both from the poultry farm a mile away – the watchman, and the man in charge of the place. And he saw his father leaning by the side of the house and talking to them.

"It was two of wunna," the watchman said. "Who was the other one?"

"You will have to find him yuhself," his father said. "All I can say is, I really sorry and I going to pay for both of them if you want me to. I ain't want no trouble, Mr Watson. I begging you not to take it no further than that. Is Eastertime, and everybody would want to eat at least today."

The boy knew at once what they were talking about, he realised immediately that his father could never have bought a turkey like that. He turned before the men saw him, came out of the yard, and walked quickly away down the beach. He would wait until they left before he returned. He hoped that nobody would hear about it, but he knew the chances of secrecy were slim, the village talked too much.

And he was right. The other fellows knew. When he came to fly his kite the next day, the boys were waiting to taunt him.

"Thief, thief!" they shouted. "You and you father is the same, all o' wunna is thieves."

"A chip off the old block, that is what my father say. Like father, like son."

But he knew they wouldn't dare to touch him and he kept on flying his kite. He was sure that there was a big difference between him and his father, and he was content.

Timothy Callender, **The sins of the fathers**

ASSIGNMENT

What kind of life do Trevor and his parents lead? Write about a page, referring to the story.

1 How much sympathy do you feel for:

  (a) Trevor;

(b) his father;

(c) his mother?

Write a couple of paragraphs on each.

2 Imagine that you are Trevor's father. Describe your actions, thoughts and feelings about:

(a) wanting to provide a turkey;

(b) Trevor stealing the kite;

(c) what happened afterwards.

ASSIGNMENT

Write about each of the sons in these three passages and show what you think about them. Do your feelings change at any point?

More suggestions for coursework

- Describe a visit home by a son or daughter who has left and feels that he or she has 'outgrown' home and the people there. (You could write a play or a story, or do a role play.)
- Write about what happens when someone wants to buy a special present but hasn't got much money.
- Write about the kinds of punishment you think are effective:
  (a) for children;
  (b) for adults.
  You could also give a talk on this topic, or have a discussion.
- Choose a physical activity like flying a kite, or mountain bike riding, or roller-blading. Give a talk or write an account of it, showing the skill required and giving some idea of the sense of excitement and achievement involved.

Family feelings

POEMS ABOUT SISTERS

My sister likes to try my shoes,
to strut in them,
admire her spindle-thin-twelve-year-old legs

in this season's styles.
She says they fit her perfectly,
but wobbles
on their high heels, they're
hard to balance.

I like to watch my little sister
playing hopscotch, admire the neat hops-and-skips of her,
their quick peck,
never-missing their mark, not
over-stepping the line.
She is competent at hopscotch.

I try to warn my little sister
about unsuitable shoes,
point out my own distorted feet, the calluses,
odd patches of hard skin.
I should not like to see her
in my shoes.
I wish she would stay
sure footed,
sensibly shod.

Liz Lochhead

ASSIGNMENT

1 Jot down all the things the poem tells you about the writer's little sister – how she behaves, what she's like etc.

2 The poet focuses on feet as a way of expressing character. Look at the references to shoes and feet and make some notes on what they suggest about both the poet and her sister.

3 Now use your notes to write your response to the poem. Make clear what the poet feels about her sister and what you think about their relationship.

4 Write a scene between the two sisters in which the older one tries to give advice and the younger one asks questions about her sister's life. You could write this as a conversation or as a playscript.

SISTERS
(for Marian)

My sister
was the bad one –
said what she thought
and did what she liked
and didn't care.

At ten she wore
a knife tucked in
her leather belt,
dreamed of being
a prince on a white horse.

Became a dolly bird
with dyed hair longer
than her skirts, pulling
the best of the local talent.
Mother wept and prayed.

At thirty she's divorced,
has cropped her locks
and squats in Hackney –
tells me "God created man
then realised her mistake."

I'm not like her,
I'm good – but now
I'm working on it,
Fighting through
to my own brand of badness

I am glad of her
at last - her conferences,
her anger, and her boots.
We talk and smoke
and laugh at everybody -
two bad sisters.

Wendy Cope

ASSIGNMENT

1 The poet gives a picture of her sister at three different stages of
her life. Write a short description of what she was like at each
stage.

2 How have the poet's feelings towards her sister changed as time has gone on? What does she feel about her now?

3 Write a scene involving both sisters, set at any point described in the poem. Make clear the distinction between the 'bad one' and the 'good one' and try to show the feelings of each.

More suggestions for coursework

- Write a story or a description which involves brothers or sisters who are very different from each other.
- Are there any advantages in being an only child? Write your response as a discussion essay, or have a discussion in your group.
- Can we learn from other people's mistakes?
- Write about someone who is 'bad' but attractive. Show the person's 'bad' qualities and show why he or she is appealing in spite of or perhaps because of them! You could write about a real person or a character in a book or film.

Fathers and daughters

Here are extracts from two plays by Shakespeare where we see the way two fathers treat and respond to their daughters.

King Lear has decided to divide his kingdom between his three daughters, Regan, Goneril and Cordelia. He is now an old man and no longer wants the responsibility of running the country. In order to gain their portion of the land, each daughter has to make a public statement about how much she loves him.

LEAR: Goneril, our eldest-born, speak first.

GONERIL: Sir, I love you more than words can wield the matter;
Dearer than eyesight, space and liberty;
Beyond what can be valued rich or rare;
No less than life, with grace, health, beauty, honour;
As much as child e'er lov'd, or father found;
A love that makes breath poor and speech unable;
Beyond all manner of so much I love you.

CORDELIA (aside): What shall Cordelia do? Love, and be silent.

LEAR   (indicating on a map): Of all these bounds, even from this line to this,

*plains
*meadows
*the children of you
and your husband

With shadowy forests and with champains* rich'd,
With plenteous rivers and wide-skirted meads,*
We make thee lady: to thine and Albany's issue*
Be this perpetual. What says our second daughter,
Our dearest Regan, wife of Cornwall? Speak.

REGAN: I am made of that self metal as my sister,
And prize me at her worth. In my true heart
I find she names my very deed of love;
Only she comes too short: that I profess
Myself an enemy to all other joys
Which the most precious square of sense possesses

*made happy

And find I am alone felicitate*
in your dear highness' love.

CORDELIA (aside): Then, poor Cordelia!
And yet not so; since, I am sure, my love's

*worth more

More ponderous*
than my tongue.

LEAR: To thee and thine, hereditary ever,
Remain this ample third of our fair kingdom,
No less in space, validity and pleasure,
Than that conferr'd on Goneril. Now, our joy,
Although our last, not least; to whose young love

*two nobleman
courting Cordelia
*rich

The vines of France and milk of Burgundy*
Strive to be interess'd; what can you say to draw
A third more opulent*
than your sisters? Speak.

CORDELIA: Nothing, my lord.

LEAR: Nothing?

LEAR: Nothing will come of nothing: speak again.

the bond of duty

CORDELIA: Unhappy that I am, I cannot heave
My heart into my mouth: I love your majesty
According to my bond;*
no more nor less.

LEAR: How, how, Cordelia! Mend your speech a little,
Lest you may mar your fortunes.

CORDELIA: Good my lord,
You have begot me, bred me, lov'd me: I
Return those duties back as are right fit,
Obey you, love you, and most honour you.
Why have my sisters husbands, if they say
They love you all? Haply, when I shall wed,
That lord whose hand must take my plight carry
Half my love with him, half my care and duty:
Sure I shall never marry like my sisters,
To love my father all.

LEAR: But goes thy heart with this?

CORDELIA: Ay, my good lord.

LEAR: So young, and so untender?

CORDELIA: So young, my lord, and true.

ASSIGNMENT

1 Write out in your own words the reply that:
(a) Goneril
(b) Regan
gives to King Lear.

2 Describe how Lear responds.

3 What do you learn about Cordelia from her aside comments?

4 Write out in your own words the reply that Cordelia gives.

5 Describe how Lear responds.

6 Write a couple of paragraphs showing what you think of each of the characters. You might like to think about:

why Lear wanted to hear his daughters say how much they loved him;

how sincere Goneril and Regan are;

whether Cordelia is right.

7 Imagine that you are a member of the court present at this occasion. Write your account of what happens, showing your response and the response of the people around you. You might like to think about the following points:

> where is everyone standing? (Remember Goneril is married to Albany and Regan to Cornwall)

> how do people react at the end of Goneril's and Regan's speeches?

> how does everyone expect Cordelia to respond? (Remember she is the youngest and her father's favourite.)

> what is the atmosphere like when she gives her reply?

Polonius, the Lord Chamberlain in the court of Denmark, questions his daughter Ophelia about the relationship between her and Prince Hamlet and warns her not to believe what he says.

POLONIUS: 'Tis told me, he hath very oft of late
            Given private time to you, and you yourself
            Have of your audience been most free and bounteous.
            What is between you? Give me up the truth.

*offers

OPHELIA: He hath, my lord, of late made many tenders*
           Of his affection to me.

*immature
*inexperienced

POLONIUS: Affection! Pooh! You speak like a green* girl,
            Unsifted* in such perilous circumstance.
            Do you believe his tenders, as you call them?

OPHELIA: I do not know, my lord, what I should think.

POLONIUS: Marry, I'll teach you: think yourself a baby,
            That you have taken these tenders for true pay,
            Which are not sterling.

*way

*passing fancy

*support

*traps to catch birds

*less free
*interviews
*talk

*a longer rope

*misuse

*command

OPHELIA: My lord, he hath importuned me with love
In honourable fashion* –

POLONIUS: Ay, fashion* you may call it; go to, go to.

OPHELIA: And hath given countenance* to his speech, my lord,
With almost all the holy vows of heaven.

POLONIUS: Ay, springes to catch woodcocks.*
From this time
Be somewhat scanter* of your maiden presence;
Set your entreatments* at a higher rate
Than a command to parley*. For Lord Hamlet,
Believe so much in him, that he is young,
And with a larger tether* may he walk
Than maybe given you. In few, Ophelia,
Do not believe his vows.
I would not, in plain terms, from this time forth
Have you so slander* any moment's leisure
As to give words or talk with the Lord Hamlet.
Look to it, I charge* you. Come your ways.

OPHELIA: I shall obey, my lord.

ASSIGNMENT

1 What does Polonius tell Ophelia she should think about Hamlet's love for her?

2 What orders does he give her?

3 What does Ophelia say in Hamlet's defence?

4 Why do you think she gives in to her father at the end?

5 Write an account of what you think Ophelia might be feeling after this conversation with her father.

ASSIGNMENT

Write about a page comparing Cordelia and Ophelia. You should discuss their attitudes to their fathers and how they show these attitudes, and comment on any strengths and weaknesses you may find in each woman.

More suggestions for coursework

- Write a description or a scene in which a dominant father tries to impose his will on either a daughter or a son.
- Describe what happens when the parents in a family strongly disapprove of a family member's boyfriend or girlfriend.
- Write a story in which someone is taken in by flattery.

Spelling check

'occasion'

Try to remember that 'occasion' has two 'c's and one 's'. It might help you to remember the two 'c's if you think of an important occasion which you celebrate with ceremony.

Other words which have a double c: accuracy; tobacco; access; accelerate

Generation clash

These two passages describe the difficulties the writers experience as a result of their parents' cultural and religious beliefs. They are both written by young women in their teens.

Life for a young Asian girl living in a western country such as England can be very confusing.

I am a fifteen-year-old Nepalese girl. I have been living in England for the past twelve years, and I have only returned to Nepal once, and that was when I was seven years of age. I find that now, as I am growing older and realising the differences in the type of life that a Nepalese girl has to live compared to a life that an English girl leads, it is hard to decide which life is more suitable for me.

Asian girls lead a very different life compared to the life western girls lead. For a start, Asian girls are not allowed to go out, they are not allowed to smoke, drink or swear, and they are definitely not allowed to go out with boys. Going out with boys means that they will ruin their chances of getting a good husband. Husbands are chosen by arrangement. Personally, I find it really silly, but back in Nepal, even if a girl is just seen talking to a few boys and being friendly with them, she is considered as something bad and ends up getting a bad name for herself. Although I have quite strict parents, they do allow me to go out, though not at night. Sometimes when my friends are allowed to stay out late at night, I must admit, I envy them a lot. I feel that because my parents are living in this country and bringing up their children in it, they must at least make a few adjustments to suit the way of life over here.

A good education is very important to Asian families, but parents usually tend to encourage their sons rather than their daughters to work hard at school (girls are more encouraged to learn how to cook and clean). Because of this, it is often the girls who study harder and want to go on to higher education. Most parents do not grant their daughters' wishes, but marry them off as soon as the suitable match arrives, but I have been lucky in the fact that my parents have always encouraged me in my studies – though sometimes, just a little too much.

Back in Nepal girls of my age are already cooking and cleaning for their family. It is because of this that I usually receive gasps of shock when I tell Nepalese visitors that I cannot cook a meal.

Sometimes I really do want to go back to my own country, as I can learn how to live my life, so I can learn about my own people, our traditions and customs. I want to go back before I, to put it in my parents' words 'ruin myself'. Already I find that my thoughts are becoming too westernised.

Another subject which I feel really confused about is equal rights. At school I am taught to believe that women are no less than men and they must have the chance of having equal opportunities; but at home, I am witnessing the fact that women are always being put down. We Nepalese girls are taught to respect the menfolk, because they have the knowledge and capability of doing everything. We are told that women are the weaker sex. Women must always stand by their husbands, whether they are right or wrong. Back in Nepal, the two words 'equal opportunities' would not even be heard of, let alone practised!

If I knew more about my own country, maybe I wouldn't feel so confused; but I don't remember a thing. The only Nepalese customs and traditions I know, are what my parents have taught me.

I have spent the whole of my life here, more or less, and hardly remember anything of Nepal. It is when my parents try to tie me down with Nepalese customs and traditions that I feel confused.

I often feel guilty about my own thoughts, and also hate having to lead two different lives. I very much want to act and feel like a Nepalese girl, but how can I when I have no experience? I often ask my parents to send me back to Nepal, but they will not. Instead they are always telling me never to forget who I am and where I came from. How can I when they won't even let me learn?

I have lived amongst English people for nearly all my life, so is it really my fault if I act and speak like one? I am not saying that I hate being a Nepalese girl, I am just saying that I wish I was allowed a little more freedom and a chance of being independent. How can my parents expect me to be and act like a typical Nepalese girl when I am brought up in a society where the way of life is completely different?

So who then is to be blamed? Who is the main cause for the confusion? The parents? Or the children themselves? Should the parents try to understand the western way of life and be lenient in their ways? Or should the children realise that they too have their own culture and try to hold on to it? I only wish I knew.

Sangita Manadhar, **Life for a young Asian girl**

ASSIGNMENT

1 What are the conflicts the writer describes? Make a list of them, then put them in order, beginning with what seems to you the most important. Compare your list with a friend's.

2 The writer finishes with a series of questions which lead out from her own situation and focus on the general topic of parents and children adapting to a different culture. Discuss the issues she raises in your group or with your partner. Jot down a record of all the points which were made.

3 Write a response to Sangita Manadhar. (This could be in the form of a letter.) Show that you have understood the feelings she describes, and give your ideas about the points in the last paragraph.

"Blessed art thou, O Lord our God, king of the universe, who hast not made me a woman."

That is the prayer a Jewish man says when he rises, and that is the first prayer I hear when I attend synagogue on Saturday mornings. I attend always with the same feelings of familiarity, scorn, mockery and guilt. Guilt is the main reason I go, as I live at home and my family are extremely devout Jews who see religion as complete obedience to the prescribed laws. They would never default from these 635 laws, not even secretly.

In the synagogue I usually sit on my own, and although I join in some of the prayers I spend most of my time in some sort of fantasy world, dreaming of what I would do if I weren't there, and of how all oppressed women in racial minorities will rise and unite!

Cooking is forbidden on the Sabbath so all the food is prepared in advance, which is an advantage in that women can sit down with the rest of the family. The rest of the week it is customary for the women to wait upon the men and then sit down and eat what is left.

We all say a short prayer then sit down to a lengthy heavy meal, with my father in the most comfortable seat. We all have to sit quietly for half an hour while he goes through all the laws relating to conduct on the Sabbath. The serving of the meal is entirely done by women, as is the clearing up afterwards. The men sit back and have coffee brought to them.

Due to the heavy meal and the lack of anything else to do, on Saturday afternoon I usually go to bed for a sleep as this helps while away the hours.

By five in the afternoon, satiated with food and sleep, I begin to feel waves of claustrophobia and terrible boredom passing through me. The strictness of the Sabbath laws limits one's choice of activity severely. The alternatives are visiting friends (girls), going for walks, or studying the books of the sages. Reading contemporary literature is outlawed because of its subversive effects. In my house and in most of the neighbours' there is no television or newspapers because of the danger of corruption by morally debauched programmes.

I have very few friends acceptable to my family as I have severed most of my childhood friendships with Jewish girls. I have plenty of

non-Jewish friends at work, but of course I would never be able to take them home. I do not know any Jewish boys, as my education was in single sex institutions from the age of 3 to 21. This is not atypical among religious Jews, and for this reason arranged marriages continue to flourish.

My Saturday night diversions are carried out with extreme trepidation. Driving a car is not allowed, nor is using public transport, or handling money. To avoid distressing my family I have to walk in an area where I am unlikely to be recognised. I usually conceal my money and make sure that I do not have loose coins as they jingle too much.

I'm usually just happy to be out and away from home and family until eleven, when I have to be back to celebrate the ending of the Sabbath and the ushering in of a new week. The oldest single girl in the family holds up a lighted candle as high as she can so that she may find a tall husband...prayers are said, frankincense inhaled...and I fervently thank God that another Sabbath is over.

Ruth, **A day in the life**

ASSIGNMENT

1 Make a list of the conflicts the writer describes and put them in order, beginning with what seems to you the most important. Compare your list with a friend's.

 2 What do you think about the way Ruth deals with the conflicts she experiences? Exchange ideas in your group or with a partner.

3 Imagine the following situation. Ruth is at home with her family. The doorbell rings. It's a friend from work. "Hi!" she says cheerfully. "You left your scarf in my car. I had to come this way to drop my brother off somewhere, so I thought I'd give it back and perhaps have a cup of coffee with you?" Continue the conversation.

ASSIGNMENT

1 Compare and contrast the difficulties described in each passage. Use your lists and mark which are common to both writers and which are different. Write about a page giving your conclusions.

2 If you had children, would you expect them to adopt your

standards and beliefs? You might like to discuss this issue first, then write an answer of about 300 to 500 words. Give examples and illustrations. Make clear which are the beliefs you hold most strongly and which are less important to you, and show where you would be willing to compromise.

3 What are your feelings about organised religion? Write 300 to 500 words on the topic, using your experience, the experiences of friends, and what you have read and seen. Remember this type of essay is a discussion, so give different points of view and come to your own conclusion. You could refer to the guidelines to help you.

4 Write a story or script illustrating the difficulties of someone living in a family whose beliefs he or she doesn't accept.

Golden years

The following material focuses on how society treats old people.

OLD AGE REPORT

When a man's too ill or old to work
We punish him.
Half his income is taken away
Or all of it vanishes and he gets pocket money.
We should reward these tough old humans for surviving,
Not with a manager's soggy handshake
Or a medal shaped like an alarm clock –
No, make them a bit rich.
Give the freedom they always heard about
When the bloody chips were down
And the blitz or the desert swallowed their friends.
Retire, retire into a fungus basement
Where nothing moves except the draught
And the light and dark grey figures
Doubling their money on the screen;
Where the cabbage tastes like the mummy's hand
And the meat tastes of feet;
Where there is nothing to say except:
"Remember?" or "Your turn to dust the cat".

To hell with retiring. Let them advance.
Give them the money they've always earned
Or more - and let them choose.
If Mr Burley wants to be a miser,
Great, let the moneybags sway and clink for him.
Pay him a pillowful of best doubloons.
So Mrs Wells has always longed to travel?
Print her a ticket to the universe,
Let her slum-white skin
Be tanned by a dozen different planets.
We could wipe away some of their worry,
Some of their pain – what I mean
Is so bloody simple:
The old people are being robbed
And punished and we ought
To be letting them out of their cages
Into green spaces of enchanting light.

Adrian Mitchell

ASSIGNMENT

1 What does Adrian Mitchell say we do to people when their working lives are over?

2 What does he think about this?

3 Describe the impression he gives of retirement homes.

4 How would he treat old people?

5 The poet uses exaggeration to make his point. Find a couple of places where he does this and describe the effect it has.

This is an extract from an article about old people's residential homes.

A recent report by Counsel and Care, a charity which provides advice on residential accommodation, found that only 36 per cent of older people in residential homes claimed to have made a choice for themselves, and 60 per cent had not visited any other home before admission. For nearly two thirds, the choice of a home – the home that is no home – had been taken for them. "If we treated adolescents in this way, "it commented, "there would be a revolution."

Few relatives have the time, or the knowledge to respect the magnitude of the decision. They may visit five homes and conclude that all residential homes must inevitably smell of urine (They don't, it's poor hygiene). They may admire the decoration or the menu, but neglect to talk to the other residents, or notice that they all seem to be wearing the same sort of neutral coloured, crimplene square-cut dresses (convenient for bulk washing). A home may have a splendid lobby, but a regimented, authoritarian regime, in which meals, baths, bedtimes are all dictated by shift workers rather than by the residents. In retirement homes, it appears, there is almost no correlation between expense and quality of care.

Almost unbelievably, there are no nationally enforced standards of care, no system of grading homes. Local authorities often enforce different sets of standards for independent and publicly owned places. Inspectors, too, will employ quite different criteria. Some like to measure floors, but are unconcerned about the atmosphere, the character of the manager, or the remarks of the residents.

Both homes and families have a tendency to treat older people as an amorphous group rather than recognise their reality as individuals. "There's this notion that elderly people want peace and quiet, and I'm not sure they do," says Dr Jan Reed, a fellow in nursing at Newcastle University who has been interviewing old people. "And there's usually a gramophone playing songs from the first world war, which none of them can remember, because they weren't even born then. I have this vision of when I go into a home, they'll still be playing "Daisy Daisy Give Me Your Answer Do.""

Why do we treat old people like that? Why do we lump them together, out of sight, in conditions of tedium and dislocation which we would find intolerable in ourselves? The shameful quality of life in many homes cannot be blamed on the staff. If they are to be paid a cleaner's wage, it is a marvel there are any good homes at all. The low status afforded to those who care for older people simply reflects the low status afforded to older people themselves.

The truth is, we do not want to know about them, think about them, or see them. For one thing their presence is a reminder of our own inexorable ageing, our own mortality. So homes exist partly for us as much as for them – to hide them away. And once they've been hidden, we forget to care about the condition of their lives. What is the point? How can the expense be justified? On average, they will only survive for another eighteen months. Effectively, they have already been relegated from the realm of the living.

Talking to older people, you realise they might feel differently. With little time left, there is all the more reason to enjoy it. A woman of 86 said, "I think you should think of it as the next chapter in your life, not as the end. People say, "Oh, retirement home, I'm finished." " They're not, you're not.""

Well, we shall find out.

Catherine Bennett, *The Guardian*

ASSIGNMENT

1 The article indicates some mistakes that relatives make when they go to check out residential homes. Make a list of what they are.

2 What examples can you find in the passage of how homes (and families) fail to treat older people as individuals?

3 The article gives some reasons for the way we treat old people. Write a sentence or two about each.

ASSIGNMENT

1 What similarities do you find in the ideas and the way they are expressed in the poem and the article? Write a paragraph about them.

2 You have been asked to give a short talk on the radio giving

advice to people who are involved in helping an older relative move to a residential home.

(a) Using the ideas in the passages as well as your own, write the text of the talk.

(b) Either record the talk or read it to your group.

Grammar box

Conjunctions

"They may visit five homes and conclude....."

"They may admire the decoration but neglect..."

Words like 'and' and 'but' are called conjunctions. A conjunction is a word which links or joins parts of a sentence.

It can be used to begin a sentence.

Example Although they were good friends they spent little time together.

Here the conjunction 'although' has been used to make one sentence from the two ideas (They were good friends. They spent little time together.).

It can be used in the middle of a sentence, often after a comma.

Example I'll finish the project tonight(,) if I have time.

Examples of conjunctions you can use after a comma to join sentences:

because; if; since; although; unless; but

Examples of words you can't use after a comma to join sentences:

however; for instance

If you want to use these words in the middle of a sentence, use them after a semi-colon.

Example Tara was worried that the photos would be blurred; however, they were all in perfect focus.

SELF CHECK

Use conjunctions to link these sentences.

He injured his knee playing football. He played in the next game. The injury became worse.

I don't usually like Westerns. I enjoyed this one. It had some humour in it.

She slipped on the ice. She fell over. She cut her lip.

More suggestions for coursework

- Describe a visit to a friend or relative in a residential home.
- Write a scene from a drama script set in an old people's home.
- "Older people shouldn't live in special homes; they should be with their families or in the community." Discuss this statement in your group. You could then write your response, showing how far you agree or disagree with it. (Write 350 to 500 words.)

Guidelines

Discussion skills

(a) Remember that even if you are in a group with people you know well, discussion is more than just chatting. There is a range of skills you can practise and improve which will enable you to be more effective in group discussion. Here is a list of the kinds of contribution which might take place in a discussion.

Positive contributions	Negative contributions
Agreeing with someone	Not listening properly
Showing you're listening	Attacking other people/ being aggressive
Asking for information or clarification	Being too dominant / taking over
Giving information / examples/ ideas	Being inappropriately flippant/ digressing
Building on what's been said	
Creating a feeling of group solidarity (showing humour, acknowledging people's contributions)	
Evaluating (weighing up what's been said)	
Summarising	

(b) Take it in turns to observe a group discussion. Draw up a chart with the names of the group members along the top and the list of contributions along the side. Put a tick by somebody's name every time you notice them engage in that particular activity. Then either give verbal feedback or show your record.

Wrinklies and codgers

This passage discusses different attitudes to old age.

There is no fixed point when old age begins. Are you old when your hair turns grey and you start to get wrinkles? This is a gradual process and does not happen at the same time for all people. Or are you old when you retire from work? Again, this is not a fool-proof test because, in western societies, people are retiring earlier and earlier. Even being a grandparent is not a sure sign: it is quite possible to have grandchildren in your early 40s, and some people do not have children at all.

Age Concern publishes an information leaflet for the elderly about 'ageism' – prejudice against old people – called How to Avoid Becoming An Old Codger. "Unfortunately it's not that easy," it begins. "That's because you don't choose when you become an old codger. It's up to other people." Old age, like beauty, is in the eye of the beholder.

Reflecting Our Age, a study published by Age Concern last year, contained the results of a survey on attitudes to old age. It showed that people's ideas of what made someone old depended on their own age. For 11-14 year olds it began in the late 50s whereas for 35-44 year olds it began in the late 60s. Even people in their mid 60s did not consider themselves elderly, believing that 'old' began only in the mid 70s.

For most people, old age is associated with a decline in one's physical capabilities. In the same report people were asked to choose from a list of qualities with which they would like to be associated. 'Happy and cheerful', 'knowledgeable and wise' and 'sense of humour' all figured in the top 10. But by far the most popular quality was 'active and energetic'.

It is, of course, quite possible for people over the age of 60 to lead fairly healthy and active lives. And there are many professions in which people continue to work well beyond the statutory retirement age.

"There is no telling what work patterns will be like in the future," says Professor Anthea Tinker. "It may well be that older people will be wooed back to work, which could be a good thing. " But this would only be positive if people did not feel they were being forced back into work because of lack of money.

Perhaps the place where we see the most positive images of old people is on television. In the Age Concern report above, people said that after the Queen Mother, Jimmy Saville represented the most positive image of old people. Their old grandmothers and grandfathers came further down the list.

Far more important than role models are practical schemes to bring the generations together. There are inter-generational projects all over Europe, which include examples of older people running workplace nurseries and leisure-based programmes.

One venture which bridges the generations is the Age Exchange Theatre Trust. Its actors gather reminiscences from older people and produce plays and books for schools and old people's groups.

The Guardian

ASSIGNMENT

1 According to the passage, when is a person 'old'?

2 What are the qualities which old people wish to have?

3 What part does television play in shaping our attitudes towards old people?

 4 In your group, discuss your attitudes to old age. You could consider the following points:

What images do you have of older people?

What words do you use to describe them?

Who do you consider to be good role models for older people?

What do you think are the advantages of bringing the generations together? Can you think of any ways of doing this?

Write up your group's findings as a report to give to the rest of the class.

Guidelines *Report writing*

There are many different sorts of report and a written report can be presented in different ways. It may be in the form of continuous prose, like the reports you read in newspapers, or it may be broken up into sections and numbered points. You should remember the following:

(a) A report is partly narrative: you are usually relating something which happened in the past.
(b) A report is partly exposition, i.e. you are setting out and explaining a number of facts to the reader.
(c) Decide which points are important and which can be left out.
(d) Group together points which are similar.
(e) Arrange your points in what you think is the best order.
(f) Keep your language concise and precise.

'Ageism'

Many words which express a belief or an idea end in 'ism'.

Examples: patriotism; chauvinism; Cubism

SELF CHECK

Match up the following 'isms' with their definitions.

hedonism	the idea that we cannot know there is a God
atheism	belief in mystical influences
agnosticism	the idea that pleasure should be pursued
occultism	the belief that there is no God

END-OF-CHAPTER ASSIGNMENT

Which people in the extracts in this chapter made the greatest impression on you? Refer to four or five in your answer.

SUMMARY

In this section you have covered the following aspects of GCSE requirements.

SPEAKING AND LISTENING

pair/group discussion
interviewing
giving a talk
role play
debate
discussion
discussion of language

READING

non-literary material
prose written since 1900
prose written before 1900
poetry written since 1900
non-European prose (complete short story) written since 1900

radio programme transcript
song lyric
extracts from Shakespeare plays
newspaper articles
autobiography

WRITING

comprehension
personal account
narrative
article
interview
discussion
argument
radio talk
report

LANGUAGE STUDY

vocabulary building
spelling groups
colons
adverbs
conjunctions
rhetoric
tone
varieties of language

REVISION AND FURTHER ASSIGNMENTS

1 Write sentences from the following notes using a colon where appropriate:

he had a house – car – good job – success – wasn't happy

making shopping list – bread – bananas – apples – tea – coffee

made plans carefully – they went wrong

2 Make adverbs from the following words:

critic; true; icy; hunger; love; desperate

3 Choose the correct word in the following sentences:

(a) You must try (more hard/harder).

(b) When the two of them were on the river you could see that Jasmine rowed the (strongest /stronger).

Out of the whole class Jamie was the one who finished (the quickest/most quickly).

4 Find three different adverbs to describe each of the following actions.

Example He was speaking hesitantly because he was uncertain of his welcome.

speaking; singing; fighting; sleeping; laughing

Use each one in a sentence.

5 Make up sentences using the following conjunctions.

although; unless; however; if

6 Which of the following would you call rhetorical questions?

What time is it?

What's the point of asking you again?

Is this the kind of society we want to live in?

7 Use the following topics as a starting point for writing. Where there are no specific instructions use them in any way you like – as the basis of a story, personal writing, script, argument....

"Young people today don't know how lucky they are"

A parent worried about a son's or daughter's behaviour

Breaking friends

What happens when your loyalty to a friend clashes with your loyalty to your family

"The family is dead"

Family reunion

The wedding

Choose an event in family life and write it from the point of view of two different family members

Breaking up

Youth and age can't live together

What happens in a family when an older relative is becoming very difficult to look after

Hard toil

These three poems are to do with people working. The first two use harvesting and digging potatoes as their focal point, and the third poem, describing a woman washing dishes, was written in response to *Digging*.

DIGGING

Between my finger and my thumb
The squat pen rests; snug as a gun.

Under my window, a clean rasping sound
When the spade sinks into gravelly ground:
My father, digging. I look down

Till his straining rump among the flowerbeds
Bends low, comes up twenty years away
Stooping in rhythm through potato drills
Where he was digging.

The coarse boot nestled on the lug, the shaft
Against the inside knee was levered firmly.
He rooted out tall tops, buried the bright edge deep
To scatter new potatoes that we picked
Loving their cool hardness in our hands.

By God, the old man could handle a spade.
Just like his old man.

My grandfather cut more turf in a day
Than any other man on Toner's bog.
Once I carried him milk in a bottle
Corked sloppily with paper. He straightened up
To drink it, then fell to right away
Nicking and slicing neatly, heaving sods
Over his shoulder, going down and down
For the good turf. Digging.

The cold smell of potato mould, the squelch and slap
Of soggy peat, the curt cuts of an edge
Through living roots awaken in my head.
But I've no spade to follow men like them.

Between my finger and my thumb
The squat pen rests.
I'll dig with it.

Seamus Heaney

ASSIGNMENT

1 Describe the scene in the poem. What do you see the poet doing? Where is he? What scene is he looking at? Write a couple of lines about this.

2 Write three short paragraphs showing how the poet uses language to give a sense of the activity of digging. Look at:
(a) the verbs he uses;
(b) the way he appeals to the senses;
(c) the way he uses alliteration.

3 What does the poet feel about his father and his grandfather? What are the differences between his life and their life? Write a paragraph giving your ideas.

4 Write a paragraph giving your response to the poem as a whole. You may find some of these words helpful:

love	tradition	admiration
guilt	continuity	respect
affection	loyalty	conflict
inadequacy	separation	distance

I AM GLAD TO BE UP AND ABOUT

I am glad to be up and about this sunny morning,
Walking the raised path between fields,
While all around me
Are cheerful folk harvesting potatoes.

I am glad to be away from books,
Broadcasts and the familiar smells
And the unending pursuit of a livelihood.

Small boys on their way to school
Trail their toes through the stripped soil,
And pounce with joy
Upon the marble-size potatoes left behind by the harvesters,
And with these fill their satchels.

One voice is raised in song,
While the men, hunkering on their heels,
Move up in a line like pirates
To uncover the heaps of buried treasure,
And transfer them to baskets.

And girls who should be playing with dolls
Unload the baskets into sacks
Which tonight or tomorrow night
Will be speeding in a groaning truck
To Karachi, a thousand miles away.

And this week or the following week,
Bilious businessmen and irate wives
And their washed and prattling children,
Will sit down at uncounted tables
And hastily devour the potatoes I see
With never a thought for these
Fields, these men and this sunny morning.

Taufiq Rafat

ASSIGNMENT

1 What is the mood of the poet in the first two stanzas? Write a couple of lines explaining why he is enjoying the morning.

2 The next three stanzas describe different people harvesting the potatoes. Find some examples of effective use of language. Write a paragraph about them saying what they are and why they are effective. (Look for techniques like the use of alliteration and simile)

3 What does the poet think about the people who will actually eat the potatoes? What contrast does he make between them and the harvesters? Write a couple of lines explaining this.

WASHING

Round and round, round and round
Circles of white soap suds.
Cleansing the plate thoroughly.
Her hands tender and soft wiping the dishes
As though massaging an oily body.

Such perfection was there in her every move.
Not a mistake, but working like a programmed robot.
That constant circular movement seemed to
Recall memories.

Yes, I recognised the movements.
It was so familiar,
It was her mother I remember who washed in
Such perfection just like her.
It was almost as if she had adopted her mother's arms.
Her tall, slim body swayed slightly as she
Continued to cleanse the plates.
The movement still going – round and round.

She opened the tap as the steaming hot water,
Steam, rose filling the air with a cosy feeling.
Tenderly she rinsed away the foamy soap suds.
They collected at the bottom of the sink gurgling down.
Another plate.
Yet again – round and round – round and round.
The same generational adopted move.

Amita (aged 16)

ASSIGNMENT

1 Describe the scene in the poem. Where do you think the poet is? What scene is she looking at? Write a couple of lines about this.

2 How does the poet use language to give a sense of the activity of washing the dishes? What words and phrases do you find particularly effective?

3 What examples can you find of repetition? Do you think they could refer to more than just the action of washing? Write a paragraph about this.

4 Write a paragraph describing the girl's feelings for her mother. You could use the list of words given in the assignment for the first extract to help you.

5 Write a description (300 to 500 words) of someone doing manual work of some kind. Try to give a sense of the person's skill or precision or pride in the work. Try also to give an idea of your attitude or feelings towards the person.

Punctuation mark

Apostrophe

'the girl's feelings for her mother'

In this phrase, the apostrophe is used to show possession. To know which word it goes in you have to ask yourself "To whom does this belong?"

If the word is singular (one), as in the phrase above, you add ' 's' to the word.

Example His friend's attempts to persuade him did no good.
Her sister's coat was still in the hall.

If the word is plural (more than one) and so already ends in 's', you just add an apostrophe.

Example The ladies' coats were piled in a heap on the sofa.
The shops' windows all along the street were decorated with coloured lights.

If the plural of the word does not end in 's', then the apostrophe goes before the 's'.

Example The men's section was closed.
The children's shoes were caked with mud.

The apostrophe is also used to show where one or more letters have been left out.

Examples

we've	=	we have
I'm	=	I am
don't	=	do not
haven't	=	have not
she's	=	she is
can't	=	cannot

would've   =   would have (not would of)
they'll   =   they will

Be careful with 'it's' and 'its'
'It's' = 'it is'. The apostrophe shows that the 'i' has been left out.
'Its' = 'belonging to it'.

Think about: his; hers; its. None of them has an apostrophe.

SELF CHECK

Add apostrophes to the following sentences.

1 We wouldve been earlier but the dogs lead went missing so we couldnt take him for a walk.
2 The womens changing rooms were crowded so they spent ten minutes watching the ladies badminton.
3 "I want six pounds of potatoes, something for the boys lunches, and see if the melons are ripe."
4 There will be five minutes delay while the timing is adjusted.

Assembly line

This is an extract from *Saturday Night and Sunday Morning*, a novel about a young man called Arthur Seaton who works in a factory in Nottingham.

The bright Monday-morning ring of the clocking-in machine made a jarring note, different from the tune that played inside Arthur. It was dead on half-past seven. Once in the shop he allowed himself to be swallowed by its diverse noises, walked along lanes of capstan lathes and millers, drills and polishers and hand-presses, worked by a multiplicity of belts and pulleys turning and twisting and slapping on heavy well-oiled wheels overhead, dependent for power on a motor stooping at the far end of the hall like the black shining bulk of a stranded whale. Machines with their own small motors started with a jerk and a whine under the shadows of their operators, increasing a noise that made the brain reel and ache because the weekend had been too tranquil by contrast, a weekend that had terminated for Arthur in fishing for trout in the cool shade of a willow-sleeved canal near the Balloon Houses, miles away from the city. Motor-trolleys moved up and down the main gangways carrying boxes of work – pedals, hubs, nuts, and bolts – from one part of the shop to another.

Robboe the foreman bent over a stack of new timesheets behind his glass partition; women and girls wearing turbans and hair-nets and men and boys in clean blue overalls, settled down to their work, eager to get a good start on their day's stint; while sweepers and cleaners at everybody's beck and call, already patrolled the gangways and looked busy.

Arthur reached his capstan lathe and took off his jacket, hanging it on a nearby nail so that he could keep an eye on his belongings. He pressed the starter button, and his motor came to life with a gentle thump. Looking around, it did not seem, despite the infernal noise of hurrying machinery, that anyone was working with particular speed. He smiled to himself and picked up a glittering steel cylinder from the top box of a pile beside him, and fixed it into the spindle. He jettisoned his cigarette into the sud-pan, drew back the capstan, and swung the turret on to its broadest drill. Two minutes passed while he contemplated the precise position of tools and cylinder; finally he spat on to both hands and rubbed them together, then switched on the sud-tap from the movable brass pipe, pressed a button that set the spindle running, and ran in the drill to a near chamfer. Monday morning had lost its terror.

At a piecework rate of four-and-six (22.5 pence) a hundred you could make your money if you knocked-up fourteen hundred a day – possible without grabbing too much – and if you went all out for a thousand in the morning you could dawdle through the afternoon and lark about with the women and talk to your mates now and again. Such leisure often brought him near to trouble, for some weeks ago he stunned a mouse – that the overfed factory cat had missed – and laid it beneath a woman's drill, and Robboe the gaffer ran out of his office when he heard her screaming blue-murder, thinking that some bloody silly woman had gone and got her hair caught in a belt (big notices said that women must wear hair-nets, but who could tell with women?) and Robboe was glad that it was nothing more than a dead mouse she was kicking up such a fuss about. But he paced up and down the gangways asking who was responsible for the stunned mouse, and when he came to Arthur, who denied having anything to do with it, he said: "I'll bet you did it, you young bogger."

"Me, Mr Robboe?" Arthur said, the picture of innocence, standing up tall with offended pride. "I've got so much work to do I can't move from my lathe. Anyway, I don't believe in tormenting women, you know that. It's against my principles."

Robboe glared at him: "Well, I don't know. Somebody did it, and I reckon it's you. You're a bit of a Red if you ask me, that's what you are."

"Now then, that's slander," Arthur said. "I'll see my lawyers about you. There's tons of witnesses."

Robboe went back to his office, bearing a black look for the girl inside, and for any tool-setter that might require his advice in the next half-hour; and Arthur worked on his lathe like a model of industry.

Though you couldn't grumble at four-and-six a hundred the rate-checker sometimes came and watched you work, so that if he saw you knock up a hundred in less than an hour Robboe would come and tell you one fine morning that your rate had been dropped by sixpence or a bob. (2.5p or 5p) So when you felt the shadow of the rate-checker breathing down your neck you knew what to do if you had any brains at all: make every move more complicated, though not slow because that was cutting your own throat, and do everything deliberately yet with a crafty show of speed. Though cursed as public enemy number one the rate-checker was an innocuous-looking man who carried a slight stoop everywhere he went and wore spectacles, smoking the same fags you were smoking, and protecting his blue pin-striped suit with a brown staff-overall, bald as a mushroom and as sly as a fox. They said he got commission on what reductions he recommended, but that was only a rumour, Arthur decided, something said out of rancour if you had just been done down for a bob. If you saw the rate-checker on your way home from work he might say good evening to you, and you responded to this according to whether or not your rate had been tampered with lately. Arthur always returned such signs with affability, for whenever the rate-checker stood behind him he switched his speed down to a normal hundred, though once he had averaged four hundred when late on his daily stint. He worked out for fun how high his wages would be if, like a madman, he pursued this cramp-inducing, back-breaking, knuckle-knocking undiplomatic speed of four hundred for a week, and his calculations on the Daily Mirror margins gave an answer of thirty-six pounds. Which would never do, he swore to himself, because they'd be down on me like a ton of bricks, and the next week I'd be grabbing at the same flat-out lick for next to nowt. So he settled for a comfortable wage of fourteen pounds. Anything bigger than that would be like shovelling hard-earned money into the big windows of the income-tax office – feeding pigs on cherries, as mam used to say – which is something else against my principles.

So you earned your living in spite of the firm, the rate-checker, the foreman, and the tool-setters, who always seemed to be at each others' throats except when they ganged up to get at yours; though most of the time you didn't give a sod about them but worked quite happily for a cool fourteen nicker, spinning the turret to chamfer in a smell of suds and steel, actions without thought so that all through the day you filled your mind with vivid and more agreeable pictures than those round about. It was an easier job than driving a lorry for instance where you had to have your wits about you – spin the turret and ease it in the blade-chamfer with your right hand – and you remembered the corporal in the army who said what a marvel it was the things you thought of while you were on the lavatory, which was the only time you ever had to think. But now whole days could be given up to wool-gathering. Hour after hour quickly disappeared when once you started thinking, and before you knew where you were a flashing light from the foreman's office signalled ten o'clock, time for white-overalled women to wheel in tea-urns.

Arthur refused the firm's tea because it was strong, not from best Ceylon tips but from sweepings-up in the tea warehouse and the soda they doused it with in the canteen. One day he spilled some of their orange brew on a bench – thus went his story – and tried for three hours to rub out the stain, and even the ingenuity of the mechanics could make no inroads against the faint testament of unswallowable tea that stayed there as a warning to all who saw it, telling them to bring their own drinks to work, though few bothered to take the hint.

"If it makes that stain on an old wooden bench covered with oil, what do you think it does to your guts?" Arthur asked his mates. "It don't bear thinking about."

He complained at the head office about it and they listened to him. A director examined the canteen tea urns and found the insides coated with an even depth of tea and soda sediment. Because Arthur stood up for his rights a big noise was made and thereafter the quality improved, though not enough to induce Arthur to drink it. He still came to the factory with a flask sticking out of his pocket, and took it out now after switching off his machine, because the light began flashing from Robboe's office, and men were unwrapping packets of sandwiches.

Alan Sillitoe, **Saturday Night and Sunday Morning**

ASSIGNMENT

1 What impression do you gain of the factory?

2 What do you learn about Arthur's character and personality as the passage unfolds?

3 Describe the relationship between employers and employees in the factory.

4 What feelings and responses do you have as you read the passage? You could think about how you respond to Arthur and the kind of work he does. Do you sympathise with his thoughts and attitudes? Is he the kind of person you would like to work with? How would you respond to working in that environment?

5 Throughout the extract the writer creates a strong sense of realism. Describe how he uses language to achieve this effect. You could look at the language used to describe Arthur's thoughts and the language used in conversation. What words and phrases give an idea of the way people really speak? Look at the way the factory is described. What use does the writer make of technical terms? What is the effect of this?

THE RELEASE

All day he shoves the pasteboard in
The slick machine that turns out boxes,
A box a minute; and its din
Is all his music, as he stands
And feeds it; while his jaded brain
Moves only out and in again

With the slick motion of his hands,
Monotonously making boxes,
A box a minute – all his thoughts
A slick succession of empty boxes.

But, when night comes, and he is free
To play his fiddle, with the music
His whole soul moves to melody;
No more recalling day's dumb round,
His reckless spirit sweeps and whirls
On surging waves and dizzy swirls
And eddies of enchanted sound;
And in a flame-winged flight of music
Above the roofs and chimneys soars
To ride the starry tides of music.

W.W. Gibson

ASSIGNMENT

1 Describe the work the person does.

2 What are the sounds he hears as he works?

3 In the first stanza, how does the poet use language and rhythm to give a sense of the nature of the work?

4 What does the second stanza describe?

5 What are the sounds he hears?

6 In the second stanza, how does the poet use language and rhythm to create a contrast with the life described at the beginning of the poem?

7 Write a description of doing work which is very monotonous. You could include some contrast, as in the passages, either by using thoughts and reflections, or by a description of what happens when the unpleasant sounds or sights are transformed into pleasant or appealing ones.

8 Both passages describe workers with a very low level of job satisfaction. What are the important factors for you, when choosing a job?

(a) Put the following in the order of their importance to you. Add to the list if you like.

enjoyable work get on with	useful work	workmates you	good pay
pleasant workplace	good facilities	job security	
uniform	appealing dress code	varied work	

(b) Use your list to help you write an account of what you look for in a job. Comment on how important or unimportant you feel the different aspects are.

More suggestions for coursework

- Choose one of the following settings and write a description, story or script based there: a cafe; a clothing factory; an advertising agency.
- Write about Monday morning. If you like you could write some contrasting accounts.

Language link

'Affability'

'Arthur always returned such signs with affability'.

affability means friendliness, warmth.

Use each of the following words, which all express different degrees of a friendly feeling, in a separate sentence.

affable; civil; courteous; cordial; amicable

Working girls

These two passages describe the working lives of young women earlier in this century.

Pre-1914 in the East End of London – drab to say the least. Two figures walking in the early morning streets. One, a woman dressed in the long dark skirt of the time and a nondescript hat. Around her

shoulders a short, black cape, not even of the time, but of some years earlier, for some traces of embroidery still cling to the somewhat rusty coloured surface. Underneath the cape, half hidden by it, the woman carries an armful of newspapers. The other figure is a girl of fourteen, though rather small and childish looking for her age, and together they deliver the papers to various houses and shops until eventually they arrive, as they do every morning, at a door in a back alley-way which is the stage door of the local music hall, the Hackney Empire. They are let in by a man who has evidently been there all night, as he is unshaven and has a muffler round his neck. Actually he is the night watchman and fireman. The three greet each other. They are my father, mother and I. Dad had just reached the stage of making an early morning jug of tea. It is hot and strong and we all partake of this exciting refreshment, which is a regular morning event.

And now it is time for the arrival of a small band of women cleaners. There are the usual few minutes of chit chat before they go to find brooms and buckets. One of them asks, "Well, Ellen, what work are you going to do when you have left school?"

This receives a vague answer. I am not very strong, my parents explain, so it must be something light and not far from home. I had done quite well at school, but they could not afford to keep me there any longer, even if I had won a Junior County Scholarship (which I had not). Mrs J says, "How about embroidery?"

She had passed a factory in Dalton Lane that morning which had a notice outside saying 'Young Ladies wanted to learn Hand Embroidery'. Now, of the things I could do, I had never been interested in needlework. I could do it very neatly, but the prospect of doing it all day, of being a dressmaker or milliner, was quite frightening. And the idea of office work was hateful. Besides, they would not take you into an office from an elementary school at fourteen. Secretly. right inside myself, drawing was my favourite subject – I always got a few extra marks for this which put me ahead in the school exams and I had been top of the school for the year before I was fourteen. But failing that, embroidery now began to seem a very good idea.

And so it was that later in the day I took my first step into the working world and found my way to the far end of Dalton Lane, where I had never been before in my life, as it was outside the beaten track of the newspaper round. The factory was a brand new building. It looked quite nice, not the usual kind of factory, and it actually had a garden in front, with flowerbeds and lots of large white daisies in them. I thought: "I wouldn't mind working there."

If I ran all the way it was only about ten minutes from home.

Next day my mother and I entered the rather imposing main door and knocked at a door marked 'Enquiries'. The clerk explained that the boss was out, but his son would see us. A tall, handsome young man invited us into what seemed to me a very richly furnished office, with beautifully polished furniture and a carpet your feet sank into. The handsome and well-dressed young man, speaking in a highly educated voice, then asked ,"Is your daughter applying as a learner?"

It is hard to imagine just what else he thought I might be applying as. But with all his obvious education, he evidently found the situation beyond him and asked us to come back tomorrow, when his father would be there.

So again the next day we found ourselves in the office of the head of the firm. Mr Thomas Muddiman was an important but kindly and pleasant looking little man, dressed in the conventional morning dress of that period with a gold watch chain and gold rimmed glasses, topped by a shining bald head. He showed us some samples of the work I would be taught to do and it was not a bit like my idea of embroidery at all; in fact it is odd to relate that in my long period of sixteen years working for this firm, I never did work like these samples.

I would start work in the mornings at 8.30 and work until 7.00 in the evenings, with lunch from 12.30 to 1.30 and do from 8.30 to 1.00 on Saturdays. That was 49 hours for 3 shillings (15 p) a week! That was sixpence a week more than my elder sister had started work with three years before. I was told I could begin that afternoon.

And that was the beginning of my working life – no thought of a career; I doubt if the word was ever mentioned. Just by the chance remark of a woman cleaner – or it might have been by answering an advertisement in the Hackney and Kingsland Gazette – work was chosen for hundreds of Hackney's poorer children in those days.

The firm, which was an old family business, established in Bethnal Green in the nineteenth century, called themselves 'Court Dress Embroiders and Textile Embellishers'. They did beautiful and costly hand embroidery for famous West End dress houses, much of it for royalty and titled ladies.

I was tremendously fascinated by all the apparatus used for winding and twisting silks and making the threads and cords and so on used in the work rooms. There were several ancient looms which still produced braids and fringes. Seeing the shuttles flying and the pattern emerging awoke the interest in weaving which I still have.

With the outbreak of the Great War in 1914, court dresses and beautiful embroidery gradually disappeared and the resources and skill of the firm and its employees turned to war work in the form of machine-embroidered naval and army badges and so on for the uniforms of those days. These were made, hundreds at a time, on huge Swiss embroidery machines, installed for the purpose.

After the war the work was never quite the same. My job there ended with the depression of 1929. I became redundant and was never able to find another firm quite like it. I believe it was unique. It really belonged to the world that ended in 1914.

Emily Bishop, **Embroidery**

ASSIGNMENT

1 What impression do you get of the family and their way of life?

2 What thoughts had Ellen had about the work she might do?

3 What made her apply for a job in an embroidery factory?

 4 What are Ellen's first impressions of the appearance of the office and the factory?

5 What change did the war bring, and what do you think Ellen thought about these changes?

It were nothing for a girl to be sent away to service when she were eleven year old. This meant leaving the family as she had never been parted from for a day in her life before, and going to some place miles away to be treated like something as hasn't got as much sense or feeling as a dog. I'm got nothing against girls going into good service. In my opinion, good service in a properly run big house were a wonderful training for a lot o' girls who would never ha' seen anything different all the days o' their lives if they han't a-gone. It were better than working on the land then, and if it still existed now, I reckon I'd rather see any o' my daughters be a good housemaid or a well-trained parlour maid than a dolled-up shop assistant or a factory worker. But folks are too proud to work for other folks, now, even if it's too their own advantage, though as far as I can see you are still working for other folks, whatever you're a'doing. Such gals as us from the fen didn't get 'good' service, though, not till we'd learnt a good deal the hard way. Big houses didn't want little girls of eleven, even as kitchen maids, so the first few years 'ad to be put in somewhere else, afore you got even that amount of promotion. Big houses expected good service, but you got good treatment in return.

It weren't like that at the sort o' place my friends had to go to. Mostly they went to farmers' houses within ten or twenty mile from where they'd been born. These farmers were a jumped-up, proud lot who didn't know how to treat the people who worked for them. They took advantage of the poor people's need to get their girls off their hands to get little slaves for nearly nothing. The conditions were terrible. One little girl I know'd went when she were eleven to a great lonely farmhouse on the highlands, miles from anywhere. The very next day after she got there the grandmother o' the household died and were laid out on the bed straight away. Then the heartless woman of the house sent poor little Eva to scrub the floor o' the room where the corpse lay. She were frit to death, an' no wonder, but she 'ad to do it. When she were cleaning under the bed, the corpse suddenly rumbled and groaned as the wind passed out of it, and to Eva's dying day she never forgot the terror of that moment.

I 'ad one friend as I were particularly fond of, called for some reason as I never did know, 'Shady'. Shady's adventures at service would fill a book on their own. She went to service when she were about thirteen, to a lonely, outlaying fen farm in a place called Blackbushe. The house were a mile or more from the road, and there were no other house near by. A big open farm yard were all around it on three sides, and at the back door, it opened straight into the main drain, about twelve feet wide and ten feet deep with sides like the wall of a house. There were no escape there. Her duties were as follows.

She were woke up at 6 am every morning by the horsekeeper, who had walked several miles to work already, and used a clothes prop to rattle on her window to rouse her. She had to get up straight away and light the scullery fire in the big, awkward old range, that she'd had to clean and black-lead afore it got too hot. Then she put the kettle on to get tea made for 6.30 am for the horsekeeper. While the kettle boiled, she started to scrub the bare tiles o'the kitchen floor. This were a terrible job. There were no hot water and the kitchen were so big that there seemed nearly an acre of it to scrub – and when you'd finished that, there'd be the dairy, just as big, and the scullery as well. Skirts were long and got in the way as you knelt to scrub, and whatever you done you couldn't help getting wet. In the winter you'd have only the lights of the candle to do it by, and the kitchen 'ould be so cold the water 'ould freeze afore you could mop it up properly.

At 6.30 the horsekeeper come in for his tea, and as soon as he'd gone Shady had to start getting breakfast for the family. If there were little children in the house, she'd be expected to have them with her and give them their breakfast while she had her own. After breakfast she washed up, including all the milk utensils and so on from the dairy, and then started the housework. On churning days Shady had to get up extra early to make time to fit the churning in. There were no time off at all during the day, and after supper she had to wash up all the things and prepare for next morning. This meant cleaning all the family's boots and shoes, and getting things ready for breakfast next morning. Farmers cured their own bacon and hams, so she would be given the bacon taken from a side 'in-cut', but the custom was to have fried potatoes for breakfast with the bacon. These were supposed to be the 'taters' left over from supper, but there were never enough left, so one of her evening jobs was allus to peel and boil a big saucepan of potatoes to fry next morning. As I'm said before, she was allowed only bread and butter for her own breakfast.

Then if she had any time before it was bed time, she had to sit by herself in the cold dark kitchen in front of a dying fire that she weren't allowed to make up, except in lambing time. In lambing time it were took for granted that any lambs as were weakly 'ould be looked after in the kitchen, and while the season lasted the old shepherd 'ould come in and set in the kitchen while he waited for his ewes to lamb. I'm 'eard Shady say 'ow she dreaded this. The shepherd were a dirty, nasty vulgar old man as no decent girl were safe with; but at the best o' times he weren't very pleasant to have to sit with, stinking o' the sheep, belching and blowing off, and every now and then getting up and straddling over to make water in the kitchen sink. The only other choice she 'ad were to go to bed, once she were sure she wouldn't be needed again, but that didn't offer such pleasant prospects either. Maids' rooms were allus at the very top, at the back on the north side o' the house. There was nothing in them but a bed with a hard old flock mattress, a table by the side of it, and the tin trunk the girl had brought her clothes in. It was icy cold in winter, and Shady weren't the only one o' my friends by a long way as told me they slept in all their clothes to keep warm.

Though 'the woman' done the washing for the family, she didn't do Shady's. She weren't allowed to do it herself, but 'ad to send it home to her mother once a week by the carrier. This took most o' Shady's 'afternoon off' because she had to walk up to the high road and meet the carrier's cart, often hanging about an hour or more waiting for him, to get her dirty washing exchanged for clean. Sometimes her mother 'ould walk the five or six mile with the clean washing, just to see her for a few minutes afore walking it all the other way. on the first time she did this she found Shady on her knees scrubbing the kitchen floor. Shady got up to greet her, and her mother lifted her skirt and said "Let's have a look at yer britches." As the poor mother expected, they were wet through with cold water and black as a soot bag with the constant kneeling and scrubbing and blackleading. It was a sort o' test to the experienced mother's eye o' what sort of a 'place' she were forced to leave her daughter in. I don't know which of 'em would suffer most, the mother or the daughter. But there were no help for it, and every girl as left home were one less mouth to feed. If she behaved herself and stuck it out a whole year, there did come a day when she'd draw her year's wages, which stood then at five pound.

Sybil Marshall, **Fenland Chronicle**

ASSIGNMENT

1 What does the speaker think about girls being sent away to service? Does she see some advantages?

2 Describe the poor conditions some girls had to put up with.

3 Describe the kind of work they would do.

4 Imagine you are Shady. Write a letter to your mother describing what your day has been like. You could include reference to your work, what you eat, the evening, the shepherd.

5 Imagine that you are Shady's mother. Write an account of your thoughts and feelings after your first visit, when you found her scrubbing the floor.

ASSIGNMENT

What are the differences between Ellen's work and the girls' in the second passage? What do you think about their situations?

More suggestions for coursework

- The First Day. Describe someone's first day at work.
- What do you think are the advantages and disadvantages of working in someone else's house, as a nanny or home help, for example?

John O'Neil

These extracts are taken from the diary of a weaver, John O'Neil. The diary was written in a cash book found on a rubbish heap. He worked in the town of Clitheroe in Lancashire. His diary describes the effect the American Civil War had on the cotton industry in England.

April 1864

10th It is nearly two years since I wrote anything in the way of a diary. I now take up my pen to resume the task. It has been a very poor time for me all the time owing to the American war, which seems as far off being settled as ever. The mill I work in was stopped all last winter, during which time I had 3s. per week allowed by the relief committee, which barely kept me alive. When we started work again it was with Surat cotton, (a coarse, uncoloured cotton) and a great number of weavers can only mind two looms. We can earn very little. I have not earned a shilling a day this last month, and there are many like me. My clothes and bedding are wearing out very fast and I have no means of getting any more, as what wages I get hardly keep me, my daughter and son-in-law having gone to a house of their own during the time I was out of work. I went twice to Preston to see my brother Daniel, but he and his family were no better off than myself, having nothing better than Surat to work at, and it is the same all through Lancashire. There has been some terrible and bloody battles fought in America these last two years...The principal reason why I did not take any notes these last two years is because I was sad and weary. One half of the time I was out of work and the other I had to work as hard as ever I wrought in my life, and can hardly keep myself living. If things do not mend this summer I will try somewhere else or something else, for I can't go much further with what I am at.

17th. I have had another weary week of bad work. I have just earned 7s 3d off three looms and there are plenty off as bad as me, and if anyone complains to the Master of Bad Work he says, if you don't like it you can leave. He wants no-one to stop that does not like it, and that is all the satisfaction we can get...

May

1st There has been some little rain today, the first we have had for three weeks. It is much wanted...I have given up my odd loom as I cannot keep two looms going, and last week I had only 5s 1d after a very hard week's work, but they have promised us better work as soon as the cotton is done that they have on hand. They have promised so often that we can hardly believe them.

8th The work at our place is beginning to mend. I have got two beams in (cylinders of wood in a loom), the best I have had for twelve months, but they are for shifting the looms out of our shop into a new shed that is ready for starting, so I hope to get on better than I have done this last winter. In Denmark the Danes are retreating and the Austrians and Prussians are advancing.

15th Whitsunday. It has been very hot all day and I have been out walking nearly all afternoon. The news from America gives an account of the defeat of the Federal army under General Banks on the Red River with the loss of 4000 men and twenty pieces of cannon, and in the course of another week we may hear of one of the greatest battles that ever was fought...At home things are much about the same. I have been shifted into the new shed and got two very bad looms and bad work in them, so I am no better off than I was. We are to have a holiday tomorrow, but I am too poor to go anywhere so I must stay at home.

22nd It has been very hot all this week, with some thundershowers. In Denmark all is quiet just now, and the Polish insurrection is over and many hundreds of families are sent to Siberia; and at our mill things is likely to get worse. The spinners turned out, and a deputation waited upon the Masters, wanting them to mend the work as it was

so bad they could scarce get a living. The Masters said they would
not mend it and if they did not like it they could leave, so they had
to go work again.

29th Another week of bad work. It is as bad now as ever it was...and
no signs of it mending...

June

19th. It has been fine growing weather this last week, and hay
harvest has commenced. In Europe the Danish armistice is prolonged
another fortnight, and if nothing definite is come to, there will be war
again; and at Low Moor things are as bad as ever. I went up to
Clitheroe last night. There was a great temperance demonstration
and procession which passed off very well. New potatoes were selling
at two pound for 3d.

26th There has been a great deal of rain this week and today is very
cold and boisterous. There was a great battle fought last Sunday
morning off the French coast near Cherbourg between the federal war
steamer Kearsarge and the Confederate cruiser the Alabama, which
had burned and destroyed one hundred merchantmen belonging to
the United States. The fight lasted an hour and ten minutes when
the rebel ship was sent to the bottom. The captain and some of the
officers escaped on board an English yacht that came out of
Cherbourg with her. They had eleven killed and twenty wounded, and
about ten or a dozen were drowned, along with the surgeon; while the
Kearsarge was very little damaged and had only three men wounded.
They picked up sixty-eight men from the sinking ship....In Clitheroe
last night new potatoes were selling five pounds for 6d so I got some
for my dinner and came home again.

July

10th. It has been very fine warm weather since Wednesday and a
great deal of hay has been got in in good condition. In Denmark the
Prussians are taking every place they come to, the Danes offering
very little resistance. In Parliament the Tories brought forward a
motion for a vote of censure upon the Government for the way they
have treated the Danish question. The debate lasted all week, and on
a division the Ministers had a majority of eighteen. There is no other
news of importance this week.

August

14th. This has been a fine warm week and we stopped yesterday as
the engine wanted repairs, so I whitewashed and cleaned the house
and today I am very stiff and tired. The latest news from America
shows that Sherman has not captured Atlanta but that he has

invested (laid siege to) it with a view to make it surrender; and General Grant has blown up a fort at Petersburg with a rebel regiment and has taken the outer line of defences. There is nothing else of importance...At our mill we have had two turn-outs for bad work. It has been getting worse all summer until we could stand it no longer, and the last time we were out we stopped out all day, when the Master told the deputation that waited on him that he would work his present stock of cotton up and then he would buy better sorts and have as good work as any in Clitheroe. It is shameful the work we have in at present. I had only 6s this last week with very hard work, and there was some had less than me; and then our machinery is running very slow owing to the great drought as Ribble is very near dry. We have had frosty nights and warm days this last fortnight, and harvest has been commenced. There were thirty mills stopped in Blackburn this last week for want of water, and will not start again until wet weather sets in.

September

11th. We have had a week of very wet weather which was much wanted...Things are much about the same at Atlanta and Mobile, but the principal news from America just now is the coming election for President, because it depends upon which of the candidates is chosen whether there will be peace or a continuance of the war, and as the position of the parties are about evenly balanced there is no knowing yet how things may be, because if there should be peace, then the price of cotton must come down 2s per pound, and that is the reason why the cotton trade is so bad just now. The merchants will not buy cloth, as they expect the price will come down one half, and the Manufacturers will not buy cotton for the same reason. There are several mills in Lancashire begun to run short time and some are stopping altogether. At our mills the cotton was done last Tuesday and no signs of any coming. There is none working now but weavers, and if no cotton comes, why then, we must stop next, so everything has a black look – and winter coming on!

18th. Another wet week and bad prospects for trade. We got as much cotton last week as kept the mill running two days and a half, and as cotton has come down 4d per pound it is thought we may get some more...The Chicago convention have met and have put General M'Clellan in nomination as President in opposition to Abraham Lincoln, so now both sides are fairly at work, and as the election comes off on the fourth of November the cotton trade in the meanwhile will be greatly depressed until the result is known.

25th. We have had some fine weather these days, and harvest is nearly over...The cotton trade is getting worse every day. There is no market whatever, and mills are closing every day. The wefts (woven threads) we have had this last week is worse than ever, but we are forced to put up with it, as we don't know how soon we will have to stop altogether.

October

2nd. It has been very fine all week and things are looking very bad. At our mill they are all working three days a week, except the weavers, who are yet on full time; but as the material is very bad they make very little wages. I have given up my odd loom and I find that two is as many as I can manage with such bad weft. There is a complete stagnation in trade, both in the cotton and cloth market, and nothing doing...

9th. Another fine week and very little doing. There has been nothing but the weavers working at our mill this week. All the rest are doing nothing, but they have got some cotton which will last three days, and all have to start tomorrow morning...There is great distress all through Lancashire at present owing to so many mills stopping, and Clitheroe will soon be as bad as anywhere else.

16th. We commenced short time last Monday, and on Thursday we stopped altogether and does not know when we will start again. The cotton that was bought last week – about forty bales – fell a penny a pound about two hours after he had bought it and he will buy no more until the market settles. I should have gone to Preston this morning but it was so wet, but I shall go tomorrow if all be well...

23rd. We have been stopped all week and likely for stopping a little longer as there is no cotton bought yet, although it has fallen 2 pence per pound last week, but in the cloth market there is nothing doing whatever. I went to Preston last Monday but only to find that my brother and family had left last Whitsuntide owing to the mill they were working in stopping. They have gone to Dolphinholme near Lancaster and never sent me word. I saw McMurray and family, who gave me all the information, so I found it was no use stopping there so I walked all the way to Blackburn (ten miles) and took the train to Clitheroe. It has been very stormy all week and we have had little pleasure. I applied with several others to the Relief Committee yesterday and got 3s, and our Masters gave every hand 2s so we are not so badly off this week, whatever they may do next week. It was the great fair yesterday, and a very poor one it was owing to the stormy weather and so many people out of work. The news from America is much about the same as last week, very little doing on either side The friends of Mr Lincoln say they are sure of winning the election by a large majority.

30th. We commenced work last Thursday and started full time, as our masters have bought a large supply of cotton which will last a few weeks; and the cloth market is a trifle better this week and it is thought that it has got a turn for the better....The public mind is taken up with the Presidential contest, both sides say they are sure of winning, but in a week or two we shall know all about it. There is nothing else of any importance.

November

6th. The weavers have been on full time all week, but the rest of the hands have only had four days and the markets are as gloomy as ever...

December

4th. There is very little news of any kind lately that I have made no note of it. Lincoln has been re-elected President of America and there has been nothing but skirmishing since, and it is likely that there will not be much done until spring. At home we have nothing but stormy weather and bad work, and a poor prospect for Christmas.

ASSIGNMENT

1 The local history society want an article on John O'Neil for their next publication. The title of the article is 'The effects of the cotton famine on John O'Neil and his fellow workers in Clitheroe during 1864.'

Select and arrange the relevant material for your article. Write about four paragraphs between 250 to 400 words in all.

2 Imagine that John O'Neil is making a speech to his employers, asking them to improve wages and working conditions. His speech will include:

(a) a description of the hardships he has had to suffer at work;

(b) the difficulties he and his fellow workers endure in their personal daily lives.

Write the speech. Try to use your own words where possible. Write about 250 words.

3 The diaries include references to historical events taking place elsewhere in the world. Write a paragraph on each of the following, suitable for inclusion in an history text book:

(a) the political and military events that took place in America in 1864;

(b) the events of historical importance that took place on the continent of Europe in 1864. Write about 150 words altogether.

More suggestions for coursework

Write a series of diary entries about your work (this may be part-time work, or the work experience element of your course). Make some reference to the type of work you do, and make your thoughts and feelings clear.

SPELLING CHECK

demonstration, procession

All the following words have either 'tion' or 'sion' at the end. Add the right ending.

conclu....   deci...   ero...   devo...
connec....   atten...   forma... explana...

Changing times

These passages describe people who work in occupations not traditionally associated with their gender.

Scott, 27, is a cleaner with Dusters domestic agency.

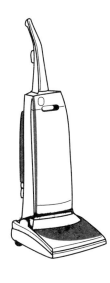

"I've been cleaning for about a year and I really enjoy it – sometimes it's just great making a dirty house clean and tidy. It's not always pleasant. I've been to some filthy houses and done some disgusting jobs. But the good thing is, you're practically you're own boss – you work hours to suit yourself and there's no-one breathing down your neck. You can amuse yourself by trying to work out what your clients are like from their taste in decoration. Occasionally it's tempting to have a bit of a snoop but it's never worth the risk. Besides, you're usually too busy.

I think you have to be quite houseproud to be a successful cleaner. If you're a bit slobby yourself, you won't know what to look for – you'll clean around the toaster rather than under it. having said that, my place isn't always spotless. When you've been cleaning all day, you don't want to start when you get home.

Sexism is rife – the female cleaners know you're capable of doing the job but some of the customers just can't hack it. Once I was even turned down for a job because I was a man! Most clients are intrigued when I turn up on their doorstep. There's still a lot of, "But you're a man, you can't be a cleaner". They expect a Mrs Mop not an Aussie in sweat pants and a T-shirt. Once you've proved you're good, the sexist comments usually stop though. They realise you don't need those feminine touches – whatever they are – to make a place look nice.

When I told my mates about my job, I had to put up with jokes about me being gay – although they knew they couldn't push me too far. They also joked about me being seduced by amorous young female clients – I wish! But a job's a job, they know that. Girlfriends think it's a laugh. They always want to know what people's houses are like.

I'll probably do this for another few years. It's a great way to make a living. There's no stress and you earn enough to pay the rent and have a good time."

More

ASSIGNMENT

1 What does Scott like about his job?

2 What are the different attitudes other people have to it?

Vyvian, 27, is a temporary secretary with Reed Employment.

"I've been a secretary for about six years on and off. I've had no formal training but picked up office skills as I've gone along. I think I've got a talent for it. I type about 60 words a minute which isn't bad – especially for someone who's never had a typing lesson.

Five years ago, male secretaries were very rare but now there's quite a few of us. I think as the 90s progress, there'll be more of a crossover between traditionally male and female jobs. Attitudes towards men and women in general are changing all the time. I might get a bit of extra attention because I'm a man but not much. A lot of sexist myths still exist about secretaries. You know, dolly birds in mini skirts who sit on their bosses' knees to take shorthand. It's rubbish. Everyone I've come across in this business has been highly professional. It doesn't matter if you're male or female so long as you get the job done. The secretary's role has changed significantly with the advent of computers and WPs, although you still have to be a good organiser. It seems slightly ridiculous that men were ever thought unsuitable for this work.

There's not a lot of difference between working for men or women bosses. It depends on the individual, you can't generalise.

I really want to be an actor but if that doesn't take off in the next few years, I'll make a career out of this. I'd quite like to be a top PA – that's the one area of office work where women still really dominate.

More

ASSIGNMENT

1 What does Vyvian like about his job? What is he particularly good at?

2 What does he say about the changes taking place in his type of work?

Lloyd, 25, is a nanny.

"I haven't had any formal nanny training. I did a leisure and community course at college which led to me going to Camp America where I was supervising kids and adults. When I came home I didn't know what I was going to do but a friend of a friend was looking for a nanny and I thought, I can do that. The parents were really cool about it, but then the dad played an active role in bringing up his kids. Fathers who regard child care as women's work would probably freak out.

The children I look after are five and two-and-a half, and sometimes I also look after a year-old baby. I love it. It's so rewarding seeing the kids develop in front of your eyes. They really do change from day to day. It's great fun, too. The children are like your little mates. I'd much rather do this than work in an office although they can drive you mad and you're glad to hand them back to the parents.

Male nannies are very rare. When you're doing the school run or going to playgroups, you don't even see many dads. Most people who don't know automatically assume you're gay because you're doing a traditionally female job. Some even think you must have an unhealthy interest in kids to want to look after them. It's such a cliché. They can think what they like, I don't let it bother me. I know why I'm doing it. My male friends think it's great that I'm doing a job I enjoy. Female friends are very supportive too. I think women like men who are good with kids. It's actually older kids who have been the most surprised to learn that I'm a nanny. Recently I went to the secondary school where my girl friend teaches and the kids had to guess my job. None of them guessed right. When I told them, the boys in particular didn't believe me. It had never entered their heads that this could be a career option for them. Afterwards a couple said they wouldn't mind being nannies. Fortunately, the nannying world seem to have no misgivings about taking men on. At last society is waking up to the fact that men can be just as good at women at looking after children.

More

ASSIGNMENT

1 What does Lloyd like about his job?

2 What different attitudes has he experienced?

ASSIGNMENT

Using the information from the passages, write an article for a similar magazine giving advice to men thinking about starting work in a traditionally female job. Include some comments about the kinds of attitude they may meet.

More suggestions for coursework

- Write a conversation between someone about to employ a male nanny and someone who doesn't think it's a good idea.
- "Women are by nature more suited to certain types of work." Have a discussion, debate or write a response.
- Do you think fathers should be more involved in child care? Write 300 to 500 words on this, and if appropriate, suggest ways in which this could be encouraged.

Punctuation mark

Dash

"I really enjoy it – sometimes it's just great making a dirty house clean and tidy"

A single dash can be used to show an aside remark, usually at the end of a sentence, or to indicate an interruption. Sometimes it introduces a part of the sentence which draws together what has gone before.

Example Silas made a good contribution to class discussion – that is, when he bothered to turn up.

Try not to use the dash too much in your writing. It's used a lot in the passage quoted above because the passage is a record of what someone is saying.

"You don't need those feminine touches – whatever they are – to make a place look nice."

A pair of dashes can be used to separate off part of the sentence from the main flow. A remark like this is sometimes called a parenthesis. Remember to use both dashes, and check that the sentence flows if you remove the whole parenthesis. This will tell you that the sentence grammar is correct.

Example When he did turn up – which was very rarely – he just made a nuisance of himself.

SELF CHECK

Insert dashes in the following sentences.

1 The main fault with the report as I said before is that it covers very little ground.
2 It was really the younger ones' turn not that that bothered Heidi.

graduates. In 1965 she left Sussex University with a degree in What's

What's it like being a female jockey in the male-dominated world of horse-racing?

Name: Antoinette Armes (or 'The Tiddler')

Occupation: Professional apprentice jockey/stable girl
Age: 24

Why did you choose this career?
I've always loved horses and being a jockey was something I've always wanted to do, ever since I was tiny. My parents aren't in this profession at all but they've encouraged me all the way, and are really proud of me.
How did you get started?
My dad wrote to Mr Henry Candy (one of the top trainers) when I was about 15, and I went to him for a month's trial to work just as a stable girl and then he offered me a job, to start as soon as I left school.

At first I just looked after three horses, mucking them out, riding them and taking them to races. then, when I was 18 he decided that I was good enough to apply for my jockey's licence and here I am now!
Do you need any qualifications?
No, I haven't got an 'O' level to my name! You've just got to be able to ride a horse.
What sort of training do you receive?
Basically you just work constantly with the horses and ride them. Once you become a jockey, bearing in mind you might be riding for several different trainers, the trainer may advise you on how best to ride a particular horse.

For example, some horses are better if they are first out of the stalls and are front-runners from the start and others you have to try and hold back until you're nearing the

end of the race and then let them go.

A trainer may tell you how to race his/her horse, but once you've ridden that horse a few times you may decide that the trainer's instructions are wrong, and this is something that we then discuss. Not all horses have the same temperament.
What sort of personality do you need to become a lady jockey?
You've obviously got to have a huge love of horses and be prepared to work really hard.
Can you describe a typical day?
It depends on whether I'm racing. If the course isn't a local one then a lot of the day consists of travelling and, of course, the races themselves. Yesterday I had three daytime rides at Folkestone, today I've got two evening ones here at Lingfield, but tomorrow will be spent totally at Mr Candy's, working with the horses.

On a non-racing day I get up about 6.30, start work at 7.00 mucking out one horse then riding him. Then it's back for breakfast, muck the second horse out, ride him, etc.

I stop about midday and then start again at 4.00, brushing them and again mucking them out. I don't get a day off because, as with any animals, they've got to be looked after seven days a week.
What are the good points?
I just love horses so it's great to spend all my time with them.

Although I get very nervous, I love the racing. I get a real buzz out of it, especially when you win. Then you just want to do it more and more.

You never forget your first. Mine was on Persian Lord at Kempton in an apprentice race. I just couldn't believe we'd won and it didn't really sink in until about three weeks later!

And the bad points?

It's hard for girls. They don't get noticed but I suppose that's because there are so few of us. In a way we don't get taken quite so seriously as the men, which is a great shame.

Do you get treated differently because you're a lady jockey?

You don't get any preferential treatment because you're a woman, but a few of the men say "well done" when I win whereas in the past I don't think they liked being beaten by a woman.

Also, there's absolutely no difference between being just one girl in a men's race than there is in an all-girl race, because the women are just as rough and tough when you're competing against each other!

Which race would you most like to win?

Without a doubt, The Derby. It's the race to win.

What are your future plans?

To just carry on as I am. I think it's going to be tough because an apprenticeship finishes either when you're 25, or when you've ridden 95 winners, so I've only got another year to go and then I become a fully-fledged professional and I go out on my own.

Do you have any advice for our readers?

Go for it, and don't give up! Take no notice if people try to dissuade you from being a jockey just because you're a girl. It's just as much our sport as the lads', and think how great you'll feel when you win!

© D.C. Thomson & Co. Ltd.

ASSIGNMENT

1 What impression have you gained of Antoinette's character and way of life?

2 What kind of insight does the interview give you into what it is like being a woman working in a male world?

3 Are there other questions you would have asked?

More suggestions for coursework

- Write a story or account of someone who faces difficulties at work because of their gender. You could write this as a play if you like.

Making adjustments

Recent years have seen enormous changes in the kinds of work people do and the way in which they work. The following material focuses on some of these issues.

Computers and word processors are now part of everyday life. This extract from a novel called *Here today* describes an office staff being trained in the 'new technology'.

The word processor was smaller than Antonia had expected. It was cream coloured with a still green screen. It didn't look as if it would do anyone any harm.

The salesman, who had DESMOND written on his badge, addressed the secretaries. "Now I expect some of you girls have seen these on television."

Somebody said, "Yeah, I saw a programme about how we're all going to be on the dole."

"The new technology," said Desmond, "is going to *create* jobs."

Liar, thought Antonia, perched on a stool at the back of the room. She didn't like Desmond. All right, if Forlex was going over to word processors and she was going to stay at Forlex, she'd have to learn to use them whether she liked it or not. She looked round at the Forlex secretaries. She'd seen some of them before: on her way to the print room, or when they came to swap magazines in Audrey's pile. Their expressions seemed to divide into two: those who hated word processors and those who would probably end up buying one.

"They're bad for your eyes," said someone. "You can go blind."

"They said that about sex a hundred years ago," said Desmond impishly. No one laughed. "Seriously though, that's a very responsible question. Flicker and glare on the VDUs on other models have been blamed for eyestrain. You should be grateful to your employers for choosing Chestnut. But don't take my word for it." *We weren't going to.* "Everybody look at the screen for ten seconds without blinking." They did. He timed them on his watch. "Now shut your eyes. Can you still see any glare? There you are, then. May I have a volunteer, please – someone who hasn't *already* got a headache from the noise of an ordinary typewriter? A girl with long black hair went forward and sat before the keyboard. Desmond picked up what looked like a record still in its sleeve and stuck it into a slot in one of the wired-up boxes. "Floppy disk," he said.

The machine whirred and letters appeared on the screen. WELCOME TO NUTSHELL. "Nutshell's the name of our introductory word-processing teaching package," Desmond explained.

WHAT'S YOUR NAME? asked the machine. The girl with the long black hair gave a little squeal and bent closer.

"Gather round, everyone," ordered Desmond. Antonia moved a bit closer so that she could see but she stayed on the edge of the group.

"Type in your name. Go on, don't be scared, it's a perfectly ordinary keyboard."

The girl typed LIZ but her hand slipped with nerves and it came out as LIZX. She blushed. Desmond said, "Don't worry, I'll show you how to delete in a minute."

GOOD DAY LIZX AND WELCOME TO YOUR FIRST LESSON. DO YOU WISH TO OPEN A FILE?

Liz grinned up at Desmond. "I don't know. Do I?"

He explained that if she called her file LIZX then forever afterwards everything she typed would be stored in the computer's memory and could be recalled in seconds if she asked for it by name. But she would have to say LIZX. The computer wouldn't recognise LIZ.

"One day computers'll know more than we know," said someone.

"They can't know anything we don't tell them," Antonia announced. "They're basically stupid and mechanical."

"Er, yes," said Desmond. "I'll demonstrate the Global Search Function. Suppose it's ten to five." Antonia muttered, "Wish it was, " but nobody heard. All eyes were on Desmond who had hustled Liz from her seat and taken it himself. He was busy fiddling with disks and keys while the screen filled up with rapidly shifting text.

"Suppose it's ten to five and you've just typed a thirteen-page report about a firm called Johnson Limited, and your boss looks at it and says it's not Johnson, it's *Johnstone*, and I can't let you use Tippex and it's got to go out tonight." All the secretaries nodded, remembering occasions when just this sort of thing had happened. Antonia said, "I wouldn't stand for it, not if he told me wrong in the first place."

"You press," said Desmond, "the Global Search key and ask it to locate all the Johnsons and turn them into Johnstones. Like this. It'll do all the corrections in the time it takes you to collect up your bits and pieces and say goodnight to your friends."

"If they haven't all been fired."

Desmond smiled at Antonia. "You haven't tried it yet, have you?"

"I don't want—"

"You can be next. Fear of innovation, you know, often arises from ignorance and inexperience." Someone laughed.

It was a QWERTY keyboard with a few extras: arrows pointing in different directions, words like DELETE, CONTROL, PAGE, ACCEPT and new things like CHAR and CURSOR. Desmond asked her name. She didn't answer. He asked her again.

"Just a minute. I'm having a look. It's Antonia."

"We've already got a file called Antonia. From the last lesson. We'll have to get rid of it." She stared intently at him while he told her how to do this. She kept her eyes hard and her mouth a tight line. She wanted him to know that she didn't mind listening to him if he had something worth saying but she didn't like him. Soon she pressed her first key on her first word processor. It was DELETE. The screen shook itself into alertness. Luminous green worms uncoiled into letters.

DELETE WHICH FILE?

"Delete Antonia," said Desmond.

DELETE ANTONIA.

ARE YOU SURE?

Antonia laughed. "Talks back, does it?"

"Yes. Like you. It's the anti-error feature. Tell it again."

DELETE ANTONIA.

ARE YOU REALLY SURE?

"Bit cheeky, isn't it?"

"User Friendly, we call it. You have to tell it three times before it deletes a file. Could be serious. There was a lady writer working on a machine without this feature once and she deleted a book by mistake. Six hundred pages. Now you can delete all the others for practice, they're only training files."

DELETE ANTONIA DELETE JANE DELETE SANDY DELETE LIZX ARE YOU SURE ARE YOU REALLY SURE DELETE SAMANTHA

"Fine," said Desmond. "It's someone else's turn now."

"But I haven't done anything except delete people."

"We'll never get her away from it now," said Desmond to the rest of the girls. "All right, you can do some standard letters."

By typing the letter only once you could produce hundreds of different versions, personalised for different people. Some of the other secretaries wanted their turn but Antonia didn't move. Desmond gave her a plastic-backed training card. The instructions were easy to follow if you concentrated. First you typed the letter. The keys yielded to the slightest touch, the beautiful green characters arranging themselves neatly on the screen.

"Now we activate the printer—" The wired-up box jolted and hummed. A tiny wheel of letters spun faster than the eye could follow. "Two hundred characters a second," whispered Desmond. Out came the sheets of paper, perfect originals.

"Wow," Antonia breathed.

"Good, eh?" said Desmond.

"Mm."

"You learned fast. That's a difficult function. You're a natural."

He showed how it could rearrange lines and pages of text to accommodate a correction. He showed how it could do underlining and italics. He said, "That's enough for today, I think." He said he looked forward to meeting those selected by Forlex for the full training course. "One last thing," he said, proffering a bottle of aspirins. "Headaches, eyestrain, anyone?" The girl who had mentioned eyestrain blushed and was nudged by her friend. Desmond gave everybody a coloured booklet to take away, called "Word Processing, a New Chestnut."

Antonia went back to the drawing office. *He said I was a natural.*

Zoë Fairbairns, **Here today**

ASSIGNMENT

1 What do you think about Desmond's attitude to the girls and the way he trains them? Do you think he is effective?

2 What is Antonia's attitude at the beginning of the passage? Remember to give references and examples.

3 Describe how her attitude changes as the passage continues.

New Job, Old Job

New job:
CD moulding technician

Kevin Benham, 32, has worked as a shift leader in the EMI compact disc production plant in Swindon for seven years. Previously, he completed an apprenticeship with British Rail before being made redundant. Discs pressed daily: 140 000

What made you choose this job?
To be honest I reckon I would have stayed at BR until the day I died – most people seemed to do that. But the closure of the factory forced me to move on and I came here by accident really. They were just setting up the plant and I thought it might take off and give me a good future.

How much do you earn?
I don't really want to say, but it's pretty good because my salary includes a shift allowance because the plant operates 24 hours a day, seven days a week.

What do you think of it?
It's great working with music because it's something I'm interested in – it's one of my hobbies. We get to hear a lot because we have it piped around the workshop. The technology can be a bit imposing when you first come into contact with it, but I've always thought of myself as pretty adaptable. When I started here we had just six moulding machines and you could almost name all the titles we were producing. Today's equipment barely resembles the old machinery and the output is enormous.

What about the people you work with?
Generally the whole place functions well as a team. It's quite a young company and we have lots of social nights out organised by the company which keeps everyone together.

What about the future?
It's a bit hard to visualise myself going any further than I am now. I would like to, but it's very hard to find opportunities. I've been studying management at college and it's just a question of waiting for something to come up. Hopefully I'll go on to study more, but family commitments are stopping me doing that for this year.

Old job: Vinyl presser

Darren Murphy, 33, has been managing his own vinyl pressing company for nine years. he also runs two dance record labels. Previously he was a member of the punk band Wasted Youth. Discs pressed daily: 6000.

What made you choose this job?
I've never done anything else to be honest. When I was in a band and making albums we used a record pressing plant in east London. One day we went there and they were in liquidation. So my father and I ended up buying the pressing plant and that's how it started.

How much do you earn?
I don't really want to say, but there's not a lot of money in pressing.

What do you think of it?
I love it. When we first started we

were mainly pressing reggae acts, now it's mostly DJs, people off the street making music in their bedrooms. We've had some famous acts come through - like Quartz who went top 30 and then signed to a major label. It was nice to watch it all grow. Vinyl is really a demo stage where people make demo records and put them out in the clubs to see what happens. If they then get signed to a major I'm delighted someone else has got through.

What about the people you work with?

There's only seven of us and I get on famously with them (he laughs).

What about the future?

Five years ago I thought vinyl was finished – the majors tried to get rid of it. But it'll be around for a while yet because although it's not the greatest carrier of music, it is the most instant. You can finish a song in the studio on Tuesday, get test pressings the following Tuesday and have it on the streets the Tuesday after. That's very healthy. Whatever happens I'm going to be into vinyl until the end.

The Guardian

ASSIGNMENT

1 Describe the way the interviewee in *New job* adapted to his new job. What does he like about it?

2 What does the interviewee in *Old job* think about his job?

ASSIGNMENT

From reading the two passages, what would you say are the personal qualities which enable someone to adapt to new working methods?

More suggestions for coursework

- Imagine you are showing someone how to use a machine they have never used before, and which makes them feel quite nervous. Describe what happens.
- Write a story or account of what happens when someone feels they can't cope with changes at their place of work. (The changes could be to do with new equipment, or different working practices, or just working for a new boss.)

Future prospects

With so-called 'normal' jobs now in the minority, this article reports on the changes in working patterns.

Only a minority of jobs in Britain now fits our idea of a 'normal' or 'real' job. We are only just beginning to understand the implications of this. In the last 15 years the labour market in the UK had undergone more radical changes than occurred in the previous half a century. The nature of these has been so substantial - but comparatively so sudden - that many people still have only a vague idea what has happened.

Many employers, too, are only now beginning to understand the variety of ways, other than 'standard' employment, in which they can get work done; and many employees and potential employees are still struggling to realise that 'normal' jobs are frequently not on offer.

Less than 50 % of the working population in Britain has a full-time, long-term job with a traditional employment contract. There has been a sharp rise in the variety of ways in which work is organised. We cannot describe it as 'the way people are employed' because many of these expanding forms of working arrangements (sub-contracting, franchising, self-employment) break the link between work and employment.

The story is one of increases in almost every form of work –

except the traditional full-time long-term job. One million people have more than one job. Part-time work has more than doubled in the last 15 years, and so has self-employment. Temporary employment and fixed-term contracts have significantly increased. And new working arrangements, such as job-sharing and annual hours contracts, have been established.

The increase in these forms of working is not just a matter of changes in the industrial structure: it is evidence of their spread into new areas. Shift-working, for example, always existed in the emergency services and where manufacturers wanted to use expensive equipment over more than eight hours per day. It has now spread into shops which stay open in the evenings to meet customer requirements, and to offices concerned with global operations which need to be in touch with people in different time zones. Similarly, sub-contracting was always common in the construction industry, but it is now common in the computing, scientific and local authority sectors.

Employees have realised that the days of a job for life have, in most cases, disappeared. Much more rapid movement in and out of work takes place now than it used to (around 10 % of the working population leave a job, and a roughly similar proportion start a job, every year). It is no surprise, therefore, to find that the job market is becoming more varied and more volatile. How we deal with this situation will be one of the touchstones of social and

economic success over the next few years.

PART-TIME WORKING

In the past two years, well over two thirds of all the jobs that have been created have been part-time jobs. Of those that are employed, about 6 million (one quarter) have part-time jobs. Women fill more than eight out of ten of these, and research shows that most people are in part-time employment because they prefer to work that way.

Part-time working enables them to fit work in with other responsibilities, such as caring for young children or elderly relatives, which may see as a major part of their lives. Employers prefer it because it allows them to match the jobs on offer to the work that needs to be done. Not all work comes in neat, seven-and-a-half hour blocks; if the work a particular employer has only last part of the day, why pay for a full day? Employers also know that if the tasks are not varied and interesting, employees find it easier to work with commitment and enthusiasm for a few hours rather than for a whole day. Nor do part-timers have to take time off for visits to the dentist or the doctor; so part-timers are more productive.

TEMPORARY JOBS

These account for well over 1.5 million employees and around 7.5 % of all jobs. Few employers can predict whether a job will continue into the next decade; none can be sure that a particular recruit will succeed in a job – so it makes little sense to make a promise of permanent employment they may be unable to keep.

OTHER OPTIONS

Shift-working is not just becoming more widespread, it is becoming less standardised. The days when nearly all shifts consisted of 10 or 12 hours are gone. 'Twilight shifts', usually for women working in shops, are now widespread. Shifts can be of different and varying lengths, brought about by increasing pressures on managers, changing employee expectations, and the advent of computer programs which enable managers to organise and check that everyone works a specified number of hours, no matter how complicated the shift patterns.

Annual hours working has taken a firm foothold in recent years. If work in places such as travel agencies, food processing firms and accounts departments is on a cyclical pattern, it makes little economic sense to employ staff for the same number of hours each day. Varying the hours to suit the work demand avoids paying for overtime in some periods - and also avoids the workers suffering boredom in others.

Jobsharing is a form of part-time working where two people share the same full-time employment pattern. Some jobsharers guarantee that if one of them is away the other will fill in for them. The employer gets full cover for only a little extra cost.

Homeworking and teleworking have grown, but only a little. Some of the wilder predictions that large numbers of us would be working this way by the end of the decade will be wrong. Although the technology would allow this to happen, the predictions failed to take account of the necessary social side of work. More and more people will work at home, but the main growth will be among those who do so only occasionally, to complete a specific report or prepare for a meeting.

Term-time working has been successful in some organisations. Female employees retain their contracts, without pay, during the school holidays, resuming their usual full- or part-time jobs during school terms.

Chris Brewster, *The Guardian*

ASSIGNMENT

1 According to the article, which form of work has not increased?

2 Which forms of work have increased the most?

3 Give two examples of areas of employment which now use different forms of work.

4 How does part-time working benefit:
   (a) employees;
   (b) employers?

5 Write a report taken from the section 'Other options' which makes clear the advantages of these ways of working for:
(a) employees;
(b) employers.

6 In what ways do women in particular benefit from these changes in working patterns?

7 What does this tell us about how women see their role in society and the family?

Language link

Radical changes

Words ending in 'cal' and 'cle' sound the same. If you find it difficult to remember which is which, think that adjectives end in 'al' and nouns end in 'le'.

adjectives	nouns
radical	article
musical	cubicle
tropical	bicycle
practical	spectacle

SELF CHECK

Add 'al' or 'le' to the following:

As a matter of princip..... I am refusing to vote on this matter.

He was very critc.....of the work, and said that from a music....point of view it was ineffective.

I think I left my watch in the changing cubic...

Breaking down barriers

This material focuses on the way both men and women can limit their career opportunities and development through set ideas about roles and behaviour. The first two passages take a look at the world of hairdressing, while the third one reports on some of the attitudes held by young people.

Short cut

The first day of my new Saturday job at the salon and I'm early, of course. Josie, the full-time girl, arrives jangling a huge bunch of keys.

The place is dark and stinks of perm solution. The floor's tiled black and white, the mirrors are surrounded by pictures of models, I'm wearing black jeans and a white T-shirt, as Robert told me to. Robert's my new boss.

"Put a tape on," Josie says, turning on the lights and nodding towards the stereo. Well, this is nothing like Romeo's, where I used to work, I decide, picking out an M-people tape. At Romeo's it was all Cliff Richard or Cilla Black, for the blue-rinse set.

Josie shows me around. Everything is black and white - the coffee mugs, even the brush used to flick hair off the client's neck. I'm starting to feel intimidated, and untrendy. In the mirror, the jeans I liked so much look baggy at the bum, and the T-shirt borrowed from my brother, looks like, well, my brother's T-shirt.

Josie makes us a coffee and sits down to do her nails.

"What time does Robert usually get here?" I ask Josie, casually.

"Oh, Robert, he's always late," she says without looking up. I brush my hair. Robert says we have to look neat, at all times.

Three Saturdays and I'm really into the job. Robert is always putting his hand on my shoulder and smiling at me. It makes me feel brilliant. In fact, I often sit in class thinking about the salon these days...

"Kay, I'm beginning to think you have a crush on him, "Josie whispers in my ear, as we lean over the twin sinks, each soaping a different head.

"No I haven't," I hiss back, bright red, terrified that Robert'll hear her as he darts past in his leather jeans.

"Well, you've no chance," she suddenly snaps. "D'you really think he'd look at you?"

"Well, thanks, Jose," I reply, feeling hurt. "Remind me to boost your confidence some time..."

"Sorry," she says, looking embarrassed. Silence reigns while I realise she's right. I do have a crush on Robert. We don't speak for the rest of the day.

A month later and I feel as if I've been here forever. Josie cut my hair and now I feel much better, with this slick style swinging round my head.

"Great," Robert approves, running his fingers through my hair. Josie is behind me, tapping the scissors against her palm. His fingers on the back of my neck make me blush. Tactfully Josie gives me an excuse to escape.

"Make us a cup of tea, will you, Kay?" she says, and I jump down gratefully.

Scuttling off to the kitchen I notice Josie turn to Robert to say something. I don't catch his reply, but in the mirror I see something I didn't expect to see - Robert's hand on Josie's waist and him whispering something in her ear. She giggles and pulls away. I put the kettle on, feeling sick.

At 6 pm we're clearing up and I

force myself to say, "I didn't know he was your boyfriend."

To my horror, Josie starts to cry: "Oh Kay, he's not my boyfriend. He was...Oh Kay, stay away from Robert. Do you know he's 30? Thirteen years older than me!"

I'm shocked. At the interview, I'd thought he was gorgeous, but I didn't think, with his long black pony tail and trendy clothes, he was more than 25.

I hand Josie a kleenex as she tells me the whole story – of how Robert started to flirt with her when she first got a job at the salon, and they'd started seeing each other. But then he began to mess her about and go out with other people. Eventually, she'd been brave enough to finish with him, at risk of losing her job, but he still refused to leave her alone.

"I look like a clown." Josie points at the mascara smearing her face.

"At least you fit in with the decor. Black and white," I can't help saying. I don't know how she will take this, but suddenly she cracks up laughing.

"Oh yes, Robert would approve," she snorts and we both splutter, trying to keep our laughter down, but it's too late, he's bounding up the stairs, two at a time, in his usual flamboyant way.

"Hi girls, nearly finished up here?" he says, seeming not to notice we're standing in a huddle.

"Yes," I mumble reaching for the dustpan full of hair.

"How are you settling in, Kay?" he asks me, giving me the full beam of his smile. "It's your first Saturday job, isn't it?"

I can feel Josie waiting for my answer.

"So far so good," I say, and the way his eyes hold my gaze makes me uncomfortable, but not in the way it would have done a few weeks ago. I can feel a blush creeping up but I'm determined to outstare him.

"It's not my first job. I used to work at a hairdressers in Barnet – Romeo's."

Josie nearly chokes on her laughter. Robert wheels round, gives her a sharp look. My blush subsides, I can feel it ebb away. A brilliant feeling.

"Well girls," he stammers, running his hand along his ponytail with a showy gesture. "That's fine, umm, that'll be all, you can go home now..."

A woman about the same age as my mum comes tripping up the stairs in high heels. "Robert?" she calls . "Have you forgotten me? The film starts at seven, darling..."

Josie and I leave together. We have a fit of giggles outside and have to hold each other up.

"Got time for a coffee?" she asks.

Over a milkshake, I hear more about Robert than I could ever wish to.

Saturdays have become even more fun now. Josie and I have a few catchphrases, for use when shampooing a stroppy client. They never fail to cheer us up. Whispered words like "Romeo" or "black and white" work like magic, sending us into hysterics. Best of all is when Josie points with the scissors towards Robert's crotch and makes snipping movements, winking at me over his head – not caring whether he sees her or not. Then we both die laughing.

Ruby Wallace, **Just Seventeen**

269

ASSIGNMENT

1 What attitudes to:
(a) work;
(b) looks;
(c) relationships;
are shown by Josie and Kay in the story?

2 Do you think these attitudes are typical of the people you know?

3 Imagine you are Robert in the story. Write an account of the situation from your point of view.

At the beginning of the course we had a lot of theory lessons – what hair is made up from, how chemicals affect it and things like that. In the practical lessons we started off practising on a block – a wax model with hair. You can't cut the hair, just play with it! After the first month you start on real people and it's much more fun. It's a cheap way to get a hair-do but clients have to sign a form saying they won't claim compensation if anything goes wrong!

One of the main things that I don't like about the course is the way we are taught to make everyone look 'nice'. We're supposed to use hair styles and make-up to enhance a woman's 'natural attributes' so that she looks more like a conventional idea of what is attractive. If a woman with white hair comes along and wants her hair dyed brown, we are told to persuade her to have a blue or pearly grey rinse, as they think this is less ageing. But to me the most important part of hairdressing is to do what the client wants. I try to spend time looking through catalogues and deciding together what would be the most interesting style to try. Since the arrival of punk fashions I think people are prepared to be a bit more experimental with hair and make-up. It's much more fun for me if the client wants pillar-box red stripes.

We don't get the chance to cut men's hair, which is a pity because lots of men are interested in having good hair-cuts nowadays, and I'm sure lots of men would like their nails done or have make-up put on professionally. There's only one man on the course, and when he walked in on the first day everyone assumed he was gay. When I asked why the college didn't allow men to come along as models, I was told, "We don't want that sort in here." They're very concerned not to get a 'bad' name – only women are supposed to look after their bodies, and most people here think it's unmanly for men to do the same.

Ideally I wouldn't choose to work in a conventional salon. I'd really like to have my own place where both men and women could come for hair cuts, massage and any sort of beauty treatment. My friend Liz and I had the idea of driving round to people's houses and doing their hair in the more relaxing atmosphere of their own home. In a way that's what I'm doing now – I do most of the women who live in my road. There would be a lot of work round here because, like most council estates, it's a long way from the town centre and there are no facilities – only two shops and a pub. Lots of women are house-tied by children and would have to catch a bus to the nearest salon. It would also make hairdressing much cheaper because you wouldn't have the same overheads.

Most of my friends are interested in my course, mainly because I do their hair for them, but at the same time I've conformed to their expectations of those friends, mainly middle class, who have stayed on at school to do A levels. They think all working class girls either become hairdressers or secretaries. I do hairdressing because I enjoy it and I don't think it's right that it should have such a low status just because it's not 'academic', and because it's traditionally women's work. Hairdressing isn't really considered to be a 'profession' by anyone, except for the few people at the top – mostly men – who are seen as 'artistes'.

Often people can't understand why I'm doing a Hairdressing and Beauty Therapy course if I think of myself as a feminist. Sometimes I do feel that I'm not living up to my own standards – I wish I could say that I was studying to be an engineer or something useful like that, but mostly I try to challenge the traditional image of hairdressing. If you want to take care of your body it's not necessarily for men's benefit, you can do it for yourself. I don't wear make-up or streak my hair to attract boys. I do it because I like experimenting with different ways of looking. It's just like wearing different styles of clothes. I'm not dependent on make-up – lots of times I can't be bothered to put it on, and I couldn't care less if I look less conventionally 'attractive' with green stripes on my face. My dad is always telling me that my hair doesn't look natural. I want it to look bleached with black roots.

Andrea, **Girls are powerful**

ASSIGNMENT

1 What is Andrea's attitude to her profession?

2 What does she think are the purposes of hairdos and make-up?

3 Write a paragraph giving your own view.

Need to be liked still blocks girls' hopes of better jobs

If school results were the key to power, girls would be running the world, but their need to be liked and worries that their appearance might put people off them prevent them from aspiring to good jobs, a study has found.

A report on the mental health of teenagers published yesterday comes to the depressing conclusion that the narrow, stereotyped gender roles of 30 years ago are still 'held with...amazing force by today's children'. The study, commissioned by the Health Education Authority, is being published on the second national Take Our Daughters To Work day.

About 250 000 girls, aged 11-15, will have a chance to see the world of work at first hand and perhaps go home with increased expectations.

The report says action is needed to combat the anxieties and negative self-images that hold back both sexes. Boys assume they will have to be the breadwinners, burdened with responsibility for a family. They expect competition and risk taking to get on or even to get a job, and worry about failure in exams or sport.

But girls, in spite of greater success at school, have lower self-esteem and worry more. The girls' overwhelming aim was to be liked. They wanted to be seen as good company, confident and outgoing but also nice, sociable and 'a person everybody likes'.

Fundamental to being liked, they felt, was looking attractive. Girls said they were very sensitive about their appearance. They continually sought reassurance about their hair, weight and skin, and felt put down when it was not forthcoming. They wanted approbation from their peers and were reluctant to assert their individuality for fear of being disliked.

Girls were particularly attracted by the image of supermodels like Naomi Campbell, who had achieved their position by their looks rather than through skills or qualifications.

Boys in the lower social classes, who also doubted their chances of a well-paid job, dreamed of achieving success through fame and fortune, like footballer Eric Cantona.

Girls had a strong awareness that they would one day have to balance work and a family. Many coped with this idea by aspiring only to undemanding careers.

The Guardian

ASSIGNMENT

1 According to the report, in what ways do negative self-images restrict young men and young women in their career choices?

2 What do you think Andrea from the second passage would say to a typical girl in the report? Write an account of their likely conversation.

More suggestions for coursework

- In your office, (a conventional, slightly old-fashioned firm) a man aged 23 comes in one day wearing make-up. Describe your response and the response of the other staff. You could write this as a story or a play, if you wish, or you could role-play the situation.
- Making-up. Write a story with this title. (Think about the different ways in which the phrase could be interpreted.)

Getting started

The following extracts focus on a selection day for a local radio journalist. Candidates had to use the information sheet and produce a demonstration tape which they scripted and recorded.

Read the information sheet and the three taped reports.

INFORMATION SHEET

Incident: Fire At Westchester Corn Exchange

Background: The Corn Exchange is an historic building in Westchester. It is used for council business, public meetings and civic occasions. It is a well-known local landmark and is also regarded as part of the national heritage.

Details: The Corn Exchange was badly damaged by fire last night. The fire broke out around midnight in the public gallery and quickly spread to the rest of the building. An emergency call from a member of the public alerted the fire brigade who worked through the night but were unable to save the building. They said the damage was so extensive because of the wooden fixtures and panels in the ancient gallery.

Comments: Chief Inspector Martin Mallory who is heading the enquiry said the police had not ruled out arson. The Exchange was the next venue for a conference on cultural unity, and there had been similar incidents at the conference's other venues. In Bromsville swastikas and slogans had been daubed on the building, and in Crossbridge the main speaker had been pelted with eggs.

Kashem Amin (23) who called the fire brigade, said, "I was leaving The Garage (a local club) with a few friends and we thought we smelt smoke as we walked down to the car park. When we turned the corner we saw flames coming from the Corn Exchange. I used my mobile phone to call the emergency service."

These are the beginnings of three tapes which were submitted.

Tape No. 1

A fire broke out in the Corn Exchange, Westchester, last night. It probably started in the public gallery and quickly spread. Firefighters were on the scene immediately but in spite of all they could do the building could not be saved. Apparently it spread so quickly because of the building's age and the amount of wood in it. The conference due to be held there today has had to be postponed. We can only be thankful no-one was hurt.

I spoke to Kashem Amin, who was first on the scene and in fact phoned the fire brigade.

Reporter: Good job you had your mobile, Kashem! The phone boxes round there are always being vandalised!

Kashem: Yes, it's often very useful. I was glad to be able to act so quickly.

Reporter: And you'd had a good night at The Garage, right? What kind of music do you like?

Tape No. 2

I am speaking to you from the site of smouldering rubble which just yesterday was the historic Westchester Corn Exchange. The building was gutted by fire which broke out late last night and quickly spread through the wood-panelled rooms. Earlier I spoke to Station Officer Nick Hambling who led the team of firefighters. He said that the fire got a grip very quickly and there was nothing to prevent the rapid spread of flames in such an old building. Local resident Sonia Raika said, "It's a real shame, a bit of history going up in smoke like this."

Tape No. 3

Towering Inferno had nothing on the fire which gutted the Westchester Corn Exchange last night. The flames shot into the sky after someone torched the building at around midnight. No-one is actually pointing the finger but when you think about the conference which was scheduled for today and the attitude the National Front have already shown elsewhere - well, you draw your own conclusions.

ASSIGNMENT

1 Which of the three tapes would you choose?

2 In your group, discuss the strengths and weaknesses of the tapes.

3 Write a report giving your decision. The report should comment on each tape and make clear why you came to your final choice.

4 Compile your own tape using the information sheet as a basis and, if you wish, the demonstration tapes. You may add details as long as they do not contradict the information given.

END-OF-CHAPTER ASSIGNMENT

You are contributing to a radio programme about work. Write a report to the producer indicating four to five extracts you would like to use in the programme, giving your reasons.

SUMMARY

In this section you have covered the following aspects of GCSE requirements:

SPEAKING AND LISTENING

pair/group discussion
interviewing
role play
giving a news report

READING

prose written since 1900
poetry written since 1900
non-European poetry written since 1900
non-literary material written before 1900
magazine articles
magazine short story
newspaper articles
autobiography

WRITING

comprehension
description
letter
article
speech
factual
conversation
drama
discussion
argument

LANGUAGE STUDY

vocabulary building
apostrophe
dash
discussion of language
language use

REVISION AND FURTHER ASSIGNMENTS

1 Re-write each of the following phrases, using an apostrophe
where appropriate.

(a) the students who 'own' the canteen
(b) the men who 'own' the lockers
(c) the women who 'own' the changing rooms

2 Insert the correct word in the following sentences.

(a) The (affects/effects) of the decision will be far-reaching.
(b) (Whose/who's) coat is this?
(c) He shot (past/passed) so quickly I couldn't speak to him.
(d) It's important to (practice/practise) every day if you want to
keep up a high standard.
(e) I couldn't see round the (stationery/stationary) vehicle.

3 Make up sentences to show the difference between the
following pairs of words:

personal/personnel

1

2

proof/prove

1

2

moral/morale

1

2

loose/lose

1

2

4 Use dashes or colons where appropriate in the following sentences:

The smallest kitten the most appealing was the first to be bought.

The creative arts faculty was very well equipped a new theatre, a recording studio and several practice rooms had been acquired.

The hotel offered everything we wanted a pool, a sauna, a gym and a free babysitting service.

I'm sorry I'm late the bus didn't turn up.

5 Use the following topics as a starting point for writing. Where there are no specific instructions use them as the basis for any kind of writing you enjoy or want to practise.

Being out of work

The new boss

The new job

My future career

What do you think about the more flexible ways of working which are becoming available?

"I'd hate to work for a woman boss."

Give a short talk about work you have done, perhaps on work experience or at weekends. Show what you enjoy or do not enjoy about it.

What do you see as the long-term implications of the rise in popularity of computer games?

Write a story in which a computer has an important part.

Raising your grade

- Read the instructions carefully. If there is a choice of question, read **all** the questions through and take a few minutes to decide which one(s) you should choose.

  If there is a compulsory question, make sure you do it.

- Plan your examination time carefully. You may be advised in the instructions how long to spend on a particular question - follow this advice.

- Look at the number of marks allocated to each question. The questions carrying most marks probably require fuller answers.

- Plan your answer before you begin writing. Jot down a key word or phrase to remind you what should be in each paragraph.

- Keep in mind the purpose of a piece of writing. If you are informing or persuading, for example, keep reminding yourself what the purpose is and angle your writing accordingly.

- Check carefully the form of writing you are asked to present. Stick to what has been asked for - a letter, a script, a story etc. Do not change halfway through.

- Leave time to read through your work and check for mistakes in spelling and punctuation.

- If you are given a variety of material as stimulus for a task remember to refer to an appropriate range in your answer.

- If your handwriting is untidy or not very clear, plan regular times through the year to practise writing as quickly as you will in the exam. Keep a copy of your practice pages and track your progress to clearer writing. Untidy and careless work can lose you marks.

- Read all the comments and corrections your tutor puts on your work. Keep a list of the correct spellings of words you have got wrong. Make sure you know how to spell them correctly. Keep testing yourself, or get a friend to test you.

- When you come across a word you are not familiar with, write it down and find out its meaning. If you are not sure about how to use it ask your tutor. You will get credit for using a wide vocabulary in written and spoken exams and coursework.

Answers

The answers listed here correspond to the symbol a in the main text.

Chapter 1
Page 11
Television's role is very important. It is a major force. It is up to us how we use it. Television is widely used as a sedative. I have seen it turned on early in the morning for very young children. Turning the set on to quieten them down is commonplace.

Page 49
plunge + ing = plunging   discharge + ing = discharging
enlarge + ing = enlarging   sponge + ing = sponging

Page 51
4
annually   busily
safely   frantically

Chapter 2
Page 66
(a) The facilities we require are en-suite rooms, cable television, a baby-sitting service, an indoor pool.
(b) The speaker was very persuasive, having a good grasp of her subject, a clear voice, convincing examples, a lively delivery.
(c) "If you are not in on time tonight, mark my words Donna, you will be grounded for a week."

Page 85
(a) whose   (b) principle   (c) whether

Page 119
4
(a) wintry   (b) noisy   (c) poisonous

6
(a) stationary   (b) principal   (c) role

7
metaphor

8
(a) self   (b) under

Chapter 3
Page 177
1

(a) chosen	(b) forgotten	(c) broken
(d) were	(e) spoken	

2

educate	describe	succeed	moisten
provide	solve	enlarge	befriend

3

(a) view	(b) ceiling	(c) their achievements

Chapter 4
Page 255
2

critically; truly; icily; hungrily; lovingly; desperately.

3

(a) harder	(b) stronger	(c) most quickly

Chapter 5
Page 227
1

(a) The students' canteen.
(b) The men's lockers.
(c) The women's changing rooms.

2

(a) effects	(b) whose	(c) past
(d) practise	(e) stationary	

Acknowledgements

The author and publishers would like to acknowledge with thanks:

Chapter 1 Taking it easy: **Geraldine Bedell**: *Why your children should watch TV*. Adapted from GOOD HOUSEKEEPING magazine/© National Magazine Company. **The Times**: for a piece by Peter Barnard on *The Big Breakfast* published in **The Times** (1992). **The Guardian** for a piece by Nancy Banks-Smith on *The Big Breakfast* © **The Guardian** (29th September 1992). **Fleur Adcock**: Poem *The Telephone Call* © Fleur Adcock 1986. Reprinted from *The Incident Room* by Fleur Adcock, 1986, (Oxford University Press). **GAH Partnership**: Data and statistics on the National Lottery. **Suzy Barber**: *"I inherited £100,000!"* /Mizz Magazine/Robert Harding Syndication. **The Sun**: for piece on boxing match © The Sun (27th February 1995). **Today**: for piece on boxing match (27th February 1995). **The Guardian**: for piece on boxing match © **The Guardian** (27th February 1995). **Bob Dylan**: poem *Who killed Davey Moore?* (Sony Music Publishers). **Louise Page**: play *Toby and Donna* (Hodder & Stoughton).

Chapter 2 Home and away: **Leslie Thomas**: Extract from *My World of Islands* (Methuen). **Quentin Crewe**: Extract from *Touch the Happy Isles* (Headline). **FHG Publications**: Extracts from *Children Welcome! Family Holiday Guide* (FHG Publications, Paisley). **University of London Examinations and Assessment Council**: Adaptation of University of London GCE Ordinary Level examination paper (1984). **Geetanjali Guptara**: *Imagining India*. **Amryl Johnson**: *Back Home* taken from *Chasing the Sun* (Simon & Schuster Young). **H.E. Bates**: Extract from *A Breath of French Air*, The Estate of H.E. Bates, (Michael Joseph Ltd.) **W.M. Thackeray**: Extract from *Vanity Fair* (Penguin Books Ltd.). **Carol Parsons and David Veal**: Extract from *Leaving Home* in the Teenage Information series (W & R Chambers Ltd.). **Catch**: *Going Solo* , "Catch" magazine (January 1994). **June Oldham**: Extract from *Moving In* (Viking, Penguin Books Ltd.). **James Joyce**: Extract from *Dubliners* (Jonathan Cape). **Stephen Poliakoff**: Extract from *Runners* (Methuen). **Shelter**: Extracts from *Speaking out against Homelessness* (Shelter). **William Wordsworth**: Poem *Lines composed on Westminster Bridge* from *Poetical works,* 1969 by permission of Oxford University Press. **Charles Dickens**: Extract from *Bleak House*. **Mark Timlin**: Extract from *Ashes by now* (Victor Gollancz Ltd., 1993). **Rukshana Smith**: Extract from *Sumitra's story* (The Bodley Head Ltd., 1982).

Chapter 3 Different voices: **Maya Angelou**: Extract from *I know why the caged bird sings* (Virago Press, 1969). **Laurie Lee**: Extract from *Cider with Rosie* (Chatto & Windus). **Subhajit Sarkar**: *Earliest memories* reprinted from *Young words* by permission of Macmillan, London and Basingstoke. **William Wordsworth**: Extract from *The Prelude*, Book I, by permission of

Oxford University Press (1917). **Anna Leitrim**: Extract from *Me and my history* from *Our Lives* (The English and Media Centre). **Carol Ann Duffy**: *Stealing* taken from **Selling Manhattan** by Carol Ann Duffy (Anvil Press Poetry, 1987). **Angela Jariwala**: Extract from *Pardesi* (Bijlee Services). **Charlotte Brontë**: Extract from *Jane Eyre*. **Ursula Bentley**: Extract from *The Natural Order* (Martin Secker & Warburg). **Oxford University Press**: Extract on Sir Richard Grenville from *The Dictionary of National Biography* Volume 8, 1917 (Oxford University Press). **Encyclopaedia Britannica**: Extract on Sir Richard Grenville from the *Encyclopaedia Britannica* 15th edition, © 1995 (Encyclopaedia Britannica Inc.). **Alfred Lord Tennyson**: Poem *The Revenge*. **"19" magazine**: Statements on cannabis. Wendy Granditer/"19" magazine/Robert Harding Syndication. **The Guardian**: for piece by Alex Bellos on Manchester rave scene © **The Guardian** (17th March 1995). **Ogilvy & Mather Ltd.**: for drugs and solvents information advertisement. **Cellnet**: for advertisement. **Hewlett Packard**: for permission to reproduce an advertisement. **Samuel Pepys**: Extracts from *The diary of Samuel Pepys*. **Zlata Filipovic**: Extracts from *Zlata's diary* (Viking, 1994). **Pauline Collins**: © 1992. Extract from *Letters to Louise* (Bantam Books, an imprint of Transworld). All rights reserved. **Wilfred Owen**: Letter from *Wilfred Owen: Collected Letters* Edited by Harold Owen and John Bell (Oxford University Press, 1967). **Scarlett McGwire**: Extract from *She's leaving home* by Shreela Ghosh in *Transforming moments* (Virago, 1989). **Irene Spencer and Vera Small**: Extract from *Ladies of letters* (Futura, 1991). **Anna Adams**: Poem *Her dancing days*. **Alan Bennett**: from *A cream cracker under the settee* from *Talking Heads* (BBC Enterprises Ltd.). **James Berry**: Extract from *Becky and the wheels-and-brakes boys* from *A thief in the village* (Hamish Hamilton, 1982). **Clodagh Corcoran**: Extract from *Ms Snow White wins case in High Court* published in *Sweeping Beauties* (Attic Press, 1989).

Chapter 4 Generation games: University of London Examinations and Assessment Council: Adaptation of University of London examination paper (English paper 05). **Roddy Doyle**: Extract from *Paddy Clarke Ha Ha Ha* (Martin Secker & Warburg, 1993). **Margaret Atwood**: Extract from *Cat's Eye* (Bloomsbury Publishing Ltd., 1988). **BBC Radio**: Excerpt from programme *Girl Gangs* broadcast on BBC Radio 4. **Randy Newman**: Song *So long Dad* © 1995 January-Music Corp. and Six Continents Music Publishing Inc., USA Warner Chappell Music Ltd., London W1Y 3FA. Reproduced by permission of IMP Ltd. **Edmund Gosse**: Extract from *Father and Son*. **Timothy Callender**: Short story *The sins of the fathers* (Thomas Nelson & Sons Ltd.). **Liz Lochhead**: *Poem for my sister* from *Dreaming Frankenstein and collected poems* (Polygon Books, Edinburgh University Press). **Wendy Cope**: Poem *Sisters* reproduced by permission of the author. **Sangita Manandhar**: Extract from *Life for a Young Asian Girl* from *Say what you think* (The English and Media Centre). **Sheba Feminist Publishers**: *Ruth - A day in the life from Girls are powerful* (Sheba Feminist

Publishers). **Adrian Mitchell**: Poem *Old Age Report* taken from Adrian Mitchell's *For Beauty Douglas* (Allison and Busby). **The Guardian**: Extracts from *You're as old as you feel* © **The Guardian** (20th September 1994). **The Guardian**: for extracts from story *Ending Up* by Catherine Bennett © **The Guardian** (8th October 1994)

Chapter 5 The nine to five: Seamus Heaney: Poem *Digging* from *Death of a Naturalist* (Faber & Faber Ltd.) **Taufiq Rafat**: Poem *I am glad to be up and about* from *Bite In 2* (Thomas Nelson & Sons Ltd.) Poem *Washing:* Language in the National Curriculum (LINC) Project, 1989-1992; based at the Department of English Studies, University of Nottingham. **Alan Sillitoe**: Extract from *Saturday Night and Sunday Morning* (HarperCollins *Publishers* Limited) **W.W. Gibson**: Poem *The Release* from *Bite In 2* (Thomas Nelson & Sons Ltd.). **Emily Bishop**: Extract from *Embroidery in Working Lives, Volume 1* (Centerprise Trust). **Sybil Marshall**: Extract from *Fenland Chronicle* (Michael Joseph). **R.A. Banks and F. Burns**: Extracts from John O'Neil's diary in *Summary and Directed Writing* (Hodder & Stoughton, 1980). **More!**: Extracts from More! magazine. **Catch**: *Horse Power*, "Catch" magazine (January 1994). **Zoë Fairburns**: Extract from *Here Today* © Zoë Fairbairns. **The Guardian**: for piece *New job/Old job* © **The Guardian** (15th March 1995). **The Guardian**: for extracts from *You've got to go with the flow* by Chris Brewster © **The Guardian** (22nd April 1995). **Ruby Wallace**: short story *Short cut* published in **Just Seventeen. Penguin Books Ltd.**: for extract *Hairdressing* in *Girls are powerful*. Text copyright © Spare Rib and Shocking Pink. **The Guardian**: for extracts from *Need to be liked still blocks girls' hopes of better jobs* by Sarah Boseley © **The Guardian** (27th April 1995).

The authors and publishers would like to acknowledge with thanks the following illustration sources: Lifeline Manchester Publications for the cartoon on page 147; all other cartoons by Mik Brown; The BBC Photograph Library for the photographs on pages 2 and 11; The J. Allan Cash Photo Library for the photographs on pages 5, 26, 30, 34, 60, 104, 112, 115, 126, 141, 142, 159, 185, 189, 218, 245, 272, 273; The Ronald Grant Archive for the photograph on page 15; The Robert Harding Picture Library for the photographs on pages 86 and 162; Hewlett-Packard Ltd. for the advertisement on pages 152 and 153; The Billie Love Historical Collection for the photographs on pages 95, 132, 180; Ogilvy & Mather for the drugs information advertisement on page 150; Tony Stone Images for the photographs on pages 34, 53, 60, 67, 90, 181, 253, 264, 270; TRIP for the photograph on page 211; Yorkshire Television for the photograph on page 76.

The publishers have made every effort to trace copyright holders, however if any acknowledgement has been inadvertently omitted this will be rectified at the earliest possible opportunity.